T0208272

I BELIEVE I CAN TRY

DENVER E. LONG
BFA, MA. DPAKR

authorHOUSE®

AuthorHouse™
1663 Liberty Drive
Bloomington, IN 47403
www.authorhouse.com
Phone: 1 (800) 839-8640

Published by AuthorHouse 07/18/2019

ISBN: 978-1-7283-1900-1 (sc)
ISBN: 978-1-7283-1899-8 (e)

Library of Congress Control Number: 2019909658

Print information available on the last page.

Joan C. Johnson-Long,
the little *"Jamaican Doll"*, who has been my
inspiration from the moment we met.

Contents

Acknowledgements

The idea of writing a book about my life was born when I was four. At that time, I had little to write about. Learning to write was my biggest challenge. I began to study and focus on words. When I wrote my book, I was going to fill it with everything that ever happened to me during my life, the good, the bad and the ugly. It was the next great American novel. To my great good fortune, I started writing short journal entries and short stories very early on. Over the years that habit of writing things down produced what I called 'my life in notes'. When I began to do research in earnest, I discovered that I had accumulated notes, letters, documents and post cards dating back to 1958, some even earlier. I counted my earliest grade school report cards. I kept every letter I ever received, many from girls. They number in the hundreds.

When I began this book, I set a solid deadline to have the manuscript completed. I gave myself six months. I planned to work eight hours a day, five days a week from nine to five, like any other job. Every daily activity would be aimed at producing a finished product whether that activity be reading, sketching, studying, talking on the phone or writing. My personal objective was to write at least an hour a day, every day, period. At that rate I would have three hundred and sixty-five hours of work. If the one hour per day could produce at least two pages of work, I could produce seven hundred and thirty pages of material in a year, enough for two books. It simply meant making a serious commitment. Once I started down that trail of commitment, I never looked back, but I had no idea how very difficult it would be. Despite the supreme challenge, the manuscript was done in six months. But revisions and preliminary editing took forever. Now it's done. Most of my life is now on paper and I learned during the process that writing is the loneliest profession in the world. What I say in these pages is written with the intention of expressing my life, unadorned and unpretentious. It is honest and filled with the joys and sorrows that have made my life the joy that it is. It is my sincerest hope that those who read it will get as much enjoyment from reading it as I had writing it. My life, like everyone else's has a story in it. And as destiny would have it, I began 'writing' mine when I was four years old. But none of it could have happened with just me alone. Though far too numerous to name, the people in my life, both living and deceased, are those I hereby acknowledge.

My late mother and father come first. Mrs. & Mrs. William B. and Irene A. Long, to whom I constantly strive to repay my debt of gratitude, I return my life to you now in these pages with true appreciation for all you have done for me. And to my one and only favorite big sister in the whole world, Jo Merriel Townsel, I offer to you my thanks and appreciation. Without my big sister, there would have been a lot less to write about. And to my one and only favorite nephew, Kenneth J. Townsel and his wife Cindy, I say: 'IPA' every day.

In 1972 at the age of thirty-one Nichiren Buddhism came into my life. I didn't know at the time that it was what I had been searching for from day one. Let me not get ahead of myself. Before joining NSA (Nichiren Shoshu of America), the precursor to SGI-USA (Soka Gakkai International). I didn't think world peace was possible. Soka Gakkai means "value creation" and I have become a world citizen as a result of the struggles I have made alongside thousands of other SGI members around the globe who are working toward achieving the same goal of world peace. The SGI has breathed hope into my life and into the world at large. It is due to the relentless efforts of three men: Tsunesaburo Makiguchi, First Soka Gakkai President; Josei Toda, Second Soka Gakkai President and Daisaku Ikeda, Third and current Soka Gakkai President. Today my mentor, President Daisaku Ikeda is leading the Soka Gakkai International in the struggle for kosen-rufu (world peace) in 192 countries and territories around the world. With his message comes hope for humankind. I celebrate and honor President Ikeda and all the members of the Soka Gakkai International around the globe.

Introduction

"As I watched with curiosity, my mother placed the delicate little cutting into a glass of clear water, then she put the glass in a shady corner on the window ledge. For days I watched as the cutting began to grow tiny roots. The roots grew longer and longer until they filled the bottom of the glass, and I wondered silently: "How did that plant know to do that?""

When I was a kid, I spent most of my time alone, in my mind, going places, exploring, looking for new adventures, thinking about life and the universe. I was seriously weird. Decades ahead of my time, there were no such words as 'nerd' or 'geek'. I was the original nerd. My mind was an ever-exciting place where wonderful things happened at my command; ideas are born, and all my wishes come true. I was the captain of my tiny ship, one that was destined to travel far and wide throughout the universe. I questioned everything-anything was possible. "How much does the Earth weigh?" "Do bears get fish bones stuck in their throats like people do?" I demanded answers. These were important issues that had to be dealt with. "Why are we alive?" If there were questions, then there had to be answers. You couldn't have one without the other. The answers would have to make sense. "Was Jesus circumcised?" "Did he ever have a girlfriend?" Because most of the answers I got were questionable at best, by age four I was having serious credibility issues with both Santa Claus of the North Pole and Jesus Christ of North Nazareth.

They were both 'good guys' but in my mind they both had questionable resumes. Adding to the mental and emotional confusion was the fact that my mom promoted both. The very day I openly declared Santa Claus to be a myth was the very same day that Santa Claus disappeared from my life. My mother simply said: "Ok, that's it; now you know the truth." And just like that, it was over. The myth had been fun while it lasted. However, Jo, my sister and heroine, didn't take the revelation so well. She wanted to keep believing in Santa and that he was going to keep coming. I didn't believe any of it. Once I understood about Ole St. Nick, my mind exploded with a vibrant new energy and an insight that I had not known before. Many things suddenly made sense. To see the light, you must brave the darkness. Suddenly it was easy to see how difficult it was for my mom and dad to provide a safe, happy home for Jo and me. Christmas costs money. They had to work hard all the time to give us the things that we took for granted. It frustrated me to know that Jo didn't understand or accept the fact that reindeers can't fly and that we had no chimney. As might be expected, I became very annoyed with her. Despite the reality before us, she chose to suffer by continuing to accept the myth. I wasn't being mean when I insisted that she open her eyes, wake up and see the light and stop living in the dark. Our arguments weren't very sophisticated but effective enough to differentiate our courses of action in the years that followed.

The question then arose as to why my mom would have us believe in such a grand fairy tale in the first place. I decided to leave that question for much later. Understandably, her reasoning would have been that she did it for our joy and our happiness. I wondered what would happen when the fairy tales came to an end. The understanding of the Santa myth fused itself into my life in such a way that life was becoming clearer to me even at the tender age of four. I was certain that my sister had a voice that spoke to her just like I did. I intended to grow up, learn everything about everything and then when I was properly prepared, go out and change the world for the good. All I had to do was ask questions, get the answers and proceed with making the world a better place to live. Most importantly I would dispel all the myths that plagued humanity. There was much work to do and no time to waste, especially on childish notions like Santa Claus and Jesus Christ.

This is the story of my journey that began in the earliest years of my life. I'm still on that journey which will last. When I think of where it started, I am always amazed. One thing I have learned is that it takes courage to be truly happy. I laugh and gasp when I look back over my past and think about some of the incredible and hilarious situations and circumstances in which I found myself in my search for the 'truth'.

CHAPTER ONE

The Porch Door Mystery

We lived second floor front in a four-flat building with a flat roof and an open front porch. Our building was at 1536 Massachusetts Street, Gary, Indiana. We didn't have a fireplace. Nobody in our neighborhood had a fireplace. A fireplace was something that we only saw in the movies. We didn't have lawns, either. The closest lawn was in the park two blocks away across 15th Avenue where the white folks lived. The stairs up to our apartment were wide and creaky but were always swept and scrubbed clean. The entry door to the building at the bottom of the stairs was so hard to open that you needed both hands to gain entry. The glass in it was so thick, breaking it was impossible. Our apartment faced east and greeted the morning sun. It shone right onto our front porch, through the windows into the living room, warming the room in the winter cold. The apartment was always bright, colorful and clean. My mother made sure that we kept the house clean, the dishes washed, and the garbage taken out. Jo was kitchen management. I was waste management. Ma was very fussy about a messy apartment so if she got angry, she would just give us 'the look'. It was a 'death ray' stare that particularly affected our dog, Big Boy. When he got 'the look', he would whimper and scamper away and hide under the bed, but Jo and I had to endure. There was no conversation from mom, just the stare of death, a look that could melt rock.

Our apartment was drafty, especially in the wintertime near the door that led out onto the front porch. The screen door on the outside just caught snow when it got very deep. The inside door had a window in it where you could pull back the curtains and look out onto the wide narrow porch. I had to stand on a stool to look out the window. I decided early on that the kids on my block who had porches and flat roofs were the lucky ones; they had landing strips for Santa Claus just like I did. I felt sorry for kids who lived in basements. With me Santa had his own private landing strip. My thoughtfulness in providing him a private landing strip had to count for something. I figured that Santa would then show his appreciation by putting something nice under the Christmas tree. It was simple: be nice to him and he'd be nice to me. However, every year at the beginning of winter, Ma stuffed the cracks around that door, especially at the bottom. She used old towels and her old nylon stockings. She filled every crack so tightly that you couldn't feel any air coming in. It worked and I was always amazed at how much warmer it felt after she had completed that chore. Stuffing the door was an annual event. When Ma stuffed the door, it meant that it was definitely wintertime. It would be spring before that door opened again and we all knew it. It got so cold that even the weather had a name; they called it 'The Hawk'. I would often hear the grownups say, "Yeah, 'the Hawk' is out tonight." At first, I thought 'The Hawk' was a big, flying bird-monster that swooped down and ate people. When I asked Jo about it, she told me that it meant the cold temperature and wind and that I was so stupid. There were no stairs to the porch. The only way onto the porch was through the apartment and through the living room. The mere idea of someone, anyone, walking through our living room in the winter to either open that door onto the porch or come in off the porch was impossible; it just would not happen. We didn't even have to talk about it.

Christmas was always a time of festive celebrations and good fun. There was magic in the air and love was everywhere. There was plenty of good food and lots of music. December 25th was one of the happiest days of my life with my birthday just two days later on December 27th. Christmas time was wonderful, and all was right with the world. What was even better was the fact that my mother worked at *Babyland*, the big toy store. That alone should have given me pause. I understood 'bad or good' and 'goodness sake' that were mentioned in the song, *"Santa Claus is Coming to Town"*. 'Bad' meant punishment and I did not want punishment. But Santa couldn't possibly know whether I'd been good or bad. His time would have been better spent figuring out how he was going to explain the slush on the living room carpet.

Jo and I always got enough toys and clothes to completely fill the living room. In fact, our living room would be literally filled from one side to the other with gifts, clothes and toys for each of us. One side of the room was designated Jo's side. The other side was mine. We always awoke in new pajamas with the footsies. We had so many toys and gifts that we had to take naps and return to finish playing. Jo's side of the living room looked like a girl's room. There were the pinks and yellows and frilly things that said 'girl'. Girl clothes, dolls, gifts and toys filled the sofa from one end to the other. It seemed to me that anything that a girl could ever want, or need was somewhere on that side of our living room; and it all belonged to my sister. The cocktail table was a boundary, a border. It cut her side of the room off from my side. My side of the room said 'boy'. The big chairs on my side of the room were full of more clothes than I thought I would ever wear. There was long underwear with the buttoned trap door in the rear and a row of buttons down the front, navy corduroy pants, bold plaid flannel shirts, new boots and lots of socks. I got trucks and cars and guns. They were toys for boys, play tools, marbles, airplanes. My toys made noise. Every year there were flannel pajamas and handkerchiefs. I can't remember a Christmas morning that I didn't get exactly the present that I wanted. The joy was exhausting. On Christmas morning even Jo seemed sweet as she opened her gifts and tried on her many new outfits. Her presents kept her mind off of me for a while. I loved her very much but still, she was a girl. Even before we could finish opening boxes, there were so many wrappers and ribbons all over the room that we had to stop and clear away the huge piles of colorful wrapping paper accumulating on the floor. Life was good.

At the same time, serious questions about Santa were stirring in my head. It was troublesome. I asked questions but nobody wanted to talk about it, especially the grownups. How did that little plant know to grow roots and how did Santa always know how to get into the living room without leaving tracks? I was just four, but I just wasn't stupid. Coming up the stairs for Santa would have been out of the question. If he had done that, then he would have had to park his sleigh in the vacant lot next door and walk up two flights of stairs. I didn't think so. If he had taken that option, then 'The Demon Twins' would have stolen his sleigh and killed his reindeers for sure. The mere idea of a little fat, white man, dressed in a furry, red and white suit, driving a sleigh full of toys and sitting in a dark vacant lot on 15th and Massachusetts at night, all alone, shouting, *"Ho!, Ho!, Ho!"* was crazy. It was a bad idea. Then there were the tracks or the lack of tracks on the porch. We always had several inches of good virgin snow to land on so not having adequate snow was no excuse not to land on the porch. And there was never any reindeer poop on the porch. Actually, I was thankful about the poop part because it would have been my job as waste management to clean it up. But most troubling was the fact that the stuffing around the porch door was always intact on Christmas morning. There was a real problem brewing and I meant to get to the bottom of it. Besides 'The Demon Twins' owned the night. They owned the day, too, but at night I was inside where they couldn't get to me. Christmas was becoming a very complicated issue and it seemed that I was the only one who was willing to face the harsh reality that confronted us all. Everyone was in a state of supreme denial, but I wasn't having any of it. It was time I took a stand.

The Demon Twins

The Plummer family lived at 1510 Massachusetts Street, the north end of the block in a front basement apartment. The two youngest brothers were twins: Calvin and Alvin. They were young, strong, frightening little black terrorists. If they wanted something, they took it, sometimes even from each other. They were not the type you spent time debating with. The reality was simple: they were predators and the rest of the kids on the block were prey. I was a just a snack, but I lived in fear. The twins devoted their waking hours to the dark side of life, the task of making every other kid's life miserable. They stalked; we fled. Luckily for me, they usually threatened and intimidated the bigger kids, those who offered some resistance. I offered no resistance. I was small fry and usually not big enough to bother with. That was little solace for me whenever I saw either of them coming toward me on the street. I had seen them both in action. So, I maintained a real low profile. In my mind the twins were life's way of telling me that the 'boogie man' was not only alive and well, but that he had a twin brother. Though they lived down the block only a few houses from me, they lived in a totally different world than the other kids on the block.

Calvin and Alvin were the scourge of every kid on our block and a few nearby blocks. They were not identical twins and in fact, it was difficult to see how they might have been twins at all. Calvin was the bigger and 'older' of the two, he was built like a gladiator even though he was about my age. Even as a youngster, he had the body of a man; his black muscles were well defined, and his actions made it clear that he was as strong as he looked. He took every opportunity to let other kids on the block know just that. He stood tall and erect with thick lips and a wide nose and skin as black and rich as crude. There was no doubt he took pride in his physique since he more often than not could be seen stalking around the neighborhood, bare chest and bare foot, his huge feet slapping against the pavement as he closed in on some hapless victim. He had hands like vices whose only real purpose was to inflict pain and suffering upon those who were unfortunate enough to fall into their grasps. His hair was short, thick, nappy and always uncombed. It stayed matted to his head that housed a brain with the IQ of a potato. It was doubtful that he could read or write; he stopped going to school when he was old enough to steal and he started stealing when he was old enough to walk. He was not my major concern. However, his twin brother, Alvin was shorter but nevertheless had a remarkably similar physique. He too was built strong with a set of muscles that indicated he was no physical weakling. Together they had inherited a code of behavior that set them apart from every other kid on the block. And as different as they were, in some ways, they were unquestionably related. Both were left-handed, both had admirable physiques and neither seemed to have had much mental aptitude. They thrived on what could only be called 'animal instincts. But what made Alvin look distinctly different from his twin sibling was that he was built low to the ground. He had a tendency to slump forward when he stood or when he ran. And like a wolf, usually bare chest, he had a distinctly animal-like appearance that perfectly complimented his intellect. He was about my height, but much stronger. Looking back, I think now how he reminded me of the character in *Altered States* who, after some experimentation, was transformed to his original primal state, that state where man's natural predatory instincts were dominant. To me Alvin was that guy. He was the closest thing I knew to a cave man that ate mayo and sugar sandwiches.

On one unfortunate occasion, when I got caught by this predator, he squeezed my arm so hard that I thought I would never use it again. His grip was a vice. My weapon was my mind. He was a real wild child. What really made him scary was that you never knew what he would do next. He was completely unpredictable. And his nose constantly ran. He'd just wipe most of the drippings away with the back of one of his ashy forearms, inhale the rest and keep going. I thought of him as the shorter half of the 'Snot Squad'. I was small in stature but that was no reason not to think like a giant. There was no way I could beat him up, but I could quietly call him all kinds of dirty names, the kind of names that he wouldn't understand even he heard them. Like his bigger sibling, his hair was a thick, matted, mass of steel wool. There was always something stuck in his hair. Things got stuck in his hair like a magnet. And together, whatever they wanted, they took. I was afraid of him and I hated him in spite of what the church ladies had taught us in Sunday school. But the church ladies didn't have to deal with him. He was the 'Bully from Hell' and unlike his 'smarter' brother, he had the IQ of a baked potato. Even so, I often wondered about him, his life, his brother's life and his family. I wondered if he was as happy as I was, especially at Christmas time. I wondered.

KING, QUEENIE AND ALVIN

It gets better. Wherever Alvin went, King followed. And wherever King went, Queenie followed; the three were inseparable. King was a huge, ugly orange/brown/gray colored male mongrel dog with hair that was thick and matted, much like that of his master. He followed him everywhere. Whenever Alvin was in Mr. Butts' Owl Drug Store on the corner, stealing whatever he could get his hands on, King sat outside motionless, unchained with his eyes focused on the door to the drug store, waiting for his master's return. As likely as not, he would come running out to get away from Mr. Butts who'd be chasing him. Nobody knows where King came from; he had been around for as long as any of the kids could remember. He was just a part of the neighborhood landscape. I can't remember a time when King was not around. If you saw one of them, you saw the others. Queenie was even uglier than King. She was a scrawny, one-eyed bitch that followed King everywhere; she was his mate. But King ruled the animal kingdom on the block and therefore no harm ever came to Queenie. There was no question in anybody's mind about that. King was clearly top dog and he did whatever his master ordered him to do. Queenie, on the other hand, always went along for the ride. There was some special kind of communication between the three that nobody else could fathom, not even the other Plummer kids. It was concluded that the three of them could read each other's minds, what little collective minds they had. Sometimes all it took was a subtle movement of Alvin's eyes that sent King into action. At other times, it was an unintelligible verbal command that King responded to. Either way, when given a command,

King acted. King knew all the kids on the block so he was never a threat to any of us so we all considered him one of us, but he was not the kind of dog that you would want to pet. As in war, the kids on the block and throughout the neighborhood were civilians and hence were off limits to King. It was a different story, however, for strange dogs or cats that strayed into the neighborhood. Rats were especially good hunting. It was at these times that King showed his true predatory skills. I saw how vicious King could be on command. Many dogs, cats and rats had perished in his huge jaws. Large or small, he simply took them in his jaws and ferociously shook the life out of them. Once lifeless, he would drop the limp carcass to the ground and sit at attention as if waiting for more orders from his master. The threesome feared only one person, Mr. Austin Plummer the patriarch of the clan. The entry way down to the Plummer' apartment was in the front of the building, under the Galloways' concrete stairs. You'd have to go down a steep flight of crooked, brick steps that spiraled into a dark, dank cave-like area at the bottom, directly underneath. A single light bulb usually dangled from a frazzled overhead light fixture, creating creepy, moving shadows as it swung this way and that in the small space. It was creepy even during the daylight hours. The few times I went down those stairs, I was always with someone and never at night. Whenever I thought about Christmas, I wondered how Santa would negotiate those steep stairs at night in the snow and ice with a big heavy bag of toys on his back. What was worse, King lay at the bottom of the stairs at night, guarding his castle. He was like a big, ugly monster, hiding down there in the dark, waiting to eat you. I often wondered why the twins were so bad and why they lived in such a sad, dark place. I wondered if they had made that place sad by the way they acted or had that place made them act the way they did? I probably would have been sad, too if I had had to live in such a dark place like that with so many brothers and sisters who were always fighting with one another. I knew what it was like just to quarrel with Jo and there were just the two of us. Being afraid of the dark didn't help me much either. The twins were bad boys, so I assumed maybe they were getting punished. I was a good boy. I didn't hurt people and I didn't like to fight. My friends and I didn't fight. We never even talked about fighting. That was because I couldn't fight. Sometimes Jo and I got into it, but she was my sister, and she was a girl and she always won. Where we lived was the perfect metaphor for our lives. The Plummers' home was a dark, gloomy place, below ground in 'Hell'. From their living room, you couldn't even look outside and see the sun. The sun would have to be nearly over head before the light could even penetrate their space. Their apartment was about eight feet below the sidewalk level. An area about six feet wide and the width of the building separated the front window from the wall supporting the sidewalk. It created a pit. From above at sidewalk level you could look over the twisted wrought iron railing and down into the pit. There were two crooked railings that ran down length of the concrete stairs. It was a hazardous journey down those stairs, especially for someone as small as I was. The pit was usually filled with all kinds of junk and their front window faced a blank wall outside. It was a dark world they lived in and I felt so lucky that I lived second floor front, facing the light of the sun, in 'Heaven'.

I WORKED FOR MR. BUTTS

In 1951 the Owl Drug Store stood on the northwest corner of 16th Avenue & Massachusetts St. in the heart of Mid-town Gary, Indiana. It was in my territory. The address, 1550, was easy for me to remember because my address was 1536 Massachusetts just two doors down from the corner and on the same side of the street. I remember when they painted the fat cement post that held up the second floor of the building. It went from a dark dirty green to a flat ugly gray. The owner, Mr. Leo V. Butts was a giant of a man who was kind and generous. He was a pharmacist. He made medicines for people in the neighborhood. He always wore a white pharmacist jacket. At the age of ten years, I started working for Mr. Butts in the Owl Drug Store. He never offered me a job; but it was clear that I was becoming responsible for chores in the store. I think my mom had a lot to do with me spending so much time' working'. My pay was one dollar a week plus benefits which included all the ice cream I could eat and a candy goodie bag on payday, Saturdays at closing. A dollar was big money for a ten-year-old in 1951.

Despite or maybe because of my little size Mr. Butts gave me a job. I sure don't remember asking for it, but I learned to love it. My initial responsibilities included sweeping the floors and emptying the ash trays in the ice cream booths. It was also my duty to make sure that the telephone booth was always clean with no gum stuck to the sides. My job description began to change as I gained a vaster range of responsibilities. During the hottest days of the summer it was also my job to wipe down and remove all of the cardboard displays in the windows and sweep out all the dead flies from the display windows. Sometimes the flies were so many that we used fly paper but that didn't look very nice.

I also brought the stack Sunday morning newspapers into the store whenever I was up that early. The nickel Coke cooler had to be filled and all of the soda crates stacked. The cooler was a big rectangular red tub filled with mostly ice and Coca-Colas. The bottle caps also had to be emptied from the container on the front of the cooler. I didn't realize it at the time, but I learned what a "rubber" was and what it was used for. Some friends told me about them, but I didn't make the connection until I discovered by accident that Mr. Butts sold them. Then I understood why all the "big boys" would always go quickly to the back of the store to the pharmacy and whisper to Mr. Butts. Life was good.

Joyce was the older girl who worked behind the soda counter, making cones and shakes and whatever. She was kind of cute and she smiled at me a lot. I started liking until I noticed the black hairs on her legs. I knew all the flavors and where they went inside the serving cooler. I made it my job to watch closely whenever the ice cream vendors came to replenish our stock. I knew where the cones were kept, the straws, the cookies and everything else. Learning to clean the mixer blades from the malt maker was fun. It was always done after a customer had ordered a milkshake. I got the leftovers. I even knew where to go in the back-storage room to find whatever was needed in the store. I was the manager. Mr. Butts was proud of me for never being rude to any of the customers even when the customers were some of my friends – except for the *Demon Twins*.

My graduation came when I found myself wearing a white apron that was way too big wrapped around me at least twice and a little white cap on my head diving down into the kegs of hard ice cream to make a customer a cone. In addition to all my other responsibilities I was now a soda jerk – and I loved it. Sometimes if a girl that I liked came in and wanted a malted milk or a milk shake I'd offer her a second package of the one chocolate/ one vanilla cookies. Customers always got cookies with their shakes and malted milks. The shakes were so big that there was always an extra serving left in the big metal blender can. As I joyfully went about my duties, Mr. Butts came to me and asked for my help. He needed my help! Of course, I would help: I'd do anything for Mr. Butts. Once he explained to me what the problem was and how I could help solve it, I went to work. It seemed that over time many customers had dropped money-both coins and bills over the counter and behind the ice cream cooler. There was a very narrow opening between the cooler and the counter. My job, if I chose to accept it was to retrieve to the best of my abilities all the money that had fallen behind the counter. It became more urgent since a customer had recently dropped a five-dollar bill behind the cooler. For me it was an adventure because the space was dark and too small for anybody but me. I gathered my tools: Mr. Butts" garden hand rake, a long stick and lots of bubble gum, a flash light and a ton of hope. As it turned out much of my extra "salary" came from behind the ice cream counter. While retrieving booty that Mr. Butts was aware of, I found many nickels and dimes and too many pennies to ignore. He knew. He also knew that it kept me busy and out of trouble-mom. I soaked most of the coins in warm water until the gunk dissolved away and then I'd clean them and count it as income. Sometimes in the summer before the sun came up Mr. Butts hosed down the sidewalk in front of the store. There was no horse playing in Owl Drugs! The place was always neat, clean and orderly. My mom even said so. By the time I turned twelve, I was making three dollars a week plus tips from the soda fountain-and free candy-mostly *Nut Chews*, my favorite. Life was good.

THE GALLOWAYS

Mr. and Mrs. Galloway were the oldest, most religious and most respected couple on the block, and they represented the good in people. They lived at 1510 Massachusetts Street in a weathered, two flat, brick structure a few doors down from us, on the same side of the street, right over the Plummers' apartment. Mrs. Galloway was in her seventies, skinny and mean. Mr. Galloway was just the opposite; he was in his eighties, fat and mean. All the kids on the block took a wide berth whenever they saw either of the Galloways coming down the street. They were just as likely to give you a short sermon as to say hello. Entering the Galloway apartment was like walking into a museum of antiquities. It was immaculate, beautiful, old things everywhere. Everything was shiny and polished. Each item commanded its place in the dignified atmosphere of their apartment. The furniture was warm and rich with years of care and attention paid to it. Each piece spoke of a time when people used their living rooms as parlors for funerals. The atmosphere was quiet, dignified. Any kid who had seen the insides of the Galloway apartment would have called their place creepy. It all came from a time in the past when living rooms were called parlors and often used for funerals. Everything was old, and precious just like the Galloways. And the apartment was dark. Gospel music always played softly on the radio, no matter the day, no matter the time.

Mrs. Galloway was a character right out of a comic book in both her appearance and actions. She looked like a chocolate version of Popeye's girlfriend, Olive Oil, right down to the bun on the back of her tiny head. She was the original 'Church Lady'. Nobody in the neighborhood was as religious or as righteous as Mrs. Galloway. It would probably have taken an act of God to separate her from her Bible. She had a passage for any and every life situation. If you got a splinter in your finger, she had a passage; if you lost your house keys, she had a passage. And nobody in the entire neighborhood was more respected than Mrs. Galloway. Unquestioned moral authority was her weapon. She represented righteous justice. The kids on the block didn't hate her; we feared her. Weighing no more than ninety pounds, she feared no one. She did not hesitate to scold any kid on the block if she caught them doing something wrong. And if any kid was bold enough or stupid enough to rebuff her, she went right to their house and reported them directly to their parents, and pretty much demanded that the matter be dealt with post haste. Unfortunately for most of the kids the parents were on her side. Often, parents would accompany her on missions of dispensing juvenile justice. Mrs. Galloway said something to me one day that remained in the back of my subconscious for years and I eventually came to understand her message probably better than she meant. I heard her say things like *"Cast your bread upon the water."* Unless I'm feeding the ducks why, would I do that? I wondered. Or she'd ask: *"If God is for you, who can be against you?"* Alvin Plummer that's who! I couldn't get the statement out of my head. *"Cast your bread upon the water."* And though she had passages for every occasion, that one stuck with me.

The Galloways were not the only grownups to guard the neighborhood and protect the children. The elders took ownership and responsibility for both the kids, and the neighborhood. The elder men were the community's the Paramount Chiefs and the women were the mothers of the tribe. The kids respected them. We lived in a real, live, thriving village. It was safe. If word ever got out that I had said or done something disrespectful to one of my elders, I'd be in big trouble when I got home. The adults would reprimand any kid they saw misbehaving. So, most of the kids didn't commit any delinquencies on or near their own turf and distance wasn't always a safe thing to rely on, either. There were exceptions. If I got a paddling at school for any reason, I got another paddling at home. Word of the misdeed would always get home before I did. At school, the teacher was the undisputed ruler, period.

One day I was playing with some other kids, a few blocks from home where none of our neighbors could see us. It was across 15th Avenue in the unfriendly white folks' neighborhood. We jumped a fence into a yard that had an apple tree and a cherry tree in it. We got dozens of apples and pockets full of cherries. We got away clean, I thought. When I finally got back home later, my mother asked me how many apples I had gotten in the raid. I was shocked. My mother would not hesitate to scold Richard, my 'big brother' from across the street or any other of my friends as quickly as she would scold me. I can't remember a time when I didn't know Richard. It seems to me that I met him around the same time that I met Jo. He lived directly across the street from us. He was at 1541 on the east side of the street. Richard was an only child. He was a few years older than Jo and me, so he played the part of our older sibling. He used to come into our apartment life he lived there and rummage through the refrigerator, looking for whatever he thought he might find. He was as much a part of our family as Jo and I were.

Mrs. Elliott, Richard's mother, whom we called, "Miss Dorothy", and who Richard called, "Little Mama" was a gorgeous and very dignified little woman. "Big Mama" was the name Richard granted his grandmother, Mrs. Danzler, "Miss Dorothy's" mother. Richard's mother had an air of sophistication about her that drew attention from all quarters when she walked down the street. She was a small, shapely and very attractive woman who doted on Richard. Mr. Elliott, who we called, "Mr. Earl" was quite the opposite when it came to Richard; he was the disciplinarian. Also built low to the ground, "Mr. Earl" was a very handsome man who also had flair about him. Together, he and "Miss Dorothy" made a striking couple and Richard reaped the benefits by having inherited their good looks. But unlike all of the other residences on the block, Mr. Elliott owned a business. He was the owner of a plumbing company which he eventually brought Richard into and trained. Compared to others in the neighborhood, Mr. Elliott made a lot of money. From as far back as I can remember, Mr. Elliott always owned a car. At first, he drove a blue 1950 Mercury but after that he drove nothing but new Cadillacs. Coming home from school one day, Richard asked me if I had noticed the new car on the block. I hadn't until he pointed out that the black four door 1952 Cadillac in front of his building was his father's. That car seemed to represent a clear dividing line between those families on the block who had money and those who didn't. The only other people on the block who drove black Cadillacs were Mr. and Mrs. Burt, the owners of the cleaning business. They were perfect black replicas of the Addams Family. They wore only black, looked and acted like zombies. However, Richard never seemed to be affected by the fact that his parents were 'moving up' financially; he was always just another kid on the block who rarely got into trouble and who I adored like my big brother.

The Elliotts were church going folks. Mr. Elliott was a strong member and deacon of Galilee Baptist Church. It was also the church Richard belonged to whenever he decided to go to church. When we weren't in church, we were in his room playing. Few if any other kids on the block ever visited Richard at his apartment. Jo pointed out to me that I was the only kid on the block who could visit Richard at his home. Until then I had never even given it a thought. Sometimes I would have sleepovers with Richard, and we'd stay up most of the night laughing and talking about everything under the sun, especially girls. There was one thing that he had in his room that always captured my attention and became my favorite past time enjoyment. I would stare and stare at it with amazement. On his bedroom wall was a huge balsa wood skeletal structure of an airplane. I was amazed at how intricate it was and how complex the inner parts of the plane were. I think his father put it together when Richard was a small boy. Sometimes I would go to church with Richard and look forward to coming home with him to see that airplane and Sunday dinner with his mother's delicious homemade dinner rolls that melted in your mouth.

To the Elliotts, I was there 'adopted' son and to the Longs, Richard was our 'adopted' son and brother. He and Jo acted so much like brother and sister that anybody who didn't know them would believe they were related. She would beg him to ride her on his big black Schwinn bicycle. He always obliged and he always rode her on top of the handle bars. Once she was aboard, he would take off down the middle of the street as fast as he could go causing Jo to scream at the top of her lungs, begging him to stop and let her off. Once she was off the dare devil ride, she would scream again for him to take her for another ride. This went back and forth. To her it was a private roller coaster ride. I had many great memories but those that stand out are few. Like brothers and kids everywhere, fights broke out from time to time. I was no fighter and even if I were, Richard was much bigger than I was. For whatever reason, I angered him one day and what he did to me I can't fathom to this day. Knowing that he had the size advantage and wouldn't dare attack me, I pressed my luck, pissed him off and he must have hit me thousand times in a split second. He hit me on every part of my body in a flurry of punches that left me stunned and bewildered. It was a scene out of a cartoon. I never saw hands, only a flurry. But strangely I wasn't hurt physically; it was just my pride that was shattered. I even refused to tell on him because I was too embarrassed. If "Miss Dorothy" had asked me where he hit me, I wouldn't have been able to tell her. All I could have said was that he hit me everywhere, all over at the same time.

My life and mind expanded immensely as result of one trip that I took with the Elliott family. It was the summer of 1953 that the Elliotts invited me to go with them to the Indiana Dunes State Park. I had heard about 'the Dunes' since I was a little kid, but I had never been that far away from the neighborhood. I felt special being invited along on the trip; it would turn out to be a totally new and life changing experience for me. My mother did not hesitate to give me permission to go, knowing that no other kids on the block had been given such an invitation. Richard and I scrambled around making the back seat of the car our personal domain as we headed out of the city on the forty-five-minute journey. At about thirty minutes into our ride, I noticed how the air smelled different the closer we got to the lake. The park was a few miles ahead, but the smell of the lake got stronger and stronger at every mile post. Then just as we reached the top of the last hill on our journey, the sky opened up before us and there was the majestic sight of Lake Michigan. I had never seen it before. It was magnificent. We had driven to the end of the earth and found water. I was awe struck, trying to wrap my mind around the amount of water that lay before me. On the map the lake didn't look so big. But stretched out before me was water as far as the eye could see. My imagination went soaring. I thought about what the ocean must look like and what it would be like to fly over that huge expanse of water, on my way to some foreign land. The lake and the shoreline of the beach held me captive and I found it difficult to put into words what I was feeling. That first time seeing the lake was permanently imprinted into my psyche. It was even more important for me to travel and see the rest of the world especially now that I had seen something so magnificent right in Indiana and so close to home.

On Christmas Eve I was at Richard's apartment. We were all in the living room which was beautifully decorated with lights and a tree and holiday music playing when "Mr. Earl" handed "Miss Dorothy" her Christmas present. It was a small case, the kind a bracelet or a watch come in. When she opened the case, there was a one-hundred-dollar bill inside. I had never seen a one-hundred-dollar bill before and right then I realized that the Elliotts were rich. I asked if I could hold it and "Ms. Dorothy" put it in my hands. I stared at the bill for a long time before handing it back to her. Again, I was in awe. Not long after that the family moved to the new house that Mr. Elliott had built on Arthur Street, on the west side of town.

The village that I lived in was alive and thriving. Kids had the absolute right of way down our streets and sidewalks. They dominated the streets. They were everywhere, playing on porches, running through gangways, climbing rooftops, screaming down the alleys, climbing trees, roller skating and racing handmade carts made from bottle crates and skate wheels called 'go-tars'. The children were the life of the community and drivers, especially, paid close attention to them. I had two very special friends when I was very young, maybe six or seven years old. One was a man called "Powder Face". He was a short, very dark, extremely soft-spoken man who was very smart. He used to tell me stories about places all over the world that he'd been and places that I didn't even know existed; he had been in the military. Powder was a veteran and a wino. He was never without his brown paper bag. I don't know how he got that way or where he got the name, but I was very safe with him; he was my friend. My parents thought so, too. They trusted him. I'm sure they knew more about him than I did. Deep inside I felt that he had suffered a big setback or tragedy in his life. Everybody knew "Powder". With a slur, he would always ask passersby: *"You wontsah wine?"* It sounded like a little song. Nobody ever accepted, but he always offered. We'd sit on the curb at the corner of 15th and Massachusetts, next to the fire hydrant, right in front of Mr. Butts' Owl Drug Store. "Powder" always talked. I always listened. On one occasion I remember he got angrier than I had ever seen him. A car came down the street too fast and he jumped up from his corner station and ran out into the street, right in front of that oncoming car, forcing it to screech to a stop as he yelled at the driver: "Goddamn it! Slow down, man! Don't you see all these kids out here playing?" The driver apologized and slowly drove off. We were all stunned. It was like he had never had a drink of wine. He seemed perfectly sober. It was really something to see. The other special friend was a very tall, golden brown, very beautiful woman who always kissed me. She looked like a movie star. I always looked forward to a big kiss that usually left lipstick somewhere on my face. It would always excite me just to see her. She made me tingle whenever she hugged me. Her name was Helen. To me, she was a princess. She was always dressed up in beautiful, expensive looking clothes and she always smelled good and I loved her for more than her Tootsie Rolls. My heart belonged to Helen. She would always ask me if anybody had been bothering me and I always thought Alvin Plummer. I got my first 'woody' hugging and smelling her. Helen was a prostitute.

I was four years old when I first thought about that little plant in the kitchen window and the experience sparked the beginning of my life's journey for understanding and 'truth' even though I didn't really know what the 'truth' was. I figured I'd know it when I heard it or saw it or tasted it. The important thing was to continue my 'search', to continue to act. Taking action was the key. I didn't realize at the time that I had begun a journey that would span my entire life. The only thing that was clear to me was that questions continued to come; the more questions I got answered, the more questions came. It wasn't long before I was asking serious questions about everything! Deep inside was an inexplicable urge to know and to understand things, all things, everything! Each answer opened a door of understanding just a little bit wider. I didn't yet understand the difference between knowledge and wisdom, so the pursuit of knowledge became my passion. There was something wonderful and profound about how the mind worked. Then I heard the 'voice' inside speak louder. I had ignored it at first because it spoke so softly that I barely heard it, but it was there all the time. It was very difficult but as time passed, I learned to quiet myself down and to listen very carefully for it. It was instinctive. The ideas came so softly and so quickly that I often had the feeling that they were just my imaginings. They came and they went. Soon I knew that all I had to do when the 'voice' spoke was to listen, listen with my heart. It became a game of follow the leader. If I second guessed and chose another course of action, other than what the 'voice' told me, I usually ended up regretting it. The 'voice' always gave the right answers or asked the right questions. I started slowly by silently asking: "Are you there," "Can you hear me?" Then I proceeded to talk, talk, and talk. I would spend the day discussing every minute detail of my life. I was nearly five years old when the 'voice' must have known that I was thinking about the little plant in the window. My sister insisted that I was weird if not downright crazy for talking to myself aloud and asking so many stupid questions. My mother did the best she could to keep up with the constant barrage of questions that I aimed at her. At one point her most uplifting comment was a verse from the Bible, and though the passage found a home in the back of my mind, it was much later in life that I fully understood the real meaning at the root of that passage: *"Seek and ye shall find"*. I intended to do just that. For every question that I got answered, three more questions appeared. No subject was off limits. I wanted to learn everything a person could learn. It soon became apparent that the very act of asking questions was the cause for getting the answer. If I didn't ask, I would not get answers. In my mind there was nothing a five-year-old could not accomplish if he put his mind to it. I was living proof of it. By age eight, I thought I knew just about everything. My idea of an exciting day was to go into my room with a stack of books, maps and music, and play my favorite piece, *The William Tell Overture*, better known to the kids as the theme from *The Lone Ranger*. It was not uncommon for me to pick up a random volume of the encyclopedia and just start reading wherever the book opened. My mother was close to insanity from the constant barrage of questions I aimed at her. At one point I decided to just start reading from A and go to Z. Jo considered me weird for staying in my room so much, reading books, listening to classical music and studying maps. My room was small, but it was as vast as the universe. In my private space I could go anywhere, be anybody, or talk to anybody, living or dead, with whom I want a conversation. The 'painting' in my head was becoming my life. I was beginning to see an image forming in my mind of what I wanted my future to look like. It was better than paint by numbers.

My mom was a goddess. She had mystical powers and could make any pain go away. She could solve any problem and she always knew exactly what words to say to make us feel better. We never went hungry; our clothes were always clean, and we said, "Yes, ma'am "and "Thank you" and "No sir.' We had the best mother in the world. Her name was Irene and she grew up in Blue Island, Illinois in the 1930's. She came from a big family of three brothers and three sisters. She was the second oldest of the girls, coming in behind her oldest sister, Aisalee. Her sisters in order from youngest to oldest: Annette, Alberta, my mom and Aisalee. From early on, my favorite aunt in the whole world from her family was Annette, youngest of my mother's sisters. Annette was a few years older than Jo and me and she was sweet. There was a quiet air about Annette that was calming. She looked just like a younger version of my mother. All four sisters were beautiful. But Aunt Annette was hot! Then when I was about eleven years old, Annette, my favorite aunt in the whole world made a left turn in life, got saved and joined the church. She was a teenager giving herself over to the Lord. I thought that was an odd thing to do. Since she had joined the church, she was not only hot, she was hot and holy.

There could not have been a more loving person in the world than my Aunt Annette despite her holy heat. Then her scandals hit! One after another the scandals were tearing me apart. In testimony it was revealed that when my Aunt Annette was a little kid, she, along with her brothers, stole cigarettes. I was devastated. Her image was getting a little tarnished as I held onto my love for her. Then another scandal hit. It was discovered that during an altercation with her older brother when they were both very young, she threw a cast iron plate holder at him. She hit him, too, right between the eyes. She had been guilty of theft and now assault with a deadly plate holder. I didn't know how much more I could take. I was reeling from the onslaught of bad news when the final arrow of injustice struck. Annette used to baby sit Jo and me. She was always willing to come over from Blue Island and spend as much time with us as possible. Jo and I suspected something was up with her, but we couldn't pin point it. When Annette came over, she always insisted that we all go outside for some 'fresh air'. She would disappear for long periods of time, leaving Jo and me together. We didn't really need her protection in the first place; we were on our own home turf. It was clear to Jo and me that she was up to something. In my eyes her third and final sin had been committed. She had stolen; she had committed assault against her brother, but this last one was worse. Annette had the hots for, of all people, our 'big brother' Richard! Since he lived right across the street, it was easy for Annette to just hang around until he showed up, which he always did. No wonder she was always so willing to come over and no wonder she always wanted to take us outside for 'fresh air'. It was Richard all the time; it was him who was making her boat float. Jo and I were just her means to an end. Then it all made sense why Annette always left Gary happier than she had arrived. Jo and I did a high five and kidded her relentlessly about Richard. Annette, our favorite aunt in the whole world was so busted!

My mother and her sisters were raised under very difficult circumstances. Both my mother and her oldest sister, Aisalee continued to study and get their educations while they attended the nearly all white Blue Island Community High School. But back home, it is alleged that her father, Mr. Thomas A. Thomason, better known to members of the family as "Dee", had more of a fancy for other women, new cars and shotguns than he did for his family. He kept a job, working at one of the steel mills along the lake shore. Every few years he got a new car and drove it to Gary to show us how well he was doing. I remember the new gray Nash he drove. I thought it was the ugliest car I had ever seen. Gone most of the time, he was demanding and abusive when he was home. My grandmother suffered heavily under his reign. One morning while "Dee" was meting out punishment to my grandmother, two of his sons, my uncles Raymond and Fred put an immediate stop to the abuse and physically put him out of the house, for good. At eighteen my mother decided that the first man with the courage to ask her to marry him, she would accept. Most young men who knew of "Dee" Thomason were too afraid to even try to date her when she was at home with her parents. The times were difficult for the family. My grandmother, Mrs. Ellie Thomason, formally, Ellie Moore, ran the house from sun up to sun down. She had a household to feed and manage. I remember, as a child when my mother took Jo and me to visit our grandmother in Blue Island, the trips were like visits to the country. She lived on 134th and Woodlawn Avenue. The little frame house was at the end of the gravel road. The street was a dead end. The canal ran perpendicular to it. In my earliest memories my grandmother had a wooden outhouse, located some yards away from the back of the house, near the field. I could never, ever forget the smell that came from the little brown shed. Jo hated it so much that she tried to burn it down. My grandmother was so angry with her that when it came time to braid Jo's hair, my grandmother braided it so tight that Jo's eyes became slits. She said it hurt like hell. I reminded her that getting braids were so tight they hurt like hell was a very small price to pay for burning down the outhouse.

Later my grandmother got an indoor toilet but for reasons I didn't understand, once it was used, we would still have to pour a bucket of water into it to flush it. That water came from the well outside the house and it served all of the household needs, except for drinking. Drinking water was purchased like milk from a white lady who lived a short car ride from the house. Right in the middle of the dining room was a big, black potbellied stove that heated the entire central section of the house. I especially loved the telephone. It was a tall, black, skinny, 'goose neck' phone that had no dial. If you wanted to make a call, you had to ask the operator. Too often, once you got your connection, there would be other parties on the line at the same time. Hence the name 'party line' came into being. There might be three separate parties on the same line at the same time, each trying to hold separate conversations. Our visits were adventures for me, like going back in time. During the summer all of our cousins came and there would be a house full of kids. Saturday night was bath night. My grandmother, with the help of the oldest girls would set up a big tin tub behind the potbellied stove for all the kids to take a bath using the same water. Girls went first. After every bath, a pot of hot water was added to the tub. By the time all the kids were bathed, the water was murky. But we were clean. It was common practice for my grandmother to use Lava soap. This soap was dark gray and so rough to the touch that it felt like it had gravel in it. That bar of soap lasted a long time because my grandmother was an expert at economizing. Once when three of us kids caught a cold, she applied one of her home remedies. First, she rubbed all our chests with goose grease. Next, she made each of us swallow a teaspoon of sugar with a drop of turpentine on it. Then heated wool flannel cloths were put on our chests and we were all covered from head to toe, tucked tightly under heavy blankets and ordered not to move. We looked like 'pigs in a blanket' as we all lay there on our backs baking like cookies in an oven and sweating like hell, not letting any air get under the covers. In the morning the colds were gone.

Early one summer morning, I had a chance to see my grandmother at work. She was standing on the back porch holding a live chicken by the neck in each hand and with a series of quick vicious twists, turns and yanks, she swung those chickens in such a way as to break both their necks at the same time. I could hear the loud 'crack'. But before she could do any cooking, we had to make sure there was enough wood to fire up the kitchen stove. First, she stuffed paper and kindling in to get the fire started. Then one by one, she lifted the iron plates that covered the top of the stove and she put wood into each opening. After a period, the stove was blistering hot and she was busy preparing dinner. The chickens that she killed that morning were on the dinner table that evening. Often Jo, my favorite aunt, Annette and I would go across the big field that extended about an acre out to the highway. To me it was a jungle safari. I imagined we were on an expedition to find a lost temple deep in the heart of Africa. The trip I remember most was when I kicked over a flat piece of a cardboard as we went marching through the tall weeds only to discover a snake underneath. It quickly slithered into the thicker weeds but that was enough to rattle me. It was a garter snake and was probably more afraid of me than I was of it. Annette just laughed at us two 'city kids. I never knew what we would encounter trekking through the tall grass but that only made the journeys more exciting. Across the field and the highway there was a service station where we went to buy the very simple things that my grandmother needed. It was the most fascinating place. On every wall and even on the ceiling, were weapons used in WWII. There were big guns and little guns, and shells, big shells. The place was filled with war memorabilia. The war had ended in 1945 and it was now 1952. I was eleven years old and everything was exciting. There were days while visiting my grandmother when I would run at my top speed for as long as I could. I ran like an antelope, just because I could. I had so much energy that when night time came around, I had no trouble falling asleep, ever. The crickets held concerts every night and, in the mornings, Samson, the rooster was always on time. Coming from the city, I thought my grandmother's house was definitely in the country.

In the late nineteen thirties, a dark-skinned man asked my mother to marry him. She accepted and left home. That man was William Beddow Long, my father. Later, when I asked my mom how he proposed, she responded, "He just said, "We're getting married, you and me." And that was it. "At first, I thought he was joking. He just walked in and said, "We're getting married."" He had the courage to marry my mother without hesitation. My father was clearly more of African descent than my mother. His nose was wide, and his complexion was a deep rich brown. His hair was short and dark. He was a tall man, standing well over six feet. His family tree had roots in Alabama from where my grandfather, James A. Long migrated. My mother's side of the family had some white and Native American blood in it. Each member of her family was fair skinned with straight hair. You could see the Native American features in my grandmother with her long straight shiny black hair. I often wondered how far back we would have to go in our family history on my father's side to find the ancestral family members who were slaves.

In 1940 my parents got married and moved to Gary, Indiana. One year later, on January 9, 1941, my sister, Jo Merriel Long was born. On December 27, eleven months later of that same year, 1941, I was born- both of us Capricorns, born during the biggest holiday season of the year, Christmas and New Year. For about two weeks Jo and I were the same age and it took me a long time to understand how that worked. I thought she was two weeks older than I was. Jo joked that for me to be so smart, I was pretty stupid. We had a happy little family, the four of us. My mother was our beloved 'High Priestess in Charge of Comfort and Miracles'. She could fix anything. She knew things. She could make me feel like there was nothing in the world that could harm me if she was around. Jo was my protector and hero in all things threatening. I ran away from fights;

she ran toward fights. She had a real penchant for getting into trouble. One day in the dead of winter, Jo arrived home without her coat. When my mother asked her where it was, she said she forgot. She had gotten so involved in a fight that she took off her coat and left it at the fight scene. Fortunately, a friend brought it to our house later. Dad was our 'Coach in Charge of Mental & Intellectual Pursuits and Challenges'. He did his best to keep up with my questions but in the end, he would usually direct me back to the books and encyclopedias. What really encouraged me to learn was my father's habit of saying, "Ask me again later." whenever I asked him a question that he didn't have the answer for. And nearly every time I asked the same question the next day, he gave me an answer and most of the time he'd be right. By the time I was twelve, I had randomly read most of several volumes of the encyclopedia and page after page of the dictionary. My passion for learning was not something that I talked about; it was my private, personal obsession, only allowing my mother a peek inside my mind from time to time. But she could only help so much; the rest was up to me.

CHAPTER TWO

Indiana Bell Telephone Company

By the time I was thirteen, it was routine for my dad and me to get deeply engaged in heated discussions about one topic or another. I was usually the instigator and aggressor in these encounters, challenging him to explain such and such and if he couldn't, I declared myself the winner. Most of the time he would prevail but often he would refer me to something that he had read in a book or in the encyclopedia. I always demanded proof from him to defend his arguments. He also expected no less from me. One discussion changed my entire outlook on life. During one of our weekly 'debates', my father, in making his presentation, used the word 'perfect'. I immediately pounced on him, arguing vigorously that nothing was perfect and that everything was in a state of change or 'becoming'. "Nothing is ever perfect", I argued. "Like this telephone directory for instance!" I said. "This Gary Telephone Directory is not perfect; it has flaws!" My father grinned, jumped at the opportunity and retorted, "Ok, Mr. Smartie Pants-then find it!", as he laughed and dismissed me forthright. I was steaming mad. At that moment I declared that I would read that entire telephone directory to find the flaw in it if necessary. Nothing is perfect, I angrily maintained.

The main thoroughfare in Gary, Indiana is Broadway; it runs right through the center of the city from the front gates of US Steel Corporation downtown from the north, right out to Crown Point south and beyond a distance of many miles. All the streets west of Broadway were named after the presidents: Washington, Adams, Jefferson, etc. The streets east of Broadway were named after the states of the union: Massachusetts, Connecticut, Pennsylvania, etc. We lived on 15th and Massachusetts, one block east of Broadway and nobody knew this better than I did. All I had to do to get on Broadway was to cross the alley behind our apartment building and I was on Broadway. I opened the telephone directory and started reading. I had gotten no farther than the city map of Gary in the directory, reading the street listings when I realized that the directory had listed Massachusetts Street at three blocks east of Broadway. Though I was prepared to read every page in the directly, I had read only a few pages into it and had found a blatant error! Nobody could argue with what I had found. I was ecstatic! With uncontrollable excitement, I showed it to my mother for verification and then with shoulders high, a gleam in my eyes and a big smile on my face, I showed it to my father. Totally taken aback, he said to me unexpectedly, "Wow, ok! Now what are you going to do about it?" I could feel my blood pressure rising as my immediate response was: "I am going to write to the president of the telephone company and tell him about the mistake." My father responded, "And what do you expect him to do about it?" "I expect him to respond to my letter, thank me for pointing out the mistake, and I expect him to correct it!" I said. My dad laughed and said, "Ok." It was clear to me that he expected nothing to come of my efforts. He was wrong. With my mother's help, I carefully crafted a letter and sent it to the telephone company. About three weeks went by then one day when I came home from school, both my mother and father seemed exceptionally excited. My mom told me that I had some mail, a letter from the telephone company! I could hardly contain my excitement as I opened the envelope. It was from the district manager of the Indiana Bell Telephone Company. It read in part:

"Dear Denver,

Thank you for your letter. It was very thoughtful of you to take the time and to make the effort to contact my office regarding the misprint in the Gary Telephone Directory that you discovered. You must be a very good student in school to be so observant and we appreciate your efforts. Please accept our apology for the error. I assure you that the error will be corrected right away and as a token of my personal appreciation, I will send you a first copy of the new directory,

Sincerely,
the District Manager."

My parents, especially my father, were proud and I know he was impressed with my diligent efforts. I was just getting started. It was obvious to me from the beginning that the little plant had some innate wisdom. It grew roots. What force made it do that? I constantly wondered; I could only think to call that force 'life'. It was there, an integral part of the plant and it caused the plant to expand and get bigger. The plant was alive! It was that simple. But what was this thing called life? The sun gave the cutting light, the fresh water quenched it thirst and my mother earned the credit for putting them all together. Life was there, in the plant, all the time, just waiting for the opportunity to show itself. How mysterious, I thought. The birds and goldfish had it for sure. There was nothing anybody had to do; life is just there. From what I could understand, it seemed to work from the inside out. Even if that plant had never tasted a drop of water, it would still possess the potential to grow-just add water. There are rules: and those fortunate enough to be alive must the rules. Life is law, I reasoned. Bad things happened if you didn't follow the law. That force is in me, too. I was alive. The mystic force was coursing through me, causing me to grow taller, just like that plant. I had not asked to be alive and I knew that the little cutting hadn't asked either. Nevertheless, I had enough fortune to be born and become an inquisitive human boy. The plant and I had a lot in common and it had answered a lot of my questions. It 'knew' better than most and certainly better than my sources, what it was supposed to do. All I had to do was observe and continue asking questions. The plant would do the rest. Having questions meant that there had to be answers. How could there be a question without an answer? I was determined to find them. It seemed somehow my life's purpose to seek out the answers to these questions. Nobody had explained it to me, but I was becoming more and more aware of the laws that made my little life function. It was simple at first: do bad things-bad things happen. Do good things-good things happen

From Plantation To Salvation

Like most black folks of my generation living in Gary, Indiana, I was born into Christianity. My family was Methodist, at least my mother was. My father had no real commitment to any religion. He was what I called an 'Eastmas' Christian. He might only go to church on Easter and Christmas. The black families in the neighborhood were either Baptist or Methodist. The Poles and Hispanics in the neighborhood were Catholic. Only one black family that I knew, the Wilsons, was Catholic. I was best friends with Vernon, my next-door neighbor, the oldest of the four Wilson children. He was my age. For all practical purposes, we were brothers. We often talked about religion. I'd ask about the Catholic Church so much that one day he invited me to go to mass with him. So, I went.

He belonged to St Monica Catholic Church, some distance from the neighborhood where we lived so we just went to St. Hegewisch instead. It was the only Catholic school and church right in the neighborhood. The school and church took up the entire east side of the block, from Seventeenth Avenue, all the way to Eighteenth Avenue. The playground sat between the school and the church. It was the biggest and best playground in the entire area but only students from that school could play there. They were all white kids. When they weren't there, the playground was locked off to the rest of the kids in the area which made me wonder about Catholics. My visit was the first time I had ever been inside a Catholic church. When we walked in, I was flabbergasted! I had never seen a place of worship that was so elaborately decorated. There were statues everywhere; even the ceiling was painted; the walls were covered in religious icons. It was like walking into a palace. I was amazed. Why were there so many holy or religious things in the church? Why so much? My mind was in a turmoil about why his religious practice was so very different from mine. He was black, my age, my friend, and he lived right next door. We had both gone on many apple raids together. We had done the same kinds of mischief. So why were our religions so different? Was his better? I wondered. He was taught to call it the Lord's temple. When my family went to church, things were simple. The churches were just churches, not temples. That word, 'temple' stayed in the back of my mind. I understood it to suggest the home of some anthropomorphic god, a Supreme Being who was peering down on us from above. Deep down inside, I had a problem with that. I never forgot about the myth of Santa Claus, so I asked: "What is the truth?" Searching for the answer to that question became my focus.

I went to church just like everybody else. Most of the kids in the neighborhood went to church and there were many churches to choose from. My sister and I had to go to church, usually with mom. Dad stayed home and read the Sunday papers. For us, it was either go to church or stay home and not go to the movies or roller rink skating later in the afternoon. It was extortion so we went to church. Even though I wasn't giving my heart to the church, I did give it my mind. I spent a lot of time reading the Bible, trying to understand what it was saying. I studied it seriously, often approaching my mother with questions. She would just suggest that I go ask Reverend Davis, my mentor and director of the Stewart Settlement House across the street. The problem with Reverend Davis was that he was the one who confused me the most. He was the one reciting the Bible; it was him in the pulpit on Sunday mornings. He knew that I was not being arrogant when I questioned the Bible but curious about religion and how life worked. He did what he could to help me understand but I concluded that religion, like anything else, if you start with a false premise, no matter how you try to justify your answer, you're going to end up with a false conclusion. So far, nobody had shown me otherwise.

Our church was just a church; everything was made of wood. There were no statues. I thought of statues that I had seen in the movies. I didn't have the vocabulary to express my discomfort but inside, I had a problem with the whole statue, cross issue. I had that same problem when I went to my church. The question remained: "What is the truth?" Searching for the answer to that question became my driving focus. As I got older, Sunday morning services were a part of my weekly routine. Going to church meant that I would see girls that I liked but was too shy to approach. If I sat next to them in church, they would never be suspicious. It meant dressing up in 'Sunday clothes, hanging out on the corner at the Owl Drug Store after services, drinking nickel Cokes and looking forward to the afternoon trip to the movies or to the roller-skating rink.

It meant that for just one day a week, Sunday afternoon most black people across Gary, across Indiana and across America were gathering together and sharing dinner, the social experience that began centuries ago when the slaves first arrived. Even in my generation Sunday afternoon meant coming home to a big Sunday meal where the entire family and sometimes relatives would sit down together and feast. It meant giving thanks to the Lord for the bounty that was on the table before us. I, too, was sharing in that long-standing church tradition of socialization, but I couldn't understand why we did it. To me it made little or no sense. I felt no personal obligation to the spirit forces that held sway over my family and other grownups. My father worked every day; my mother worked every day and they took personal responsibility for my sister's and my wellbeing. If neither made the effort to provide for their family, what help would the Lord have offered? Summed up, I thought: "The Lord is my effort".

CHRISTIANITY

I imagined a slave family, four or five hundred years ago, sitting down to the same dinner table with meager rations, scraps from their master's table, giving thanks to the Lord for their sparse bounty. Why would they do that? Why be slaves? None of it made sense to me. One reading says: "*The Lord is my Shepperd I shall not want.*" It occurred that:" *The Lord is my Effort; I shall not flaunt.*" It is no secret that Christianity forced itself upon African nations all along Africa's west coast and deep into its interior by missionaries. It went on for generations. Africans were taught Christianity and then enslaved, or they were enslaved and then taught Christianity. This does not count for the millions who were killed. History has shown that the continent of Africa was fodder for the powerful European colonial powers —of whom, many were Christian. France, Spain, Portugal and England decided that the 'Dark Continent' was one big pie that they were going to carve up and share between themselves. The ten million Congolese who were mutilated and murdered by the 'Butcher of the Congo', King

Leopold of Belgium, were just a footnote in the history of the suppression of black people, especially in Africa. Africans were not Christians when they were stolen and taken across the ocean from villages in Sierra Leone, Liberia, Senegal or the other pillaged countries. Once they arrived in the west, ironically Christianity became their 'escape'. Sunday afternoon was usually the only day hey had free to spend with family, eating and sharing stories. Understandably they had begun to use the church as a haven. It was one of the few times they could congregate and socialize without raising the suspensions of their white masters. The focal activity was the family gathering around the dinner table. It seemed reasonable at the time that by adopting Christianity the slaves saved themselves tremendous social pressure and at the same time gain some degree of confidences from their owners.

Generations later Africans were becoming Christians of their own accord. Over the hundreds of years since their arrival in the west, they adopted their captors' religion. Over generations the strong religious traditions of Africa began to fade into memories as the older slaves died and younger ones replaced them on the plantations. More and more Negroes became Christians and bore children who also struggled as Christians to survive in a land that kept them in shackles. From one generation to the next, they supported the black community's only viable road to salvation, the church. One would argue that they did it solely for survival. And that would suffice for a time, but much time has passed since the 'official' abolition of slavery. We could question such rationale, not so much because of actions of the many but because of the validity and credibility of the teachings themselves. Doing whatever it takes to survive is understandable. What does it say about a religion that condones or even advocates slavery? How valid can those teachings be if its practitioners are doing so according to gospels that promote an 'eye for an eye' mentality? Slavery was not just a reflection of various religious practices. It was the law of the land. *"Slaves obey your earthly masters with respect and fear, and with sincerity of heart, just as you would obey Christ."* (Ephesians 6.6)

I was made to go to church and look at Jesus up there nailed to the 'old rugged cross' before I could go see Tarzan up there on the screen swinging in an 'old rugged tree'. I wielded my intellectual curiosity like a skilled surgeon with a scalpel. Nothing intellectually questionable escaped my scrutiny. It was important for me to understand what there was about Christianity that held so many people, especially black people captive. And if I went to church on the first Sunday of the month, I got a chance to 'drink of Jesus' blood' and 'partake of his body'. I reminded some people that there was a word for people who ate other people, even if symbolically. But to say that word aloud would have meant a real fight. All these things were going through my mind and nobody could offer me any reasonable answers. The good thing about the 'blood' in the communion ceremony was that I knew it was Welch's Grape Juice. The ceremony's real significance stuck in the back of my mind and would not go away.

In the past, certain warrior tribes in South America would consume the bodies of rival warriors. Their reasoning seemed fundamentally sound. If defeated in battle, in honor of their courage, the victor would consume the defeated warrior's heart so that he could take on that warrior's bravery. Likewise, his brain would be consumed so that the fallen warrior's intelligence would go to the victor. To both the winning and losing tribes it made perfect sense. It was a sign of respect and honor to consume your nemesis. Christians still think it makes sense even though it's just 'ceremonial'. You consume the body of Christ and drink his blood so that you may acquire his 'divine' qualities. Seems logical enough, but however you look at it, it's still cannibalism. The question remained: Why would anyone want to even 'symbolically' eat somebody? In the old black and white movies, the good guys shot the bad guys and together they would go and shoot up the Indians, but they never showed blood. A scalping only meant that you had to imagine the gore; you needn't worry about seeing it on the screen. I could even sit through a *Werewolf* movie and not see a single person bleed. *Dracula* was the closest thing to gore; and even he produced only two little drops. But again, the choice was either to go to church in the morning or stay home from skating or the movies in the afternoon. That choice was always easy: give Jesus a chance, especially since he was up there bleeding for us.

For the most part church time was fun time. During the height of the services, the minister bellowed phrases from the 'Good Book', the older members encouraging him on with soft, rhythmic chants of *"Yes, Lord"*, and *"Amen"*. The men dozed off, giving themselves away with their jerky, bobbing heads. The older women and mothers sat straight, alert, listening to every word, fanning themselves vigorously during the hot summer months. Most of the time I was with Richard, often deciding whether to take a dare and fart during the services or pretend to drop my psalm book on the floor so I could look under some girl's dress. Sunday service was the social event that brought all the church-going members of the community together in the name of brotherhood. There were always banquets and celebrations going on and always plenty of food. The music and the choir singing at a pitch kept you focused. Sometimes the music made us want to dance. Sometimes we did. Easter Sunday was the big day. Even adults wore new 'Sunday clothes' on that day, though many had not been to church since the previous Easter Sunday. When asked about the significance of that holy day, I was told that it celebrated the resurrection of Jesus, his rising from the dead to ascend into heaven. My head exploded. It was the story of the *Ascension of Jesus into Heaven*. How could anyone believe such a story?

In defense of that myth, the *Shroud of Turin* was offered as proof that Jesus rose from the dead. The shroud in which the body of Jesus was allegedly wrapped has imprinted into it, an image of a man which believers say is the image of the body of Christ. Upon his resurrection, Jesus' body passed through the cloth, leaving the image because the shroud was allegedly found folded, just as it had been when Jesus was wrapped in it. *"He ascended into Heaven and is seated at the right hand of God, the Father."* It's taught that forty (40) days after his resurrection, Jesus, in the presence of eleven of his disciples, on Mt. Olivet, outside of Jerusalem, physically floated into the air and up to heaven where he sat next to God, his father.

I was not buying it!

"Amen!" "My rock!" and *"Can I get a witness?"* were the phrases of the day and for just that day, everybody seemed to be paying homage to the Lord. As hard as I tried, I could not understand why. Nevertheless, church was fun unless you had to sit next to your mother or Mrs. Galloway. The absolute best time to play undetected and at the same time develop your delinquency skills was during the sermon. The height of accomplishment was not to laugh when a friend did something stupid or funny during services. And of course, the more you resisted laughing, the funnier it got. On one Sunday in particular, Richard and I were in church. We sat on the same row but on opposite sides of the center aisle. Neither of us sat on the

aisle seat, so we had to somehow communicate in front of the people sitting next to us. Richard's head would pop out intermittently and spontaneously from the other side of the audience. Back and forth his head would pop with me never knowing exactly when to lean forward and look down the row. This went on for some time. It would be my turn, then his turn. We never knew exactly when the other's head would pop out. But when his head popped out the last time, his finger was in his nose and he quickly gestured as if to put a booger in his mouth. We both nearly got put out of church because we both lost it, breaking out into uncontrollable laughter. And on other occasions while the congregation paid tribute to the Lord, I honed my penny pitching and jackknife skills out back on the playground. After services, the evening gospel music programs flooded the radio waves but by then we were always off to the movies or the roller-skating rink.

THE BIBLE

As I grew older, I began to look at religion more seriously. A little jackknife throwing incident scared me back into church. One bright, sunny Sunday morning, as services were going on, a group of us guys were sitting in a circle on the grass, outside playing jackknife. On my turn, I took the knife, slowed down the game by 'praying' for a perfect throw and then I threw the knife as hard as I could. It was a perfect throw. The knife miraculously split the sole of a friend's gym shoe. There the knife was with a blade about six inches long, completely embedded inside his shoe. His toes were lying on top of the blade. It looked like it belonged there. Only the handle was visible. It looked like a butter knife separating a stack of pancakes. For a moment there was absolute silence as we all processed the unbelievable sight. Then we all exploded into laugher. For months afterwards we laughed about it. The incident ended my knife throwing days forever.

Back in church I had more questions. I began seriously studying the church's practices. I began to read and study the Bible. I read with the intensity of a student studying for an exam. Month after month I read. A year went by, then two. My attitude hadn't changed. I still felt that a question deserved an answer and not just any answer. I was still getting answers about a god, life, heaven and hell that did not fit reality. I wanted to believe in something, but the Bible was not it. Those churchgoers around me who professed absolute faith in the Bible were no better at explaining. There was only impatience and intolerance with my constant questioning of the gospel. From my perspective, everybody was subject to the same laws of nature that I was subjected. I was not special in any way. There were never any exceptions to the laws in real life but there were many exceptions written in the Bible. I had a big problem with that.

By twelve, my body was slowly beginning to change. Words that I knew to be associated with sex were popping up more and more in the conversations around me. Boys were awkwardly talking about it, snickering aloud to disguise their ignorance. The girls already knew everything. They were way ahead of us when it came to understanding things like nature, girls or sex stuff. For me, someone who had earlier thought his sister was two weeks older than him, the talk of sex seemed to add fuel to the fire of hormones and the confusion of my awkward pre pubescence. Girls started looking good. I gave them more and more of my attention. The gesture was not usually returned; I was not deterred. I thought about Helen and I felt when I hugged her. That feeling was much stronger now. In no time, I began to understand that my 'ding-a-ling' was to be used for more than just taking a pee. I wasn't quite sure what it was, but I knew I was onto something. Accordingly, girls and talk of sex got my absolute immediate attention. By the time I was a full-fledged teenager, anything that had hair on it, had my attention. One day I put it all together: one plus one equals three, boy plus girl equals baby! Girls were everywhere; I allowed them to demand my attention. I felt a sexual attraction for every girl. I began to see life through white cotton panties. And then I was introduced to the quiet Christian couple named Adam and Eve.

ADAM AND EVE

As a teenager, I prided myself on my seeking mind; I was learning at a rate that surprised me. I was the super computer brain. It was ignorant for me to think that I could know everything back when I was only eight years old. I had to be at least thirteen before I could know everything. Even more importantly, I knew about sex! How could I not be the coolest kid ever? To prove my awareness, if a girl had the nerve to suggest it, I'd have shown her 'mine' if she had shown me 'hers'. I found myself having to negotiate two seemingly unrelated subjects: puberty and religion. When the time came, I gave a big *"Hooray"* for Adam when I read Genesis. My sympathies were with him because I could honestly say to Adam that in my current hyper sexual condition: "I would have 'boinked' Eve, too. If you don't, nobody is ever gonna' have sex!" I imagined Eve was a hot chick, a thirty-four double D with nice nipples. She'd have a nice bush. But Adam put all of humanity on the road to damnation when he smoked the first cigarette afterwards. She 'rocked his world'. That was fine.

The problem with the fraternization of Adam and Eve, the progenitors of humanity, were the consequences of such a unity which apparently nobody considered when they wrote about it. Where 'the First Couple' came from was another problem for me. The scene is set in Genesis, in either Testament, it doesn't matter. In the scene a serpent (as in snake) in the Garden of Eden spoke to Adam and said something like: "Psssssss, yo, Adam, don't do it. You'll be sorry". But Adam went on and did-the-do with Eve and got her pregnant: she was officially 'the First Pussy'. Eve gave birth to a healthy son name Cain. Then another, Abel. And because of jealousy, Cain killed his young brother, Abel. Just suppose they had not come to such a tragic ending. What if Cain and Abel continued to live? If this family is the progenitor of the humanity, they are off to a very bad start. With two growing sons, Adam and Eve would have to keep 'going at it' until they got a girl who would have to keep having girls to supply the boys, their brothers. Then all of the older sisters would have daughters who could later mate and have sons and daughters with their other brothers, sisters and cousins, nieces and uncles. It would be one big happy incest orgy.

For the 'Adam and Eve Family' to have survived, they would have had to give birth to girls and boys. Even that brings this issue closer to the genealogical facts of the situation. One family inbreeding over the entire period of humanity, say since Genesis, would have produced a race of feeble minded, maladroit knuckle draggers.

On a more serious note, if I were a prophet and wanted to pass down my message of salvation to all posterity, the best way I know to do that would be to write it all down, sign it, date it and make sure my closest disciples kept my documents safe and protected them so that there could be no questions as to the legitimacy of my message. In this way there would be no doubt. It would leave little room for speculation or random interpretations. Hypothetically, the true written word would come from me, not my devotees. Documentation counts. Who can argue with that? We know what happens to a message when it is conveyed verbally or sometimes even in written form. Before long the message has completely changed. The same problem would occur if, again hypothetically, two hundred or so years after my passing, my devotees decided to write down what they thought I meant when I was alive, what my beliefs were. With the best of intentions my twelve closest devotees would produce at least twelve different versions of what they thought was the 'truth'. Perhaps because of my analytical mind and lust for reason and rationality, my tolerance for anything short of reason, is limited. And it appears that I am in very good company. Plato also promoted the dialectical style of inquiry in which the pursuit of truth is sought through questions, answers, and additional questions.

One of the strongest reasons that would have prevented me from documenting my ideas if I were a prophet was that I couldn't read or write. Even if dictated to another, my message would still be secondhand at best. If I couldn't read, then how could I proof what was written? It would seem unkind to mention Jesus and illiteracy in the same sentence, but that is a reality of Christian history. Scribes did the writing and the research. The greatest works of literature, music, and science have shown this to be so. Failure to do so provides ripe opportunities for misunderstanding, misinterpretations and worse, misguided uses of that theology. Strained social, political and religious relationships around the planet speak to the travesty of wars and human suffering, based on misinterpretations of religious doctrines. Under such circumstances peace and harmony are unachievable. It seems to me that one blatantly obvious reality about life is that it is governed by laws, not mysticism. One such life law states that in time everybody will die, period. It is law because it applies universally, always, at all places. Nobody can skirt around or cheat this fundamental reality. To argue otherwise is folly. Another fundamental law of life is gravity. Science says that people cannot walk on water, unless it's ice, because it defies the law dictated by gravity and the density of water. But in church I was taught that the laws could be defied. I was told that Jesus, the Son of God, could do all these things. How or why would He shape my life but not teach me or anyone else how to perform miraculous deeds, too? If I had that power, I know plenty of people who could use those skills. The problem was that humanity was not supposed to perform those deeds; miracles are reserved for only Him. I wanted to know how Jesus could save me and humanity when he could not or would not and certainly did not save himself. If He did it for our sins, then it was a wasted effort because sins continue. It defies logic. It would have been better to have survived and show others how to do the same. Suicide in my mind is not a heroic course of action. What's more troubling about the idea of placing one's faith in an entity outside of oneself, it renders you powerless.

One may ask, even plead for forgiveness and receive it, but that in no way exempts them from the consequences of his or her actions. Then I remembered the passage from the Bible that said, *"Seek and ye shall find"*. It was becoming clear that to seek was the cause; to find was the effect. Life worked that way. Make a cause and in time, the effect is manifested! It had nothing to do with any deity outside of oneself. Understanding that changed everything. It also infuriates Christians.

To Rome With Love

I was fourteen years old, reading about Rome, Italy. My father listened as I went on talking about the magnificent monuments and buildings along the streets of Rome. Food, I continued was highly regarded around the world. On and on I went. A voice inside my head said, "I'm going to Rome." My dad must have heard it too. "I'm going to Rome", the voice repeated. Only this time I heard the voice come from my mouth. My dad was surprised when I told him that I was not only going to Rome but when I got there, people were going to love me. I was also going to have mad, passionate love affairs in Rome with beautiful girls from all around the world. They were going to love me. Some of these girls were going to fall so madly in love with me that they won't want to leave. I was going to dance the nights away in romantic and exotic splendor in hangouts throughout Europe. But before I do any of the partying, I was going to send you a post card. Rome, here I come. One the way, I was also going to find my life mate, my soul mate, 'The One'.

My father laughed and laughed. It might have been my delivery. I went on to tell him that there was a good chance that one of my romantic interests would be rich. It wasn't costing me a dime to dream, so why shouldn't she be rich and beautiful and want me? That comment sent my father over the edge laughing. That could happen. My dad was hysterical; he was in stitches. I was serious as I went on and on in minute detail. He could not contain himself. He laughed so hard that I started laughing. When I get to Rome, people were going to know it and welcome me with open arms, I reassured him. His laughter was uncontrollable. He even had my mother laughing. Then he jokingly reminded me that Rome was in Italy, across the Atlantic Ocean in Europe. He questioned how I was going to get there. At that moment, in my mind the whole picture was perfectly clear. I was living in Rome. It was just a matter of time before it all became real, just a matter of time. I vowed to my dad: "I am going to go to Rome if I have to walk to the east coast of the United States and back stroke across the Atlantic Ocean. And the first thing I do when I get there is send you a post card." On later reflection, I realized that my he knew exactly what he was doing with me. He knew that I would accept any challenges that he put forth and that I would be victorious in the end. I reassured him that I was also going to become a designer, known around the world for my contributions to humanity. "I want people from around the world to see my art and be moved by it", I proclaimed. People were going to talk about my work for years to come. I wasn't bragging, just reading from the script that rolled through my mind. The 'voice' dictated everything. The things that I said were simple realities. It was like saying "Today is Tuesday". I understood early that if I was determined enough to never give up on my ideas and dreams then they had no choice but to become real. What other possible reason could there be for even having dreams? I felt that deep in my heart. Something had occurred in me that I had never felt before. I knew that I could accomplish anything in the world that I set my mind to. Life was showing me that there was a purpose in being able to 'see' what you wanted. I couldn't convince anybody of my determination, but I knew as surely as I was alive that I would be victorious. From that moment forward, my life was set upon a path to get a college education and to go to Rome, if only to buy my dad a post card. I didn't realize it at the time, but it was faith. Intuitively, I knew that by focusing on that main goal, all the other dreams would also be realized. I remembered once 'traveling' to Egypt and Brazil when I was in my room, dreaming and listening to music.

Getting to Rome became so much a part of my psyche that I secretly started learning Italian, just a little at a time; I had years to learn it. "Become Italian", I told myself. I started becoming 'Italian', still black, a' *Blactalian*'. I began to study the streets, the clothes, the monuments, and the transit system of Rome so that I could get around easily when I arrived. I read about the food, the history of the neighborhoods and ethnic groups. I was interested in anything Italian. My biggest desire was to visit the Coliseum and sit there, alone, where, hundreds of years ago, gladiators fought and killed. Sitting there in the Coliseum would be my crowning achievement. I would sit there among the throngs and scream," Kill"! Oh, yes, I was going to Rome alright; it was my destiny. I was laser-focused. Fourteen years old and I had no idea when or how; all I knew was that some rainy night in the future I would be landing at the airport in Rome, Italy. I would be alone, and I'd send my father a postcard. Then I would always wake up. I had never been so certain of anything before. Beyond my understanding was a burning, desperate urge to move forward, to lay the foundation now for what I wanted to happen in the future. Methodically I put all the pieces together to create a grand picture of life. I kept it all to myself and built upon it block by block. It made life exciting to know that I could plant a picture in my head and in time see it realized. Certain that if I shared my thinking with anyone else, they would simply laugh at me and tell me I was crazy or maybe even steal my dream. It didn't matter, holding the picture in my mind was fun and there were no limits to what I could put in the frame. From time to time my mother suggested to me that maybe God was talking to me. "Ma, I don't think so".

The John Stewart Settlement House

There was a group of nine of us loitering in the lobby of the Stewart House at the same time. Somebody decided to take a picture of us. In an instant we all bunched together struck our poses as the flash went off. A moment in my life's history was frozen in time as we stood there. It was the fall of 1956. Above me were *"Big Nate"* Moore, next to him was *"Chilli"* Smith, Charles Suggs, Lenrow Smith, Alvin Smith and Percy Bell. Kneeling were *"Little Charles"* Carter, Charles Blair and me. We all felt the moment was special. Then Reverend Arthur W. Davis, "Reb", walked in and we all scattered. I worked at the church, Delaney Memorial Methodist Church right across the street from our apartment on 15th and Massachusetts St. The church supported the Stewart Settlement House that was housed on the lower floors of the same, huge, five story Georgian structure. I spent many of my waking hours there, either on its playground, in the basement or somewhere within the inner sanctum of the mysterious and spooky top floors. I knew every room, hall, closet-every hiding place in the building. I knew the building better than Rev. Davis. It was like my own private haunted castle, only I wasn't afraid in it

On one of my adventures, I discovered a storage room on the very top floor, hidden away from everything else. When I looked inside, I found a stack of green, folding, sleeping cots that had been used for the nursery school kids many years earlier. Those were the same cots that Jo and I took naps on when we were tots and went the Delaney Nursery school.

If I wasn't in school, I was at the Stewart Settlement House. "Reb" was Minister of the church and Director of the Settlement House. Reb came into my life when I was about eleven years old, the same age I met Mr. Butts. I met Mr. Butts first. Reverend Davis would come into the drug store often. When our paths crossed, we became fast "buddies". Reb had his 'business' (the church and settlement house) on one end of the block and Mr. Butts with the drug store was on the other. The neighborhood was alive. Soon I was spending my time across the street at the settlement house, playing baseball basketball, and my favorite, horseshoes. Reb was born in 1907 and raised in Indianapolis, Indiana where he attended public high school. I kidded him about being just one year younger than the city of Gary. He received his A. B. degree from Fisk University in Nashville, Tennessee. He was a very smart man and for nearly his entire career he was dedicated to the church, having held many different leadership positions in various churches throughout the country. We bonded instantly. I was already living on the block when Rev. Davis first came to town. His assignment was on my turf. It wasn't long before "Reb" knew every kid in the area and every kid for blocks around knew him. He took no back talk, period. He had a very pleasant disposition, often laughing and joking with the kids who swarmed to the recreational facilities at the settlement house. Whether inside during inclement weather or outside on the vast playground, "Reb" was always on alert. He was a very handsome man with a ruddy brown complexion and salt and pepper hair. He was short and fat. Like in a cartoon, he resembled a chocolate bowing ball with legs. But his size was deceptive because he was fast, very fast. If any kid said something smart to him, they had better be standing a safe distance away from him because he would pounce with amazing speed and put that offender in a vice like head lock.

By age sixteen, I was working at the Stewart Settlement House part-time, running errands and sweeping floors. As I grew older, my job responsibilities grew until I was partly responsible for opening the facility. It was also my job to make sure all the sports equipment got turned back in at the end of each night. I unlocked the basement recreational area when six o'clock rolled around and made sure it was locked up at nine o'clock when the evenings ended. I was even in charge of the sound booth downstairs where we played records for the many dances that Reb permitted. The dances were free, fun and without fear. Nobody came into the Stewart House, let alone to a party, with alcohol on his breath. It would attract Reb like a bear to honey. If any kid got out of line and used foul language, Reb would physically headlock 'em, pick them up and carry them out the front door. All bystanders were behind Reb up, not that he needed any backing up. The offender would have to come and apologize to the other kids for being an ass before he could back into activities. One summer night Reb gathered all the kids together and offered us what he considered a treat. He seemed more excited about what was in the box than the kids were. There were three huge, flat boxes. I thought that was odd. Inside was an enormous round crust with tomatoes and cheese and sausage and more cheese. What the hell was that thing, I thought without uttering a sound. I tasted it and, asked, "What is this?" He looked at me smiling and said, "It's called pizza".

Reb trusted me with all kinds of tasks, even his bookkeeping records, I felt comfortable talking to him about most topics, but God was usually the main topic of discussion. I asked Reb: "How was Jesus any different than Santa Claus?" He admonished me mildly for the comparison then said Jesus had performed miracles; he had given sight to the blind and he fed the multitudes with a loaf of bread and a few fish. Jesus was the son of God who died for our sins. He was our savior and when his work was done here on Earth, he rose from the dead and ascended into heaven to be with God, his father. My head exploded. But Santa performed miracles, too, I argued. Anybody who can raise reindeers that fly and who can bring toys to millions of children around the world by coming down their chimneys, even when they don't have chimneys and do it all in one night, was definitely performing miracles to me. He shook his head and laughed dismissively. Initially my attention during church services was somewhere else. I daydream constantly. It didn't matter if it was Delaney Memorial Methodist where Reb was or my mother's church, it all said nothing.

Either sit through a sermon or miss the new *Tarzan* movie at the Roosevelt Theatre. One day while I was working at the Stewart House and Delaney Memorial Methodist Church, sweeping the main chapel floors making sure it was clean and orderly, I discovered the 'wine' used for communion. It was left in the refrigerator after services. It was my favorite: Welch's Grape Juice. Once a day, I would take a little drink and replace the amount I drank with water. It didn't take long before the juice started looking like grape Kool-Aide. What I was learning in school and what I was learning in church did not match up. There was a problem with one of them. Intuitively God never made sense to me. And the more thought I gave it, the more I questioned it. That was how I felt, but I never said anything. The older I got, the bolder my questions got. I spent time searching for answers. It was clear: Christianity was not the answer. I concluded that the teachings themselves were flawed. There was no getting around the fact that I was being taught one thing about God, but my experiences were giving me different messages. I received real life messages that completely contradicted the ideas that I was being taught in church. There was a huge elephant in the room. Life always functioned according to strict law. Therefore, I reasoned, the conflict must lay in the teachings that arise from the Christian point of view. How does one rationally ignore the laws of physics that present themselves whenever some part of the Bible is questioned?

I was frustrated. How could people follow a system of belief, faith aside, and not ask fundamental questions about its teachings. It takes courage to seek the truth and question everything that is not understood. It became clear to me that 'universal' laws governed my life and no matter what I thought or did, those laws never varied, and they applied to everybody, regardless of color, gender, age, social status or religious belief. The little plant cutting had proven this to me a long time ago. Life is inherent in the universe, waiting to come forth, to come to fruition in its multitude of forms. The life force that allowed the little plant cutting to manifest its destiny was the same life force in me and everybody else. Life comes into fruition and then declines. The unavoidable conclusion is death. The law dictates that all living things will die! There are no exceptions. No one would truly deny that all things age as they pass through time The life cycle is birth, maturity, old age and death. Nothing escapes. There had to be another dimension that preceded birth. At one end is birth and at the other end is death; they must be connected. Can't have one without the other. I saw two sides of the same coin. If that be the case, then life must manifest itself in either one or the other of these two dimensions; we are either alive or not alive, but always existing in the universe. Repetition is the word that clarifies it all; life repeats over and over and over.

One argument from a critic for an 'exception to the rule' situation might say that there are places in the world where it does not get dark at all for three months out of the year; the day lives on and on, disagreeing with the repetition position. For such an argument it would be logical to contend that just because one's eyes are open does not mean that they can see. The seasons come and go regularly, bringing with them the years, each season knowing exactly when to arrive and when to leave. The planets rotate regularly according to their rhythms. Birds head south and return at the right time. I awake, full of vim and vigor, fill my day with activities, then I slowdown in the evening and rest at night. Even the casual observer can see that life has its own rhythm or multitude of rhythms, manifesting in myriad forms, all subjected to very strict guidelines which exclude no one and form our collective 'life experience'. In church they used to say that when you die, you go to heaven and live forever. My opinion is that such a rationale is an abandonment of reasoned thinking, supported by science. Living in heaven for eternity is another way of saying that we 'flatline'. That notion simply contradicts the basic cyclical rhythm of the universe. And if going to heaven was so important and wonderful, why do so many of its profligates cling so tenaciously to life?

In all my life experiences, I've never known, or ever seen anyone rise from the dead. To say that you had seen someone rise from the dead-after three days, either puts you in the category of a loony or the deluded. When my parakeet died, I wanted nothing more than for it to come back to life, but it never did. My dog never returned. My grandmother and grandfather never returned. The Bible says that Jesus *"Rose from the dead, ascended into heaven and sat on the right hand of God, the Father Almighty; from there he should come to judge the quick and the dead."* Not that it is the ultimate test, but the kids and especially the adults that I grew up around would never admit to following a man who claims a life of celibacy and could not read or write. Reason and forethought are much too difficult to deal with; it is much easier to just go to church and pretend. Pretend that Santa Claus is still coming to town. Pretend that Jesus was literate. Ask a church-going Christian about the sex life or literacy of Jesus, you would get either no answer or one shrouded in mystery. That is not to say that an illiterate cannot lead the people. Illiteracy, alone, is not the problem. In my opinion the problem appears when we don't consider the consequences of not documenting a teaching. I asked myself: Why are there so many different types of Baptist and Methodist churches? What would Jesus say about the broad spectrum of diversity that exists in both the policies and practices of the modern houses of worship? Why are race relations in America the same, if not worse than they were decades ago?

America is a Christian country, whether we admit to it or not and that fact is the foundation of American thought and its value system. Why is America constantly engaged in war? Why do we support death penalties? The general rebuke to that is the Christian response: 'an eye for an eye'. Let reason prevail. Christianity commands a powerful grip on the minds of many Americans who, due to their own absolutist attitudes about their beliefs, refuse to step out of the darkness and into the brilliant light of reason. It is not my intention to discredit Christianity but to shine a light on ignorance that shaded my early life. I had the very good fortune to never stop asking questions.

ON THE PATH

The 'voice' had always been positive and had taught me from the very beginning how to live life and live it happily; I didn't always understand or sometimes even obey. The voice did not teach me how to die or to worship the dead. Either way, I was seriously seeking. Who should I trust, my mother, the reverend or the 'voice' inside? I don't hold it against her, but it was my mother, it was she who had turned us on to Santa Claus. Reverend Davis worked for Jesus, so I knew where he was coming from. The problem on the surface was simple. I was in school, living and learning about science and how the world worked. Many laws of nature are clear. There were the cycles: hourly, weekly, monthly and annual cycles. There also life cycles. These things don't change. I understood that. I was seven years old when my parakeet flew into the clear glass window of our dining room door and broke its neck and died. Jo and I held our mother totally responsible for the tragedy. While we were in school mom had removed the curtains from the dining room door so that she could clean the glass. Before she completed the task, Lulu, flew right into the glass. Jo and I held a solemn private ceremony in the vacant lot down the block. Lulu never flew back. I felt then what death was. It was all an accident, but our bird was still dead. Life can be harsh, but ignorance does not invalidate the workings of the law. In time life is reborn into the universe.

Life and death represent two sides of the same coin. It was my reasoning that the 'coin of life' consists of heads and tails. Heads is life; tails is death. Flipped by karma, life expresses itself to us. At some point in time the down side of the coin will be the up side. The two sides are inseparable. These were my conclusions and I was sticking to them. In church I saw Jesus nailed to the cross, blood running from his wounds. My question was: Why would I worship a symbol that represented such suffering? It's easy to die. Everybody is going to die, and they won't even have to do anything special except be alive. The difficult thing to do is to live and to live happily. Life appeared amazingly like the cycles of a 24-hour day. A part of the time is being spent in dormancy. That is our sleep cycle and the other times, in our awakened state, a time when we go about our daily activities making causes that continuously affect our lives and our futures. I concluded that if this cycle existed in the everyday phenomenal world, it would be totally inconsistent for human life to simply stop short, never to go again. According to the gospel, if we lived the life of Christ, we would even have everlasting life in heaven. Even hypothetically that did not work. The coin has two sides, not just one. In one instance, I was experiencing life firsthand, deciphering phenomena as I lived from day to day. In another instance, I was being told to ignore these basic instincts and laws and believe something that was in direct contradiction to what I knew to be true. At first it was confusing, then infuriating. My search continued. I should not believe my lying eyes. The person who bore the brunt of my questions was my mother, who, after listening to my exhaustive perspective, simply replied, "I don't know the answer to those questions, sweetheart. You should ask Reverend Davis." My head exploded-again! That was of little consolation since I knew his answers were based solely on the basis of me questioning the credibility of the Bible and he was right. I was doing exactly that. It was the minister and his church services that had confused me in the first place. When children are old enough to ask questions, they are old enough to get answers. "Reb" had suggested that I "Have faith in the Lord". I remember clearly how frustrated and annoyed I felt with that response.

By the time I was seventeen, I was totally disillusioned with Christianity. It was still my opinion that a simple, straight forward honest question deserved a simple, straight forward honest answer. How could you learn if you didn't ask questions? It made perfectly good sense to me that if what a person believed didn't fit with the realities of what that person experienced, then the belief system should be called into question.

The teaching should fit the physical laws that govern life; in my opinion they should explain them. There should be a harmony between belief and reality; one should actually reflect the other. Faith should equal daily life and practice. I eventually lost all interest in church and started reading about other religions and philosophies. But I wasn't mad at anybody. My search intensified.

I read Plato, Socrates, Aristotle; I read Kant, Descartes, Sartre, Kierkegaard, Schopenhauer, some of whom directed me to an inner awareness that I had not known before. I read about the religions of India and Africa and found myself particularly fascinated by the eastern traditions, particularly Hinduism. At first especially interesting to me was the Hindu view that opposing theories are only aspects of one eternal truth, like my two-sided coin analogy. The idea of 'one eternal truth' sounded a lot like my notion of a universal law, a law from which all others derived. It was unusual indeed, though, that Hinduism, the world's oldest faith, had no one founder and no authoritative scripture such as the Christian Bible or the Muslim Koran. I wondered how such a religion could remain intact after such a long time and still affect the lives of so many millions of people. My conclusion was that it had to have been the validity of the teachings themselves that made it work. I was on to something. I was getting closer.

Kim Of Destiny

In 1958 I was a sophomore in high school. I still wondered what my purpose in life when one little girl made it very clear to me that I had no purpose in life. I was sixteen years old and she was three. We had a love/hate relationship. I loved her. She hated me. Her name was Kim. She was one of seven children. Her oldest brother, Michael, a high school basketball player, was about my age and one of my close friends. Kim had gray-green eyes and soft, shiny sandy, blonde hair that touched her shoulders with strands of it always in her mouth. Her complexion was like a light chocolate milk shake. She reminded me of a tiny mermaid. She was beautiful. My heart belonged to Kim. There was only one problem. Kim refused my existence. I tried bribery, flattery, promises, anything just to get her attention. She always kept her distance and just stared at me. Her entire family knew that she and I had this weird, non-relationship and they thought it was funny. I wondered how I had developed such a strange relationship with this beautiful little girl. Michael and I were good friends and he knew how much I was enraptured by his little sister. Under no circumstances would she speak to me or acknowledge me in any way, except to stare. And she kept her distance even in the presence of her brothers and sisters, even when her parents were around. She flatly refused to allow me into her world, and I couldn't fathom why.

I had never experienced anything like that before and I was baffled. When I spoke to her, she just kept her distance and continued to stare at me coldly. She had no reason to dislike me; I had always been nice to her. Candy that I offered had to go through one of her sisters before she would accept it. Nothing I did ever made a difference. Why my relationship with a little girl named Kim was so important to me was a mystery. Who was this little girl? And for whatever reason, it only made me think about my life even more. Why was Kim even in my life, I wondered? I wondered what there was about my life that repulsed a little girl whom I had known all her life. She was Kim Morris and she had imbedded herself deep into my consciousness. I doubted that I would ever forget her. Often when I was able talk to her from several yards away, I'd make little promises and tell her that one day we'd meet again and be friends. I told her that in the future when we meet that she was going to be sorry she treated me so mean and made me cry. Nothing. She just stared at me with an amplified indifference. She made it clear to me that the world could function without me. I tried to put myself in her position and see what she might see and feel. Try as I might I saw no reason for her indifference to me. She knew that I was friends with her brothers and sisters. Her parents even knew me. I made myself content with the idea that Kim was just a part of my life that only life itself could and probably explain-in time. I carried her in my heart though she never spoke a word to me.

CHAPTER THREE

The Art Institute Of Chicago And
The University Of Chicago

As far back as I can remember, getting a good college education was always a major desire of mine. Learning was my passion. My parents didn't have the money to send me to college, but I was determined to go regardless. In my focus and dream for the future I'd attend a very high quality, regardless of cost. Again, I found myself determined to accomplish something that seemed impossible. Little did I realize that right across the Indiana/Illinois state line was one of the finest universities in the nation, the University of Chicago.

During my senior year at Froebel High School, I visited an Industrial Design exhibit at the School of the Art Institute of Chicago. After seeing the incredible student product renderings in the exhibition, I knew then what I wanted to do. Industrial design combined engineering technology with art and design and I loved both. I had just designed the cover of the Froebel High School 'Steeldust' '60-'61 yearbook.

Mr. Roger Gilmore, a very tall wiry character who reminded me of Ichabod Crane from the story of the Headless Horseman, was dean of the School of the Art Institute. When I applied I was rejected. I took the rejection personally. Gilmore told me that my portfolio was not strong enough. I was devastated, but not deterred. So, for months I worked diligently day and night to improve my design and rendering skills. I would have to meet with Dean Gilmore again for my second admissions critique. I was rejected again. This time I was pissed. I was even more determined. Dean Gilmore in particular, might as well open their doors to me because I was going to be an industrial design student and graduate from the School of the Art Institute of Chicago-period. The clear picture was in my head. No matter how long it took, I was going to get into the school. When I went back for the third time Mr. Gilmore was there again when I made the presentation it was the charm. I not only got accepted, but he offered me a scholarship to defray most of my costs. I thought about the earlier experience with the Gary Telephone Directory and how I had been victorious. I felt that way again. It was important to have the courage to dream, to work hard and make dreams come true. I was learning to always be victorious no matter what. Never give up on a dream.

THE DiNOVO SANCTION

In the fall of 1963, I became a full time undergraduate industrial design student at the School of the Art Institute of Chicago. Along with that victory was the fact that my academic courses would be at, of all places, the University of Chicago. I was going to be a student at the University of Chicago! I was no slouch. "Watch out, world," I thought: "I'm coming through." I was one of only two African American students in the ID department. The other student never really seemed focused on school. His attendance was always poor, and his design assignments were never in on time. I became convinced of his laxity when he offered to share some weed with me on numerous occasions. Whenever possible, he would go out into the park and smoke some weed and then come back to class. I always refused. I was in my twenties and had never smoked any weed and wasn't about to start while I was in school.

My dearest and closest friend, Fred Mackey, however, was the 'poor little rich kid' back home in Gary, who promoted all of the bad habits among the guys in our 'gang'. He taught me a few naughty tricks. Younger than me by about four years, Fred was a master of mischief. Oftentimes when I went home to Gary and hung out with Fred and some of the other guys, we'd ride around town in one of Fred's new cars, usually the red and white Ford Thunderbird or his father's big boat-like Lincoln Continental. We'd ride all over town with the windows rolled up and the car filled with marijuana smoke, but I refused to smoke a joint, for fear of getting high. We would all laugh hysterically. I had never laughed so hard in my life. I was the joke. I was getting high and didn't even know it. My ignorance was magnificent.

Fred's father owned property. On the southeast corner of 16th and Massachusetts, Mr. Mackey owned the two two-flat buildings that were adjacent. On the corner at 1601 on the first floor was the Gibraltar Insurance Company. Above it on the second floor was the Mackey apartment which occupied the entire second floor. The adjacent building to the south was a hotel. Mr. Mackey was rarely around but Fred had keys to nearly everything. When he didn't have a key, he found other ways to get at what he wanted. His imagination for mischief making was astonishing. Maybe to impress me or to show how much he trusted me, Fred took me on an excursion, the likes of which leave me dumbfounded even today. We were at his apartment preparing to go out for a Saturday night of partying. Fred told me to follow him, so I did. We went out on the back porch of his apartment, behind his bedroom and through a little door that stood way to the side of the main stairwell. The opening was so small that we had to bend over as we traveled through the tight space. After a few turns, we were next door on the second floor of the hotel. We went down to the first floor of the hotel and then to another door that led us down to the basement of the building and crossed back over to the other building.

Fred unlocked a storage bin, climbed up on a ladder and opened a floor door under the insurance company. I didn't realize where we were until I climbed up into the office from the basement below. Not only were we in the closed office, but we were in the accounting room where all the money was counted. Fred had obviously done this many time before because he immediately went over to the corner of the room where there stood a large, waist high barrel filled to the top with torn and crumpled paper money. Fred grabbed a couple of handfuls and began stacking the bills accordingly as he smoothed out each bill. He must have smoothed out three or four hundred dollars right in front of me. Then he offered me a handful saying, "Here, you want some? Take some. All they're going to do with it is take it to the bank and burn it." I stood there, rattled to my bones, realizing what we had just done. I absolutely refused to take the money. I was furious with Fred for taking me into a closed office and burglarizing it. We had broken the law and I did not find it amusing in any way. Fred's argument was that it all belonged to his father anyway and he wouldn't care even if he found out. We didn't see each other for a while after that incident. But interestingly Fred and my father were buddies so he would still come around. They used to wrestle one another just to see who could be pinned down. Whenever my dad used to sit back in his recliner and fall asleep, Fred would take a handkerchief and place it over his face to see if he would wake up. He never did. When not occupied, Fred would claim the recliner, something I never did. Fred's visits became rarer after the insurance caper.

Fred's father, Fred Mackey, Sr. was a syndicate man. He ran the biggest policy operation in town; he owned the only black owned insurance company in the city. He also had various other lucrative enterprises. Mr. Mackey was a big handsome man. He looked like a Mafioso. There was an air of strength about him. Because of his businesses, he was rarely around. The few times he was near, he would talk and joke with me as if I was just a part of the family. I got the sense that he trusted me. He was impressed with the fact that I was serious about my education. Fred's dear grandmother, "Baby", however, was an entirely different story. She didn't like me; she didn't trust me, and she thought I was too old for "Freddie" to be hanging around with. Fred thought it was funny that his grandmother had me pegged as a bad influence on him when it was, he who taught me things that I dare not share. Asked why he doesn't tell her the truth, he argued it was more fun watching the two of us go at it. Eventually Fred slipped deeper and deeper into the world of drugs and we began to fade from each other's lives.

Back at school in Chicago, the other African American student eventually dropped out completely. For me, my studies came first. Everything else had to wait its turn. My firm determination was to be the absolute best student I could be. I had dreams to fulfill; the world was out there waiting for me and I would not let it down. Anyway, during my second year at school, I met Kay, a little cutie pie freshman fashion design student who also worked in the administration office. She was short, a real cutie with a dark, beautiful smooth complexion and long hair. And she had a body to kill for. Her hair was shiny and dark. She was a doll and full of an energy that you'd feel immediately when she was around. Many guys at school were trying to date her but she was perfect and meant for me. One morning I invited her to coffee as we stood near a coffee machine. She accepted and we found a table and began a conversation. We hit it off immediately. I liked her from the very beginning, and it wasn't long before our regular morning routine began with us having coffee together.

We started flipping coins for morning coffee. Whether she flipped the coin, or I flipped it, I won. On some mornings Kay would have another student flip the coin for us, to avoid any chance of my cheating. I still won. It was crazy. Students began betting on which of us would win the tosses and most of the time I won. For nearly an entire term it went on like that, me winning coffee nearly every morning. It was absolutely crazy, but it brought Kay and me closer together. Laughter became our language. We both admitted to looking forward to meeting each other every morning.

It was an exciting time in my life. I was in college. I had a job and I was working on a degree, something that I had always wanted. The environment was new, the people were new, the languages of intellect and art were also new. I had imagined things being like this when I was younger, but not to the extent it was happening to me now. The world was waiting for me. Nothing was going to prevent me from getting my degree in industrial design, nothing. I even challenged death to take a vacation until I completed this goal. Countless days and nights over weeks, months, years, I spent in books, on the drawing board, rendering, reading, studying, learning, growing, thinking, focusing and perfecting my skills. I was crazy focused.

Kay was the same way. She was completely absorbed and focused on fashion design and photography. We became good friends initially because we admired and respected each other's work ethic. Neither of us got in the way of the other's studies. She often invited me to her department to watch her work. On those occasions, I didn't talk; I just sat and watched. She would initiate any conversation and explain to me what she was doing. Sometimes the silence would go on for extended periods of time. They were quiet, golden moments. Other times she came to my department and watched me work. She would sit next to me, quietly, as I worked on a rendering, explaining to her what I was trying to accomplish rendering. She seemed fascinated at my ability to create such realistic looking product on a flat sheet of paper. Most of the other guys in the department weren't exactly happy about the fact that our relationship had grown so much in such a short time. One guy disliked me intensely because, as I learned later, he was hot for Kay.

Eventually Kay and I started dating and then going steady; we became a couple. We were told that we looked like the perfect art school couple, always together, holding hands, laughing and having fun. Tears of laughter constantly flowed with us. We were big fun together. Students often told us how happy we seemed when we were together. Like kids, we were alive, and madly in love. And like love stories in the movies, whenever our schedules permitted, we would steal away and spend time, both summer and winter, in Grant Park, across the street from campus. When we were together, we were together. We both knew, too, without much conversation, that our relationship would probably be over when I graduated. I was scheduled to graduate at least a year before she was and I would be going one way, she the other. We understood that and we were fine with it. Her name was Katherine "Kay" DiNovo. Kay was Italian.

During our years at school, usually on Saturdays, Kay made visits to Gary with me to see my folks and to spend some quality time away from the hectic school environment. Little did I know the path that our lives would take once Kay met my family. My mother and sister loved her from the very first meeting. It was uncanny the way they all took to one another like they had all been friends before. My sister pretended to be amazed at how much Kay liked me. She joked about how any girl could find me attractive. She got vulgar and suggested other reasons why Kay might find me likeable. They all laughed at that. The three of them, my mother, my sister and my girlfriend became instant friends. I thought it was unusual, but it was comforting. My father even coined her nickname; he called her "Shorty". He was well over six feet tall so to him, everybody was "Shorty".

On one visit, the three of them struck up a conversation in the kitchen that was just simply crazy. Whenever they got together and started talking, there was no end to what their conversations would encompass. They talked about food; they talked about fashion; they talked about personal experiences; they talked about everything. Then the subject of family histories came up and that's when the mysteries of the cosmos began to unfold.

Kay was living in, of all places, Blue Island with her parents while she was in school. My mother had attended predominately white Blue Island Community High School with her older sister, Aisalee, from 1935-1939, the year they both graduated. In school my mother's name was Irene A. Thomason. Hearing this, Kay shouted out, "My father went to Blue Island Community High School at that time, too." My mother asked Kay what her father's name was and to spell it out. Kay said, "Frank, Frank D-i-N-o-v-o". "AAhhhhhhh-h-h! You're kidding! I knew him! He had the 'hots' for me in high school!" my mother screamed. "He was the quiet type and had a birthmark on the left side of his face. He was Italian and he didn't like Aisalee because she always looked so unfriendly." She went on to describe him perfectly, right down to the way he walked and talked.

"That's my father! That's my father!" Kay shouted. "My father had the hots for my boyfriend's mother!" she screamed. The three of them were all screaming. "Ahhh-h!" "He wanted to take me out. But you know that wouldn't happen. My folks wouldn't have allowed it back then and you know his family wouldn't have approved. But he let it be known that he liked me. Aisalee would just stare at him whenever he came around, so he kept his distance from us. She would even get on my nerves sometimes with that stare of hers. I guess he saw her as my body guard. Most of the students knew about him," my mother continued.

The three of them were in stitches laughing. They couldn't stop laughing. Kay's father had wanted to date my mother in high school. What were the odds? My mother and her sister were small and fair-skinned. From their high school photos, they looked almost white. Almost! Kay's family, especially her father, never approved of our close relationship. Once they learned that I was black, it was all over. They wanted no part of it. Her parents had never met me; they had never seen me, nor had they ever spoken to me. They knew that my name was Denver, I was black and that was enough. Kay's sister, whom I met on one very testy occasion, apparently felt the same as her parents. Sparks began to fly as soon as I met her. I told Kay that one day I would meet her father and shake his hand, like gentlemen do. She assured me that would never happen. I assured her it would. Who could have imagined her father liking my mother in high school and then years later them both having children who ended up in an interracial relationship? I figured if that could happen, anything was possible. Nobody could remain so narrow minded his entire life, I argued. Kay assured me that her father would never shake my hand. He had brought his daughters up in a very conservative, Republican, Catholic tradition and was not likely to ever change his views. Kay was a Catholic by birth, but she had difficulty as I did with some of the tenets of the church. Like so many other things we agreed on, religion was near the top of our lists.

She helped me to understand that at the root of her father's disapproval of our relation was his deep-seated religious belief that somehow blacks were inferior to whites. It did not strike me as a particularly new attitude. Then we learn that he personally had had a 'hardon' for my mother, a black girl, in the 1930's. He was clearly a hypocrite of the highest order. To Kay and me it really didn't matter in the least that he or the rest of her family didn't approve. I was an African-American; Kay was Italian-American; we were a dating couple and that was that. As long as Kay and I were happy with one another and wanted to be together nothing else mattered. It was a time of social unrest in the country but to us, blissfully in love, everything was as it should. The year was 1965.

THE DATING YEARS

"Make love, not war" was the national anthem of Americans who hated the idea of sending young men to die. It was a time of war, demonstrations, drugs and free love. The Rolling Stones were on top of the music charts with *"I Can't Get No Satisfaction"*; it blasted on music systems and radios everywhere. Big social change was in the air and the colleges across the nation were nurturing the angry voices of descent that emanated from students around the nation who opposed the devastating war in Viet Nam. Thousands of young Americans were dying in a land far from home, in a war that they had no part in starting. Rebellion was in the air. America was in turmoil. The Viet Nam War dominated the news. Uncle Sam kept constant vigil on potential recruits, and I kept constant vigil on my selective service status. Stay in school or you would increase your chances of getting drafted-by tenfold, if you were black. I did whatever necessary to avoid an A-1 status. As long as I was in school full time and making good grades, I was relatively safe. I lived with the reality that I could easily become draft eligible, but my mind was made up; school or no school, I was not going to war, any war and not to Viet Nam.

Living in Chicago, I was the country boy in the big city. I was an industrial design student at arguably the best art school in the country, doing quite well. What made it even better was that my two best friends, Bobby Hannum and Lorenzo Turner, who had been attending school before I arrived, both lived in Hyde Park, my fantasy land. Hyde Park was where the action was, and I was in it up to my drawing board. In the 1960's Hyde Park was magical; I loved everything about it.

I had only known of one interracial relationship in my life and it was back in my neighborhood in Gary when I was growing up. A boy I grew up with had a white girlfriend. They had met at the roller-skating rink, the teenagers' house of worship. It was attended more religiously than church. Their relationship was no big deal. They were just as much a part of the neighborhood as anybody.

At the Art Institute of Chicago, however, Lorenzo and Bobby both played musical instruments, were artists and both were in interracial relationships. Students came from all over the world to study at the school and mixed couples were more common here than anywhere else that I had ever seen but I had to constantly remind myself that I hadn't seen much. My two mentors had a magnetism that attracted girls, or maybe it was just the times. Maybe it was just me. There I was, wide-eyed and anxiously learning how to fit in. The parties were always interracial and always punctuated with the strong, pungent smell of marijuana smoke but I never indulged in it. One party stands out. It was a Halloween party at the University of Chicago that Kay and I attended together. The future would reveal the irony and cosmic forces that prevailed upon me to go to that party dressed as a nerdy Cub Scout. There I stood in long, skinny pants that were way too short for me. They didn't even reach my ankles. I wore a Cub Scout cap that was a size too small and around my neck I wore the scout scarf, neatly folded and correctly tied. In the photo, I was saluting either valiantly or comically, depending on how you interpreted it. Next to me with her arm around my waist, stood Kay; she was my sexy little 'den mother/drill sergeant'. She wore an officer's cap with a fatigue jacket that extended down to her mid thighs. Underneath she was decked out in all black leotards that started at her neck and ended over her toes. The fatigue jacket was kept open for effect. Around her neck, on a long string, hanging nearly to her knees was a plastic whistle, as big as her hand. As the photograph was being taken, we stool there, arms around one another's waists, looking like characters from a Marvel comics movie. This was all new to me, having come from across the border in Indiana. I had never smoked marijuana, but it was all around me. I had never dated outside my race, but here I was in an interracial relationship. The University of

Chicago was right at the heart of the activities. Fortunately, not all of my academics were at the downtown U of C campus; many were on the Hyde Park campus. I was meeting foreign students, graduate students, doctoral candidates, artists of all sorts and professors from every discipline. It seemed that every third person in Hyde Park was somehow affiliated with the university. It was a very intellectually stimulating and dynamic environment and I was a part of it. It was exciting. I was going to college, meeting new people from around the world, partying with intellectuals and artists alike, but most importantly, I was getting a good education. 'The Denver' was 'in the house.

Kay and I were like kids when we were able to be together. From time to time we did stupid things at school, just to see what would happen. One time we both sat on the floor, underneath the telephone directory stand that was attached to the telephone booth in the student center. We just sat there, drinking our coffees, peeking out from under the ledge, waving at friends as they walked by. Another time Kay stood right behind me, front to back, body to body, very close and had me tie a giant bow in the yards of red ribbon that she had wrapped several times around us. We were like Siamese twins, walking in perfect lockstep wherever we went, causing uproars of laughter from students who noticed. Some never noticed. Tears of laugher flowed. The funny thing about our antics was that many students acted like those were the most normal things two people could do together. Some students even told us that together being who we were, we were making a social statement. We agreed. But the only statements we were conscious of making were statements that showed how absolutely, absurdly stupid we could be. We had crazy fun together. We danced, studied and laughed together more than most. Often, we talked about the future and what it held for us. From the beginning of our relationship, I had always told Kay that one day she was going to be famous, but jokingly, not too famous. She was going to be a leader of people, but jokingly, not too many people and a mother to many, but not too many. I assured her that one day her name would adorn some monument or a building somewhere. She was always moved by these words of encouragement. I also assured her that her monument would not be in the black community. She was going to be the idol of every little girl in her presence, the envy of every mother she encountered and the wet dream of every teenage boy who saw her, and maybe even a few dads. As I expected, she was in stitches laughing at that idea. We constantly encouraged each other. Other students, mostly fashion design students, were always gathered around Kay. I often kidded her about what might have happened had her father and my mother had actually gotten together. I suggested that instead of her being my cute, sexy little girlfriend, she'd be my clumsy, stupid little sister. My mother even thought that was hilarious. I could see even from her activities in school, that Kay was a leader in the making. Our relationship was pure and wholesome and good; we made things happen. We were so happy together. But there were times when people outside of the school environment let us know that they didn't really approve of our relationship, but we didn't give a damn.

THE SETUP

Back in the kitchen, the laughing and screaming continued. Jo, Kay and Mom were having a ball. Then Jo came up with a wonderfully devilish idea. She suggested that Kay take home some of my mother's old high school photographs and let her father find them. It was a devious idea and we all loved it. Once he found the photos, Kay would interrogate him about the woman in the pictures to see what he would say or how he would react. His initial reactions would tell her everything. Two of the photos were of my mother when she was sixteen, another at seventeen and one of her in her graduation cap and gown. Kay agreed to do it. The three of them could hardly contain themselves. They were the "Three Crazy Amigas."

THE STING

Weeks later we were all together again. Kay could hardly report her findings because she was laughing so hard. When she finally got it out, she reported that she had 'hidden' the pictures at home in plain sight and waited to see what would happen. Her father eventually discovered the photos, but never knew he was being surveilled. Kay said that when he first looked at the photos, his expression went from curiosity to confusion to panic in quick succession. At that very moment, when asked about the woman in the photos, she said he nearly had a 'heart attack'. He didn't realize that Kay had been watching him staring closely at the photos. Her intense questioning had caused him to stutter and fidget. She was having a difficult time getting the details out to us; her laughter interrupted her narrative over and over. Finally, her father said, "I think she's a girl I went to school with at Blue Island High School. Her name was Aileen or something like that. I think she had a sister, an older sister if I remember correctly. They were always together," he added. He was clearly very uncomfortable about the questioning. "You remember her?" Kay asked. "Yes, I remember her", he responded. Then Kay said, "Her name is Irene; it was Irene A. Thomason when you were in school". "Where did these pictures come from? How did they get here?" he asked. "I got them from her. Her name is Irene Long now; she's Denver's mother", Kay said. He looked confused for a moment and then asked, "Denver?" Kay was having difficulty holding her tongue but then she added, "Denver, my boyfriend at school, at the Art Institute, the one you refuse to meet. Denver Long, Irene Long; she's his mother you went to school with and she told us that you had a real crush on her at Blue Island High School. Is that true?" she asked. His face went beet red as he avoided eye contact and refused to answer the question directly. Again, she queried him on his relationship with the woman in the photograph. Again, he avoided a direct answer as he began to fidget with the photos in his hands. "She was a nice girl." he responded warmly. Kay knew right then that it was true; her father really had held a crush for my mother back when they were both in high school. We all laughed aloud at the profound irony of this situation. What were the odds of our parents having met and possibly dated when they were in school? It was an incredible series of events that had led to this moment and it left us all dumbfounded. Yet Frank D-i-N-o-v-o, disapproved of my relationship with his oldest daughter. He was so busted.

The Peace Corps

Near the end of my junior year of college, the U.S. Peace Corps visited the school to do some recruiting. I had no clear plans for what I would do right after school, but I knew I was not ready to go into the work force. That was coupled with the fact that my design professor strongly suggested that I attend the Peace Corps presentation since I was a junior and it would be the 'polite' thing to do. After the presentation, applications were distributed, and we were all asked to fill out the forms as completely as possible. The application asked, "If selected by the U.S. Peace Corps to represent America abroad, where would you like to serve?" Without the slightest hesitation, I blatantly wrote across the page: *"Africa or Bust!"* When the meeting ended, it all became just a memory until some month or so later when my mother started receiving strange phone calls from neighbors, my high school, my former employers and parents of my closest friends. The neighbors were concerned about me perhaps being in some kind of trouble. My mother seemed just as concerned as I assured her that I had had no trouble with drugs, or the law and nobody was pregnant!

Months passed before I received an official letter from The U.S. Peace Corps, Washington, D.C. I had been accepted into the program as a volunteer and my assignment was in Sierra Leone, West Africa. My parents realized then that all the mysterious phone calls had been from the government, checking my background. I immediately checked my world map to locate Sierra Leone and sure enough, it was in West Africa, neighboring Liberia to the south and Guinea to the northeast. My assignment was teacher at Union Teachers' College in a village called Bunumbu. For the remainder of school, I planned and prepared for my trip to Africa. I had to take a series of vaccinations and exams that would protect me from some of the dangers of jungle life. But I was excited! I began to plan my ultimate route on the maps. I was headed for the Mother Land.

TRAINING

By June of 1967 I was a college graduate, having earned my bachelor's degree in industrial design. As we had agreed, Kay and I began slowing going our separate ways. I was Africa bound and she was still in school, pursuing her ambitions in the world of fashion and photography. Our parting was bittersweet; Kay was proud to see me head off for fun and adventure. I was happy to see her work towards her goal with so much determination. She had even gotten some very promising job offers during her last year in school. I had promised to write from all the places I planned to visit. It was an exciting time for both of us, but the real world lay ahead now. I had only two more weeks left before taking off to begin Peace Corps training. My mind was racing; it would be my first time to the capital, the first time on a plane, the first time anywhere! When the time came to leave home, I felt both excitement and sadness. It was an opportunity of a lifetime and the first time I would be away from my family. If I was going to travel and see the world, it was now or never.

The training program started during the steamy summer in the nation's capital, Washington, D.C. When I first arrived in D.C., I got a temporary room at the New Dunbar Hotel near 15th and U Street. The room was $8.00 a day, clean, comfortable and adequate. I was only going to be there for two or three days and only in the evenings when I crashed. Fortunately for me the hotel was centrally located within six or seven blocks of all the places I needed to go for training. For the next couple of days, I had to get passport photos taken, get fingerprinted and get the last of my vaccinations. I was having a wonderful time. A big part of the program that the volunteers understood upon signing up was that they would be living with families in the city while they completed their summer long training. The Peace Corps office had made prior arrangements with families in the city that were willing to be a part of the program. The families received stipends for the room and board that they provided each volunteer. Across the city families were opening their homes to recent college graduates of all ethnic groups, races, genders from around the country, who were about to embark on journeys that would affect the rest of their lives. I lived at 550 23rd Place, N.E. with the Trawick family, an elderly couple who 'adopted' me the first day I walked through their door. They lived in a well-kept two-story row house that was immaculate. I had two rooms on the second floor, both air-conditioned with a big new television in the adjoining room, all for my personal use.

For whatever reason, Mrs. Trawick urged me to be careful and not to rush into marriage too soon; too many young people, she protested, were getting married and not thinking about the consequences. I assured her that I had no intentions of getting married any time soon. The Trawick's children had all grown up and moved away and started their own families. Mr. and Mrs. Trawick were very impressed to see that a young black man, a college graduate was leaving home to go live in the 'jungle' in Africa for two years. She was the typical grandmother type. I couldn't leave the house until I had eaten breakfast or dinner, which she made for me every day and she stayed up at night until I walked through the front door. Mr. Trawick, age 75, was a character right out of the comics who always wore a tie. He was a cantankerous, skinny little man who reminded me so much of Percy Kilbride, better known as the comedic character, "Pa Kettle", opposite Margorie Main in the old black and white *Ma and Pa Kettle* films. He didn't believe in much of anything, especially claims made by scientists. Nothing was funny to him and he was anti-everything. The three of us often got into conversations over dinner and I just listened to him as he went on and on about whatever subject was at hand. Mr. Trawick had some clear cut ideas: "Most people ain't worth a damn", "Ain't no man ever gonna go to the moon"; "Preachers shouldn't be educated"; "More people get killed in air planes than in cars" and "Dr. Martin Luther King, Jr. is a crook." When I explained to him that I had just flown to D.C. in a plane, he told me that I was just damn lucky. His closing argument was that everybody should agree with him. Asked why everyone should agree with him, he said simply because he was right. Being perfectly serious all the time, he kept me laughing and I don't remember ever seeing him smile or laugh at anything. Mrs. Trawick would just roll her eyes back in her head when he labored on.

Washington, D.C. in the summer of 1967 was hot. It was one of the hottest I summers I remember anywhere or maybe it seemed that way because I was away from home in another city. The daytime temperatures remained in the nineties every single day and the humidity was so high that I was sweating constantly. Fortunately, as recommended, I had packed plenty of light weight summer clothes that made my days and night bearable. The weather was a sample of what was to come when we landed in the tropics. The nights were no better. The heat and the humidity together made every physical effort a challenge. My air-conditioned room at the Trawick house was a treasured relief.

The trainees were assigned teaching positions in the public schools during the day and language classes, either Mende or Temne in the evenings and 'culture' classes on most weekends. My overseas assignment was in a part of the country where both Mende and Temne were spoken. It was a college campus village near the small town of Segbwema called Bunumbu. Further north Temne was the dominant tongue. From sun up to sundown, all day, every day was filled with activities and meetings. Some volunteer trainees dropped out, claiming that the program's schedule was excessively rigorous and exhaustive. It was a hot, grueling summer program. But it stood to reason that the program would and should be intense. If stress in the capital of the United States was too much to bear, I tried to imagine what it would be like 'up country', deep in the bush of West Africa and freaking out because of a lack of familiar resources. I was proud of myself and the others who had stuck it out and gotten accepted for the next phase of the training which was Jamaica, Puerto Rico and/or The University of the West Indies and perhaps a few stops along the way. I taught art and English classes at Eastern High School during the summer. Another black volunteer from Philadelphia, Ron Jackson, taught classes there too and we often planned field trips and exhibits together for our students. The classes were all made up of African American students who pretty much thought Ron Jackson and I were the two wildest, funniest, smartest art teachers that had ever come to Eastern High School. Both Ron and I had just graduated from art schools and were anxious to put our skills to work in a class room. Together we made it a magical summer in the class room with our ideas and those that came from the students. Together we created an exciting atmosphere that had the whole school talking. Ron and I were a team. On one field trip we went to the movies and saw a movie starring this new good/bad guy named Clint Eastwood in what they called a 'spaghetti western'. Eastwood impressed me with his bold, daring handsomeness and cold demeanor. Without even looking up, you could tell when he was on the screen; it was the music that said everything. I think the movie was *"For a Few Dollars More"* or *"A Fistful of Dollars"*. Clint Eastwood was immediately my new screen hero. He was in my head.

Then, as quickly as it had all started, the summer was over, and it was time to move on. At the end of the D. C. summer program, the ambassador gave the volunteers a going away party. For most of the volunteers, including myself, who had come from college, without much money, if any, thought it was the most fabulous party any of us had ever attended. It was like no party I had ever attended. I quickly reminded myself again that I was from Gary, Indiana so what would I know about a real party? This was D.C. where parties were just a part of life, especially for the politicians. This was the government's way of thanking us for our dedication, for spreading good will and democracy around the world. It was a grand affair. There was champagne that flowed all night and food fine enough and plentiful enough to feed an army. There was live music, all night. Everything was free, all night. It was a special night for another reason. During the celebration, our special commemorative United States of America-Peace Corps Volunteer passports were to be distributed. The passports celebrated the fourth anniversary of the Peace Corps since President John F. Kennedy created it. We were just the fourth group of volunteers to go abroad. It was a special honor from President Johnson for us to get one of the newly designed, limited edition passports. Names were being called and one by one the volunteers walked up to receive their passports. It was as touching as college graduation. One after another, trainees proceeded to the stage and were handed their package. Every volunteer in the ballroom got a passport and a handshake, every volunteer-except me. My name was never called. I was stunned, shocked, disappointed. When I brought it to the attention of my supervisors, I was told that they had a record of my papers but for some reason the actual passport was not there. I was crushed. They assured me that my passport would be ready by flight time on the fourth, the fourth of July! It was Sunday night, July second. Everybody was scheduled to leave in two days. Then it occurred to me that if I didn't get my passport in one or two days,

I'd be stuck in D.C. for the holidays. I was told to be on standby because I could get a call at any time. The next day was the only day left to get my passport. On Tuesday, everybody was due at the airport early in the morning so my chances of leaving with them were slim and none. My passport didn't come, and they all left the country without me. I couldn't believe it. Five days later, on Friday, July 7, (07/07/67) I was notified that all of my documents were waiting for me in the immigration office at the airport. I was to fly from Washington, D. C. to New York where I'd board an international flight to Kingston, Jamaica. When I boarded that Pan Am 'Clipper' in New York, I had fifty cents, two quarters in my pocket. But I had my special commemorative United States of America-Peace Corps passport and a lot of faith. I was told that a driver would meet me in the airport terminal in Kingston. I figured that the worst that could happen was that I will have gotten two free plane rides.

JAMAICA SCHOOL OF AGRICULTURE

When I stepped off the plane in Kingston, I immediately understood what the word humidity meant. I gasped as the heat and dampness assaulted me. Then the realization hit me that I was officially in the tropics, another country, out of the United States! I saw palm trees. This was not Gary anymore. Childhood memories flooded my mind I as I stepped off the plane into the caldron. For a moment I was ten years old, back in my room at home, looking at the world map on my wall, imagining myself in all the places shown on the map. When my dreams began, I had not even thought about living in Jamaica or Puerto Rico, for free, but here I was. I was going to have to share these thought s with my dad when I got back home. I was met at the airport in Kingston by a Peace Corps country supervisor, a brother from the D. C. area whose name was Marty. My fears were all allayed. He seemed to be about my age or a little older and I liked him right from the beginning. He had a quiet, peaceful demeanor but he exuded a sense of confidence. I was very impressed with the fact that he had obviously been around, a former volunteer and now working for the U.S. Peace Corps driving his way around this country. I was going to be just like Marty when I 'grew up'. Marty was also an artist. We laughed and bonded on the way back to the Jamaica School of Agriculture in

Spanishtown where the training was being held. During the ride to the school, the fact that I had just arrived in another country with only fifty cents in my pocket came up. Marty asked what I would have done had he not been there at the airport, I just smiled at him. He laughed hysterically, as we continued the white-knuckle ride. It was the first time I had ridden on the left side of the highway, but Marty was driving the Jeep and seemed as comfortable as if he were back home in D.C. I could not get used to the right turns from a left-hand lane.

By the time we arrived at the school, I was frazzled from the ride, but Marty had laughed most of the way back. He told me that I was lucky to have arrived when I did because the hectic crowds from the first few days were over and that I could take my time registering for a dorm room. It was midafternoon. And just as Marty had said, most of the trainees I had gotten to know in Washington were going about their daily routines, some lounging lazily, some out in the fields, others hanging out clothes to dry in the hot sun. Many of them called out to me as I walked onto the campus, heading for the office to register for a dorm room. Some joked that it was about time I arrived; there was much to be done, duties to perform, routines to learn and enroll in classes. I was excited and anxious to get settled in; but first I had to go to the office. Marty directed me to the school registration office and that's when my life changed-for the better. The office was quiet and empty except for one young lady who was sitting at the front desk. I stood in the doorway as the bright sun behind me cast my long shadow across the floor and up the side of the desk. It blocked the light in her eyes as she looked up at me, my face in shadow. There I was, young, handsome, proud and feeling every bit Clint Eastwood. I could hear his music in my head as I proudly strode into the open office. The young lady's job was to register me and answer questions about the school. She assigned me a dorm room. She was a tiny young woman and I knew instantly, before I said a word that she was 'The One'. Her accent only added to the exotic nature of her presence. She smiled politely as I sat down next to her desk. There was a moment of small talk before she began to ask me questions to complete the registration form. I asked a few questions and she answered quickly, avoiding my obvious drooling stare as we talked. She continued filling out the paper work. I just sat there quietly, looking at her as she worked and then I said, "We're getting married!" She completely ignored me and continued writing on the form in front of her. "We're getting married", I repeated. Again, she ignored the statement, although I noticed the smile that was beginning to form across her little chocolate face. I could tell it was getting harder and harder for her to continue ignoring me, so I pressed forward. She was about to crack, and I couldn't let her off the hook. "You and me, we're going to get married, to each other and live happily ever after!" I stated flatly. Everything stopped. She stopped writing, looked up at me with a look of utter amazement as she broke into a state of uncontrollable laughter and said, "You're crazy, Yankee-boy!"

It took quite a few minutes for us both to stop laughing and calm down enough to attempt to hold a decent conversation. I had known her now for about twenty minutes and I knew deep inside that she was going to be my wife at some point in time. I assured her that there was absolutely nothing she could do about it; the fact was, she was going to marry me, period. "Say yes. Go ahead, make my day", I whispered, projecting my Clint Eastwood manner. My confidence sent her back into hysterics for another five minutes. But I was never more serious. Her name was Joan Cynthia Johnson, and this was her first job out of high school. She was about to celebrate her nineteenth birthday in August. When she told me that, I informed her that I was her birthday present that had just arrived for her, early special delivery. We laughed together for the remainder of the interview and she finally got me registered into a dorm room.

My room was on the ground floor of a building not far from the office where I had just registered. The room was small, bright but simple and clean. There were two sizable beds in the room and enough closet space for two people. One closet was filled with someone's clothing. I threw my bag aside and flopped down on the bed, resting my head on the soft pillow. I didn't notice them at first but then I realized that the huge insects on the walls were mosquitoes, the size of humming birds. They were the largest mosquitoes I had ever seen in my life and they just clung there on the wall as though the room was theirs. It didn't seem like a wise thing to disturb them, so I just kept an eye on them. Fortunately for me, both beds were housed inside mosquito netting. After a few minutes, a big, hulking, vibrant, smiling, six-foot white guy bounded into the room and said he was my roommate. He was jovial and friendly; I liked him right away. He was John "Ciba" Shuster, from Phoenix, Arizona. He had studied law in college. His family members back home were staunch Republican conservatives who all thought that John's idea of joining the Peace Corps was a waste of time when he could be running for some political office. We both laughed when I suggested that his parents must be eating their hair at the idea of him hangin' with the 'brothers' in Africa. He exploded in laughter and agreed with my analysis. John had a big, good heart and it was hard not to like him. He got the "Ciba" moniker from one of our African language instructors while in Washington, D.C. In Temne the word ciba means onion. They called him that because he liked to eat onions, like apples, raw. To me that said everything about the character of my new roommate. When I asked him about it, he just laughed hysterically and said, "I love onions." When I asked him how people responded to his breath, he just laughed again and blew out a big breeze of 'onion breath' at me and said, "They hold their breaths!" To say John was a character was an understatement. We became fast friends. Earlier in the day I had been lying across my bed in Washington, D.C. and now I was lying across my bed in a dorm room on the campus of a college in another country, having just found 'The One'. I took a nap and awoke refreshed a couple of hours later. It was early evening when I awoke; the mosquitoes appeared much bigger than I had remembered. I felt very thankful for my mosquito netting.

Over the next few days and weeks, Joan and I became good friends. I walked her to the bus stop in the evenings when she got off from work and I looked forward to having lunch with her when she was at the office. By late summer, we were an item. I did all I could to promote the relationship. First, I spread the word among all the volunteers that I was engaged to the girl who worked in the office. As volunteers began to see Joan and me together more and more, they took it for granted that she and I had developed a serious courtship. They were right. Our romance was well under way. On what might have been called our first 'date', I was invited to her house in Kingston. We were getting comfortable with one another. It was a beautiful night. We sat out on the veranda, close together talking about Jamaica, the U.S., world affairs and whatever topics struck our interests. Our first date turned out to be a quiet, very pleasant and memorable evening under the stars. Next and probably the most fortuitous thing I did was have other volunteers take lots of photos of Joan, my

'Jamaican Doll', and me together, often in ridiculous poses. Every week I'd send home a letter stuffed with crazy photos of us together. I let it be known to my parents back home that I had found 'The One' and that we were 'engaged'. They seemed delighted. By the end of the summer Joan and I were pretty much going steady.

I knew I was winning when, at the end of our training program, and around her birthday, Joan and her family invited me and other trainees to her house for a going away party. She lived with her family in a big beautiful house at 42 Mountain View Avenue, Kingston. Her aunt, whom she called "Goddie", loved young people and enjoyed our company as much as we enjoyed hers. The dance of the day was reggae, *"Rock-Steady"* and we all danced and partied until we could hardly stand, due to the rum punch that was served all during the festivities. Joan and I both quickly and eagerly adopted the *"Rock-Steady"* as our official dance. Suddenly it was all over.

UNIVERSITY OF THE WEST INDIES

The time had come for us to leave Jamaica for the final phase of training, after which we'd all be heading to our overseas assignments. I left Jamaica heading for San Juan, Puerto Rico. Some of the initial group of trainees had already been training in Puerto Rico but they didn't see Jamaica. I saw both. From Puerto Rico, we headed for Port of Spain, the capital of Trinidad and Tobago, commonly known as 'the true Caribbean' because the island is only seven miles off the northeast coast of Venezuela. It's true South America. Our remaining weeks of training were at the University of the West Indies in St. Augustine, one of the four campuses of the University. The St. Augustine campus had opened in 1960. The first campus, the University College was established in 1948 in Mona, Jamaica. And in 1962 the Cave Hill campus was established in Barbados. The campus was sprawling, laid out across a luscious green landscape. The weather was always perfect, and the sun shone brightly every day as the soft breezes swept across the campus from the sea. We all worked to refine our language and social skills. It was during our stay in Trinidad that many of the trainees were afflicted with dysentery, including myself. For days many of us were unable to do anything but stay close to our dorm rooms.

By now not only was my stomach beginning to ache, but I was developing hemorrhoids. I was miserable. The thought of getting on a plane heading in the opposite direction of home didn't ease my suffering either. I left Jamaica with Joan C. Johnson, the girl of my dreams, on my mind, and a severe hemorrhoidal pain in my ass.

WHAT DREAMS ARE MADE OF

Luciann Powell was a striking redhead California girl who caught my eye the first time I saw her in Jamaica. She was a picture of health and youthful beauty, and I wanted to boink her. Whenever there was a big meeting on campus, she somehow ended up sitting, or standing near me. Or maybe it was me always getting closer to her. We had good, strong positive vibes and I liked her. We felt like immediate friends. She thought I was smart and funny. I thought she was hot and hot. We enjoyed each other's company whenever a few minutes of spare time presented itself. Our conversations never lasted more than a few minutes, her usually heading in one direction and me in another. Luciann was slender and vibrant with beautiful legs which she had no trouble showing. Her hair was very short, curly and flaming red. Her face was filled with freckles that sparkled in the bright warm sunlight. She reminded me of the little Annie character. Whenever I was around her all I did was fantasize about was her bush which I imagined was a soft, lush fragrant, red bush. Luciann was exactly my height minus the wedge heel shoes that she wore. I loved the way she always smelled fresh and minty. Did I say, she was hot? I was drawn to her heat: *"Punish me with your body! Make it hurt so good! Spare me not the lust!"* It was difficult to stay focused when I was near her. More than once she looked right at me just as I was having real kinky thoughts about her. It was like she was reading my mind, like she knew exactly what I was thinking. When it happened, she smiled at me. Never a word out of line did I say to her, but I suppose my wagging tongue pretty much gave me away. Our schedules kept us busy all during most days and evenings. Whenever there were a few hours of freedom, everybody was usually too tired to get active again-especially on weekends. There was little leisure time. We smiled at one another whenever our paths crossed on the big campus.

Of all the trainees travelling in our group somehow Luci and I flew together from Montego Bay, Jamaica to San Juan, Puerto Rico. How that happened is a mystery. It was meant to be. We became travelling buddies and throughout the entire summer with the closeness we developed, all I could see was her being naked. In my fantasy she'd come to my door; I'd invite her in and close the door behind us. We'd slowly walk toward each other longingly, undressing as we got closer. She'd show me her red bush and tease me. Closer and closer our lips got. With a gentle hand I'd reach out to touch her softness and—wake up! In my condition even fantasies were painful especially if an erection was on the horizon. She was an unknowing comfort to me during my painful travel experiences. She had no idea of my constant agony. My body had taken a severe blow because of the drastic change in my diet, and in my daily rhythm. There was also the challenge of fighting off the effects of immunization shots we all got. I was twenty-seven years old, fresh out of college and off seeing the world. It was an exciting time; We were travelling, meeting new people, seeing new places, even learning new languages. The whole world was wide open for me. Adventure was my driving force and it hung heavy in the air. And I had hemorrhoids.

It was unusual for someone to be knocking on my dorm door at seven thirty on a Sunday morning. It annoyed the hell out of me. Everybody else on campus must still be asleep. I was not sleep but neither was I fully awake. I heard the rapid taps at the door. Again, and again they came. In major agonizing pain, I dragged myself towards the sound of the annoying sound, wondering who could be in such a hurry. My hemorrhoid condition was now at a new critical level. My agony had spilled over into my attitude and behavior because I was really pissed at whomever it was knocking on my door at this hour. It had been to my benefit that the past two days had allowed me to remain lying in my bed, in relative darkness not having to move. Just the thought of walking was agonizing.

I opened the door to the blinding glare of sunlight that poured down. At first, I couldn't tell who it was standing in front of me. It was a girl. Her body blocked the sunlight as she stood there in complete shadow. When I looked closer at her, she was smiling. She was standing in my doorway and dangling from her hand was what I initially thought was a pink handkerchief. I was wrong. They were panties, pink panties. In a flash before I could react, her other hand dropped to the hem of her tiny pink cotton dress and lifted it way above her waist, exposing her entire body. She held it there. She was stark naked. Her two pink nipples smiled at me as the dress exposed them to my frenzied frantic gaze. It was the most beautiful slender body in the world, a magnificent ivory sculpture. I unconsciously looked down between her thighs and there it was – the bush that dreams are made of. It was the kind of bush I had dreamt of meeting someday. That day had obviously come, and the glistening gift literally came to my door. It all happened in a flash. I fought hard to maintain my composure, but the bush got bigger and brighter. I was mesmerized, as it spoke to me. Suddenly with a slight movement, she parted her legs just enough to make me gasp aloud. The bush stared at me; I stared back. With a soft smile on her face, she leaned forward and said, "Good morning! Can I come in?", Luciann said as she kissed me on the cheek, dropped her panties in my hand, stepped past me and went inside.

During our training, we were put into situations with new instructors whom we had not met previously in the program and who all spoke Mende, Temne and Krio. Though English was the official language of Sierra Leone, spoken in the schools, businesses and government, nearly a third of the population spoke Mende; nearly a quarter spoke Temne but about ninety percent of the population spoke Krio, a mixture of English and various indigenous languages. You could get by anywhere in the country if you spoke Krio, so we all had to learn to speak it. In the training we were judged by the fluency and use of intonations that we had learned. We were put in situations that could have been lifesaving, depending on our abilities to communicate. The proficient volunteers learned all three languages. Luciann was one of those.

The weeks that followed were filled with more language classes and field work, learning how to grow vegetables and live off the land. By the end September the training programs were just about finished, and it was time again to either head for overseas destinations or home. It was that time when we all had to make a final decision. Some trainees changed their minds at the last minute and decided to abandon the program and return home, not ready to face the challenges that surely lay ahead. It was a very tense time for many. It was made clear to us at the end of the training that once we boarded that plane and took off, there was no turning around.

Those with the courage to take on the challenge excitedly chose to move forward. I was one of them. I figured that if I could leave the country with only two quarters in my pocket and get as far as Trinidad, I was good to go. As departure day drew nearer, the more excited we all became until it was that final hour. We arrived in the late evening at Piarco International Airport, and boarded a PanAm World Airways jet, chartered just for us, Peace Corps Volunteers specifically for this trip to West Africa. We were all about to cross the Atlantic for at least a two-year stint in the bush of Sierra Leone. At first it was solemn and quiet on the plane, the atmosphere calm and subdued but once we were an hour or so into the flight, things started to loosen up and the celebrations began. The cabin of the plane became one big party room and we partied late into the long night. When we awoke the next day, we were touching down at Lungi International Airport in Freetown, Sierra Leone, West Africa.

BUNUMBU OF THE BUSH

Lungi International Airport is in the coastal town of Lungi, outside of Freetown, the capital city. By the time we arrived in Sierra Leone, we had been to Jamaica, Puerto Rico, Antigua, Barbados, Trinidad and Tobago and Caracas, Venezuela. From Lungi, we had limited options as to how we'd get into town. The quickest way was to take the ferry across the Sierra Leone River. An alternative was to take the long route by taxi which would add hours to our travel times. Most of us decided on the ferry; riding two or three more hours in a crowded taxi didn't appeal to any of us. Little did we know what was in store for us. Once we finally arrived in the center of Freetown, our gazes all focused on the famous "Cottonwood Tree", Freetown's most visible landmark that sat right in the center of town.

The story goes that the tree was a resting place for slaves when they arrived in the city in 1787. Along with the splendor of the enormous cotton tree, the sights, sounds and smells of the city were a constant assault on our senses as we struggled to adjust to all the hustle and bustle that went on in the center of the city. Our first stop in Freetown was the U.S. Peace Corps office. It was vital that every volunteer entering the country check in and make sure the office had a listing for them. At the office our assignments were double checked, we were given cursory checkups and all our information was gathered to make sure we could be reached at any time, especially in an emergency. Once all the paperwork was completed, the volunteers were ready for the final leg of the trip, heading up country. Some volunteers going in my general direction up country, so they loaded up with me and my newly acquainted roommate, Rick from Philadelphia. After some time, palavering (arguing) with the dozens of lorry (truck) drivers who were assigned to take us to our respective designations, we were off again. We all departed Freetown around three o'clock in the afternoon. The lorry ride up country was the most grueling, tortuous, uncomfortable, painful ride any of us had ever been on in our lives. What might have taken us an hour at home took us over twelve merciless hours over rough, bumpy, dusty roads that rambled through the bush without any concern for our comfort. And what made it worse was that every hour or so, the driver would stop at some small shack on the side of the road and take a break and talk to vendors who had small ramshackle huts alongside the road. They took their time, laughing, joking with the other men who were traveling in the other direction and who also stopped to have a rest and share stories. It was as though we weren't even there. It was infuriating to us who had not had a shower or sound sleep since leaving Trinidad. The partying on the plane had caught up with us. By now it was late into the evening and volunteers were being dropped off at various points along the way. We were all totally exhausted. Each one who got off the bus or lorry, was being instructed by the driver on how to reach their respective destinations which were oftentimes a considerable distance from the road. Finally, the driver shouted out, "Bunumbu!" He stopped the lorry right there in the middle of the road and shouted out again, "Bunumbu!" I responded with "Yes, Bunumbu!" As I grabbed my luggage, climbed over other passengers and stepped off the lorry, I heard the driver say in heavily accented English, "Your house is up there!", as he pointed in the general direction we should go. It was so dark that we couldn't really see what he pointed to, so we asked him to use his torch (flashlight). My roommate, Rick, who had gotten off the lorry with me turned his torch on and then I followed suit. We focused our lights in the general direction that the driver had pointed. "Up there, not far!" he shouted as he climbed back into his vehicle and started back down the road and faded into the black nothingness that was the night. The lorry rattled off as we watched its lights slowly disappear down the road.

There we were, standing in the middle of a road in Africa, in the bush, in the middle of the night. The darkness was consuming. It was three thirty a.m. and it had taken us twelve hours to get to our destination from Freetown. It is funny when I think back at how we must have looked at that moment, standing in the middle of nowhere, holding flashlights. Had it not been for the torches that were part of our equipment, we would have been in real trouble. We both realized at that moment how much we had taken street lights for granted. Without the flashlights, we could literally not see our hands in front of our faces. Slowly and carefully we made our way to a small foot path that wound its way up a slight winding incline. My biggest concern was stepping on a snake. My mind took me back to my childhood days in Blue Island when we crossed the big field to go to the gas station and I saw a garter snake. I was sure that if I stepped on a snake now, it would certainly not be a garter snake. In our training we were told about some of Sierra Leone's most dangerous snakes, the Gabon Viper and the mambas, both black and green. The black mamba was a particularly nasty little snake. It is a very thin, black snake that looks, ironically enough, like a long garter snake, but it lives in trees and it is poisonous. But what makes it so dangerous is the fact that it will bite you in the head. It was strange how all the training information about snakes was forefront in my mind as we clumsily wound our way up the dark slope. We finally reached the top to find a little house. It was our new home. Carefully we entered and found the kerosene lamps that sat on the table just inside the door. Once we found the bedrooms and decided who would take which room, we dropped down on our respective beds and fell into comas.

My first full day in Bunumbu was magnificent. I awoke having momentarily forgotten how we had arrived there the night before. It was bright; the sun shone so brightly that for first few days, I had to wear sun glasses all day. My first memorable experience that day was how I felt when I walked down my incline to the road below and looked across to the college campus. On the other side of the road, past the campus, you could see as far as the horizon. We had been standing in pretty much the same spot last night when we arrived and had no idea there was so much open space right across the road from where we stood. The sky had never been so big. Our side of the road was bush from either direction as far as the eye could see. We lived on the 'wild side' of the road. Our accommodations were comfortable considering we were in thick bush country. Our little house was made of painted cement blocks. There was one step up from the ground with a gate to prevent unwanted creatures from invading the house. The house had a sheet metal roof that made music during the rainy season. As you entered, there was a big, open room used as the living/dining room. To the left of the big room was my bedroom. To the right, as you came in, was what turned out to be my office/studio. Near the back of the big room, to the right was Rick's room. Across from him was a room he used for his office. Between his office and my bedroom was the toilet, which also led outside. It was a regular, enamel toilet with flush ability. The shower was outside. It consisted of a big bucket that you filled with water and lathered up from. It was simple: lather up and when ready, empty the cold water slowly over your head to rinse. That kind of shower wakes you up in a hurry. At the very rear of the house, on the north side was the kitchen. It had a one basin sink with one faucet nozzle. There was only cold water so no need for two nozzles. There was a small refrigerator in the corner and an ample supply of cabinets and a stove. It was a very adequate kitchen. Out back lay cement across the width of the house. You could go outside from either the bathroom exit or the kitchen.

Behind the house for the first hundred yards was knee high growth with a faint footpath leading away from the house. Beyond that was dense bush! Some mornings if I was quiet enough and looked carefully into the trees, I could see the chimps coming down to forage on the ground. The house had no glass in the window openings. Instead each window was cross hatched with heavy metal wiring. Each square in the window openings was about eight inches in height and width, large enough to get plenty of air and sunshine. The living room had two stiff stuffed chairs and a dining room table and four chairs. The floor was scattered with throw rugs. My favorite was a big round, skin rug that lay the center of the living room opening. We had electric lights. The entire campus was on a grid; and at nine o'clock sharp, all the campus lights dimmed twice. That meant it was time to fire up your kerosene lamps because the generator was about to go offline for the night. Each of our beds was draped in comforting mosquito netting. It was like in the *Tarzan* movies. The house was very comfortable for the two of us, mainly because we were hardly there at the same time. Rick was a math teacher. He had his rhythm and I had mine. We spent the first few days unpacking and finding our way around the house and the campus. We settled in quickly. Even before we could get our bags completely unpacked, two young boys showed up at the door. One was about twelve, the other was about eight. They lived in the village down the road and went to the grammar school on the campus. The older one's name was Samuel Alpha. His little sidekick was Lammie Saffa. Rick, my roommate, introduced himself and said he was from Philadelphia, Pennsylvania. When I introduced myself and mentioned Chicago, they both laughed aloud and simultaneously shouted, "Chicago! Al Capone! bang!" They offered their services in exchange for school books and fees and at least one meal a day. Samuel even volunteered to be my personal 'social secretary', one who could get me in with all the students and villagers since I was a stranger and spoke a little Mende or Temne and poor Krio. He eventually became my official spokesman/interpreter and teacher. He was very diplomatic, and I was impressed. They agreed to clean the house, do the laundry and the shopping when necessary and other duties as agreed upon. In return for their services, Rick and I would pay for their school books and pay all school fees. If necessary, they would also take care of our eating arrangements. And if we were happy with them, we could, from time to time, throw in a pair of sneakers for the two of them. "Sneakers" was the magic word. It would be sort of a 'bonus' if they did a good job. We all agreed.

BUYING BUSH BEEF

It didn't take long before Sam and Lammie were running the house. And they did a damn good job. In the beginning Rick and I put their honesty to the test and left small amounts of money and small valuables lying around. Watches and belts were of special interest to the kids. Transistor radios were gold. Rick and I would consult from time to time on the results and nothing ever came up missing. They became the true protectors of the house and we felt very comfortable with them. So, we 'adopted' them. Sam talked to Rick and me like he was holding a seminar. He always had talking points. The first thing we had to learn to do was to go down to the village on Fridays and buy fresh 'bush beef'. That meant six o'clock in the morning on Friday one of us would have to go down to the village about a quarter of a mile down the road and stake a claim to the cut of meat we wanted from the butcher. Meat didn't get any fresher than 'bush beef'. I agreed to go to the village with Sam to see how things were done. I was also interested in meeting the villagers. Sam beamed as we walked and ran down the road to the village and meandered through the throng of people milling about the market place. From time to time, Sam would bark out some Krio phrase and his friends would respond accordingly. Sam was introducing me to everybody as "Meestah Long from Chicago, Al Capone, bang! bang!"

The atmosphere of the marketplace was vibrant as the villagers engaged in animated conversations. I asked Sam where the butcher was, and he led me to a big crowd that stood surrounding some activity that I couldn't see from where I was. Sam weaved his way through the crowd with me in tow until we reached the opening. We stepped out of the thick crowd and into the opening just as the machete came crashing down. With one powerful blow, the cow's head fell to the ground, leaving the body still standing for a moment. Blood gushed like a faucet. Two legs folded, then the other two as the animal dropped to the ground. It was a scene from *Apocalypse Now* where a villager beheads a cow. I had to catch my breath. Sam didn't tell me that we'd be ringside at a beheading.

That's when I realized that Sam was not standing near me but some feet away in the crowd. He was looking at me with a big smirk on his face. Sam had planned this whole thing from the beginning. I was holding it together as best I could until I turned away abruptly, choked a bit and caught my breath. The cow had been completely beheaded only a few feet away, right in front of me. Sam laughed like crazy; I wanted to kick his little ass. Then the palavering started in earnest. Shouts in Mende, Temne and Krio abounded. The atmosphere was hyper as the villagers squabbled for each cut of the cow. The flies were in paradise. I was in hell, stuck with Sam. The scene looked like total confusion. But everybody knew exactly what they wanted as they left the area with paper bags, dripping blood, containing their fresh cuts of meat. In less than thirty minutes, there was little of the cow remaining. Sam bought a cut of the meat and promised me that I would like it when it was cooked properly. I had trusted Sam up to this point, but I didn't know about bush beef. After the visit to the butcher, I stepped way back from meat for a long time and made fish a main part of my diet. Back in the states if I wanted beef, I went to the market and bought it-already packaged. I was learning fast. I had taken for granted all the conveniences we had left behind at home, again.

While we were still getting settled, Rick and I decided that the house needed a good sweeping and cleaning out before the term started. The floors were concrete, so it was easy to scrub them down with soap and water with bleach and get behind every nook and cranny in the place. Strangely, Sam politely refused to help with the task advising that there were other chores and tasks that we should be focused on other than 'cleaning' out the house as we planned to do. When we started mopping, some roaches started to come out. Suddenly there were hundreds! These roaches were huge! They came from everywhere. The more we cleaned, the more the roaches appeared. It was a scene from Hitchcock. Rick and I were flabbergasted. I thought we had roaches in Chicago but nothing like these. These roaches could eat Chicago roaches. A three-inch roach was no big deal. Part of the problem too was that the roaches were too big to spray; that would have left an even bigger mess, so we fought the cleanup battle as best we could. Sam and Lammie were in hysterics, laughing throughout the entire ordeal, not lifting a finger to help. Sam told us in so many words that we got what we deserved by stirring them up. If we hadn't started cleaning with detergents, then the roaches would never have come out. We would have never even seen one. We dumped buckets of roaches soaked in kerosene. It was a lesson learned. Sam two. Denver & Rick zero.

Rick and I were invited to the college headmaster house on campus, Mr. Gwynn-Jones, an elderly man I guessed was in his late sixties, who had requested replacement teachers for those who were leaving. We were replacing a Canadian and a British volunteer. Gwynn-Jones was bald, very British with an accent that was difficult not to laugh at. I was from Gary, Indiana. Gwynn-Jones had been in Sierra Leone for two decades. From conversations and inuendo from the other Brits, his assignment suggested that he was a failure back in England and was sent to the wastelands. He always wore a crisp, short sleeved white shirt and British shorts worn up to his lower chest with khaki shorts halfway down his legs resembling a skirt. He looked like what a typical English headmaster might look like.

His white knee-high socks always accompanied the shorts. We never knew what his first name was, but Gwynn-Jones lived alone on the other side of the campus away from where our house sat. He had a reputation as a disciplinarian. Next to him lived another elderly gentleman Brit, Mr. Cubison, whom everybody called, "Pa Cubison". He was Gwynn-Jones' bookkeeper and fellow countryman. I guessed Cubison to be in his seventies. Together with an amateur British tennis player, tiny Miss White, and a married British couple, Gwynn-Jones and Cubison gave the campus a distinctly English atmosphere. The college and grammar school were all funded by the Christian church. They were all Christian faculty.

Most of the students were Christians with a few exceptions; some were Muslim. Consequently, as required by the college, all of the students had to attend regular prayer services every morning before classes. It was an all-male student body and they were all there to get their certifications to teach in the Sierra Leone school system. Gwynn-Jones advised us at the brunch that all the teachers were also expected to attend the morning services with the students. I don't think so. "Houston, we have a problem!" Gwynn-Jones soon realized he had a rebel in his midst. The issue with attending the services arose one day when I was in a conversation with Gwynn-Jones and Mr. Cubison. They had brought their colonialist views and attitudes to the bush and were quite comfortable with those ideas, but they expected us to be openly accepting of them. I was not in keeping with that program. The two men relayed a story to me of a native religious figure that the people of Bunumbu had believed in for generations, sort of an African mystic prophet figure. According to legend, hundreds of years ago, that prophet walked back into the river and disappeared, after he had quelled conflicts in the land. He promised to return from the river in the future if the conflicts and wars started again. The people of the village pleaded for him not to leave them, but he departed, leaving the village in deep despair and causing them to pray regularly for his return. They were still observing the tradition when Gwynn-Jones arrived in Sierra Leone. Students had told me the story and each time I heard it; I was struck by the consistency of the story. However, Gwynn-Jones, Pa Cubison and Phillips, the tennis player, who also taught classes on campus, disputed the entire story, arguing and trying to convince the students that the story made no sense and that it was irrational and impossible for a man to walk into the river and live for generations and then one day walk back out. Instead, it would behoove the students to put their faith in the Lord Jesus Christ, the Savior. They were furious when I posed the question about dying on a cross and rising from the dead three, four days later. Which story was more believable? I asked. It was no surprise to them when Rick and I both flatly refused to attend the morning prayer services. We were in no way obligated to do so. In my head I could hear "Reb" back home defending his position on the Resurrection. I had to go to church when I was kid when I had little or no choice.

Oftentimes the students and I discussed religion. I gave them my view; they gave me theirs. Almost to the student, they would have preferred not having to attend services in the mornings. It was a must for them. Even during our conversations about Jesus and God, the rote learning techniques showed up in their language and conversations. Analyzing anything was not something they seemed capable of doing. They all repeated their beliefs line and verse, without variation. My challenge was to teach students how to become critical thinkers. I was determined to do my best.

THE NEW ART STUDO BUILDING

Within a month I was into my regular routine. The school had recently constructed a new art building on the campus. It had just been completed when we arrived. Like our little cement block house, my art building had no glass in it. It was an open-air structure with wire mesh covering the huge window openings. It had two heavy wooden doors and a sheet metal roof. The floors were concrete and fresh air and sunlight constantly penetrated the open space. I had two dozen desks and a storage room with an ample supply of powdered paints, brushes, papers and various art supplies. The building was a short distance down the road and across the campus. On my first morning's walk to class, I passed women going about their regular morning business, talking and laughing as they passed. "Bua!" I heard from them as I passed. "Bua!" I responded. I walked past a woman who at that very moment of addressing me, was reaching down to grab the bottom of her dress and throwing it up high over her back, exposing her butt to the wind. "Bua, Meestah Long!" she shouted as she squatted and began to take a leak by the side of the road. "Bua! Beesia!" I shouted back. It became my morning routine to walk down my pathway, cross the road, the campus and down a short footpath to my classes. Every morning as I walked past the dorm rooms of the students, I would hear in unison, "Bua, Meestah Long!" I always replied, "Bua!" When I first met my students, I was accepted immediately because they all thought I was one of them, a Mende, until I opened my mouth. They couldn't believe I was an American because I looked just like the typical Mende man, short, brown and without much facial hair. And it wasn't long before I heard one of them say, "Chicago, Al Capone, bang!" As the weeks passed, my life ran smoothly. I had created a great relationship with the students. I was an oddity of sorts. It was obvious that I was the first African American volunteer teacher to ever come to Union Teachers' College. Students took pride in which of them knew me better. There were about two hundred men students on the campus. They were from all over the country, but most had never met a black American man. One day I learned exactly what my students thought of me. It was another cultural learning experience.

MANFRIENDS

It was comforting to walk out of the art building into the sunlight. I always enjoyed the sights, sounds and smells of the campus. It was alive with singing, music and dancing. On one afternoon as I ended the class, several of the students were slow getting out of the building. Most of the time the students wanted my opinion on some topic that they had argued about. I could settle an argument between them. Most of the time I obliged. One student was on my left, the other on my right as we all walked out of the art room and down onto the footpath on our way back across the campus. One student took hold of my hand and continued to walk. We were walking along holding hands like two little girls and I silently asked myself: "What's wrong with this picture?" My mind was racing. My natural instinct was to pull my hand away and protest. But this was Africa.

We continued to walk along the path holding hands. I thought maybe I had missed something important during the extensive training program. My head was spinning because I had no idea that there was such an open atmosphere of homosexuality on campus. At the end of our walk each student, stopped, said his goodbye, turned and went on his way to his respective dorm. They had clearly not even been conscious of what had just happened. I was a nervous wreck when I ran to see my friend Abdul Kanu, a Sierra Leonean faculty member who lived on the campus. Abdul was one of the first people that Sam had introduced me to when I arrived. He was a few years older than I was and had come back to Sierra Leone, having been educated in England. Abdul taught me the ropes; he was my mentor. I reported to him any time had a question. Abdul wasn't home so I went on to my house to talk to Sam about the hand holding incident. Sam listened attentively as I related my experience and future concerns. Out of nowhere he and Lammie broke out into hysterics. Sam asked, "Meestah Long, do you like men?" In an instant I replied, "No!" He responded with: "Well, they like you very much!" They laughed uncontrollably. I didn't think it was funny. Thankfully Abdul was home when I returned to his house. He could see that I was very upset. He listened intently for a long time as I spilled my guts to him about my experience, explaining that I was not gay. I told him that I had mentioned it to Sam, but that Sam had just laughed and made fun me. When I finally finished, Abdul looked me right in the eye, paused for a moment then went into a state of uncontrollable laughter; he laughed for five minutes. Then he explained to me that in Sierra Leone and other African countries men who are close friends hold hands. My students held my hands because they considered me to be one of them. It was an acceptance gesture; they really liked me. He told me to pay more attention to what's happening around me when I am on the campus. I began to study the movements around the campus more closely, who was usually with whom and to my amazement, I noticed lots of guys walking around holding hands. I had not noticed it before. I started to understand relationships better. Abdul let me know that Sam was just having some fun with me because he knew I was unaware of the custom. Abdul also promised not to mention the incident to anyone else on the campus.

Back at my house, when Sam and Lammie saw me racing directly toward them, with my fists balled, they both took off running, laughing like two madmen as they fled. From then on, I had no problem holding hands with students as we walked from one place to another around the campus. By the time our first Christmas rolled around, I had gained so much respect from the students that two of them invited me to accompany them to their villages for the Christmas holiday. In attempting to outdo the other, one offered that if I went to his village for the holidays, I could have his sisters if as long as I was in his village. I asked, "What do mean, I can have your sisters?" "Meestah Long, are you a virgin?" he shot back as they belted out laughter. Another life lesson learned.

During my early months in Bunumbu, I received an archery set from my Aunt Katherine back home. I had plenty of space and I thought it would be a great way to pass some down time. Sam helped me make a solid, stable target with a big bull's eye. When I had it all completed, Sam and Lammie gathered around and made some wages on how well I'd do. Neither of them thought I could hit the target, let alone the bull's eye. After extensive trash talk, I took my first shot. The arrow not only hit the bull's eye dead center but went right straight through the target and back up into the bush yards behind it. We all screamed in excitement as I bragged about the shot. Sam led the way into the bush to find the arrow. He was a few yards ahead of me when he shouted out, "I found it!" He found the arrow alright. The problem was that it had a little dead monkey on the end of it. I gave up archery.

MISS WHITE

Miss White, the little British history teacher who lived on campus had the cutest little dog. She was a tiny woman with snow white hair and wire rimmed spectacles. It seemed fitting that her name was White. She was white, her hair was white and her constant companion, her dog, was also white. She walked briskly, taking short quick steps always with her head down. Once spoken to, she always looked up, smiled and greeted me. Her tiny dog, Duchess, had the very same manner. It was short legged with white hair, walking in lockstep with her mistress and always with her head down and always wagging her tail when spoken to. It was hard to tell the two of them apart. I passed Miss White nearly every morning as we greeted each other on the foot path, she is going one way with Duchess in close pursuit, me going the other way. Often times we crossed at the low point on the path where it flooded during the rainy season. During those months a temporary foot bridge of long boards was laid across the sometimes two-foot-deep water, allowing us to continue without detouring. It was especially during the rainy season that we were warned to avoid walking through standing water. A nasty bug called the Tuba fly could infect us by laying its eggs in our skin. It became instinctive for me to follow the footpaths to avoid snakes, standing water and a host of other nasty little bugs. Word was spreading around campus one evening that Duchess had not been seen for hours and had been reported missing. Everybody knew the dog because it was the only one that lived on the campus, so it couldn't have been stolen and it would have been impossible to miss. Students and faculty formed a search party and spent the evening looking for the tiny dog. We had no luck. The next morning, on my way to my class, there was a big commotion at the bottom of the hill at the foot bridge which now lay over a considerable amount of dark, murky water. I asked a student what was happening. Just as he began to tell me, the men on the bank started shouting loudly as they began pulling from the water, a huge twelve-foot boa constrictor with Duchess locked in its jaws.

Little White Corvette

It was during a visit to the capital, Freetown, as a few of us volunteers were walking around the city, that I saw what I thought could only have been a hallucination. It happened so fast that I couldn't be sure. Then several others in the group claimed they had seen it, too. A few minutes later my suspensions were confirmed. Going down the street right in front of us was an African American man, driving a white, convertible 1967 Chevy Corvette. A white Corvette in Freetown, Sierra Leone didn't seem real. Not long after first seeing the car, I met the owner. His name was Lou, from Minnesota. He was a contract employee, like Peace Corps except that he got paid, a lot. Lou was about the age as most of the volunteers. He was also in town for a party that was being thrown by one of the Peace Corps officials who lived and worked in the capital. Lou was a true Renaissance man. He had all the attributes most guys would kill for. He had them all and still he was a very likeable guy. He was the proverbial, 'tall, dark and handsome' guy but humble, compassionate and funny as well. He looked like an athlete. He could sing. He could play the guitar. He could play the piano. He could even dance. This was truly a brilliant guy and he could make you laugh. But he always seemed to have trouble getting the girl. I figured if Lou couldn't get a girl, there was something wrong. He was not gay; he was just very picky. We bonded immediately. I even learned how to use a darkroom in Lou's second bedroom at his house in Makena. He taught me how to develop film and guitar lessons came with the friendship. Lou was the envy of every guy at the party. All the guys wanted to be him. Yet oddly enough, of all people, Lou admired me. He said that I had an easy way with the girls.

The party was a blast as it went on late into the night. Then it was over. Couples assembled and began to leave, most standing out front and dispersing into the distant darkness. Suddenly from the side of the residence roared the little white Corvette. Behind the wheel was Lou, revving the engine loudly and tearing away from the premises. Sitting next to him with her hair blowing back in the wind was Beth Everson. Beth was the young lady that many, if not most, of the guys wanted to be with during the holidays. This was Lou's get even scene, like in the movies when the good guy gets the girl in the end, where they drive off into the sunset with victory music blaring in the background. Most guys would have given a lot for that 'fifteen minutes of fame.' I couldn't wait to see Lou after that so that he could tell me what happened with Beth. I knew he had lots to talk about, even boast about if he saw fit. When I was finally able to question him about Beth, he seemed reluctant to talk about it. I pressed him for details. After much insistence, he finally relented and told me that the two of them had been together for well over an hour before they parted and during the entire time, they had been together, all Beth did was ask him questions about me. I was shocked; Lou was pissed, not at me but with the way things turned out.

Beth and I met the next day and hung out together for the next few days. The night before we were all to leave Freetown and head back up country, Beth and I spent the evening on the beach. It was extraordinary. We laid our blankets on the warm sand and watched as the sun slowly faded into the ocean. We made a fire that began to crackle to life after several efforts to get it started. The difficulty in starting that fire was what made the experience so memorable and funny. We fumbled around for a long time before it came to life. It was a transcendental moment. Behind us and over our heads, strewn for yards down the beach in either direction were jagged boulders, disappearing into the darkness. High life music played softly off in the distance. It was our beach; it was our memorable moment. We lay there in silence as I recalled painting this picture in my mind when I was a youngster telling my dad about my future adventures. Every aspect of my dream was real, the location, the setting, the music and the beautiful girl. It had been the most romantic evening of my life. If Dad could just see me now.

During another of those festive occasions, volunteers from different parts of the country all came together again for holiday celebrations. It was at another party, a big, lively, 'international' party this time. Food was being prepared all evening and the smell of the rich, exotic dishes permeated the dense summer air. Delicacies of all kinds were available just for the taking. The music was intoxicating. Just to be safe I had decided to stick with the salted, dry roasted 'nuts' that smelled like popcorn but tasted like peanuts. As the party activities increased into the later hours, I went out back where more festivities were happening. There was something going on that I had not seen since I had been in Sierra Leone. As I got closer to the large circle in a clearing, surrounded by dozens of shouting, cheering children, I could see that they were having a wonderful time. A big fire was blazing and the sweet smell of something roasting permeated the air. On each side of the fire were the kids, all with pales and pans partly filled with water. The children were screaming with delight as they frantically ran around, swatting the air furiously, and trying to fill their pales and pans with the thick cloud of insects that billowed from the huge mounds. Then I realized what was happening. The light was shining on a huge termite mound. It was the only night of the year that the termites flew out of their mounds to mate. For the termites it was that night or never. As the millions of termites rose from the mound's many openings, the children batted them down into their containers of water, soaking their wings so that they couldn't fly. They jumped up and down, screamed and tussled as they used anything available to swat down as many termites as possible. The bounty would not last all night, so they had to move quickly. The children then gathered the soaked termites, dripping with water, and spread them all out on paper, allowing excess water to drain. When the termites were sufficiently drained and the wok was sufficiently hot, handfuls of the insects were dropped into the hot palm oil that lined the wok. The wok was so hot that there was an instant huge plumb of steam that rose from it as the delicate wings were seared off. The termites were then deep-fried until they became golden brown and crunchy. They were poured into paper lined baskets and salted. It was right then that I realized that these termites were the dry roasted 'nuts' that I had been eating all day. It was another lesson learned.

Curse Of The Bundus And Poros

Back in Gary, Fred used to say, "It in but not of it." By now I was well established in the village and on campus. I was 'in it'. I learned that I wasn't 'of it' when a curse was put on me by the villagers. It was serious to the villagers but not to me, initially. In my mind it had just been one big misunderstanding. Every fall around September or October the surrounding villages initiate the boys and the girls into their respective secret societies. It's a coming of age ritual. For the girls it's the Bundu society and for the boys, it's the Poro society. I learned that perhaps akin to freemasonry, the Poro is an organization, made up of tribesmen who hold power within the tribes, its highest-ranking member being called Kashi in Temne and Taso in Mende. I had met the leader in the village when I went with Sam to the market to buy bush beef. The Poro is responsible for carrying out the annual initiations for the boys. The entire initiation process is very secretive. Everyone in the region knows that during the night ceremonies, especially during the night march, foreigners should shutter their windows and not come outside or look outside until the end of the night's ceremonies.

But I had already scheduled a 'meeting' with the young lady next door which was only a few dozen yards over the footpath from my house; I knew the path blindfolded. I had showered and sprayed on some men's cologne that Sam had bought at George the Lebanese's roadside store. It smelled like a blend of bacon, perfume and ammonia. Anyone could smell me coming yards away. But after a few minutes and with the wind blowing softly my nose got used to it or became so numb that I couldn't smell it on myself. I turned down the kerosene lamp and I cracked one of the shutters just wide enough peek out. As far as I could see into the dark distances were torches for miles, winding their way to the ceremonial grounds in the far distance. It was a sight to behold. The distant sound of drums filled the night air. It was a magical experience. I closed the shutter and tip toed across the yard and onto the footpath. All I could think of was helping my neighbor 'test' her mosquito netting. I knew every step of the way. Follow the footpaths. Snakes hate footpaths. It was pitch black. Quietly I counted the steps to her door but just as I counted up to the halfway point, somebody touched me. I immediately heard what I recognized as a mixture of pissed off Krio, Mende and Temne coming from all around me. I was surrounded. Someone was holding onto one arm, then the other. I wondered why anybody other than me would be walking around in the dark during secret society ceremonies. It could have been my cologne, but I knew I blew it when I opened my mouth and said, "Hey, what the #@!^$%!" That gave me away for sure. Someone lit a torch, revealing all of our faces in the bright orange flickering light. "MEESTAH LONG!!!!", someone shouted.

There was quite a commotion as more bodies gathered around me, bringing more and more torches to the area. In only a couple of minutes it became quite a scene. My mind was racing. Before long it was a major scene. Then I recognized one of the men. My dear friend Adbul Kanu was taking part in the ceremony and was one of the bodies surrounding me. He discreetly directed me to turn around and quietly go back into my house and he would talk to me later. As I turned timidly and began to tiptoe away, I asked nervously, "Hey, Abdul these brothers ain't gonna' kill me for trying to get some pussy, are they?" When I saw Abdul a few days later, he was angry with me as he informed me that the village had collectively put a curse on me. I felt relieved. I had expected the penalty to be more severe. I didn't believe in curses anyway. They're superstition. I thought even "Reb" and I would agree on that. I didn't worry or even think about it anymore until the night chanting started. Every night at sunset women from the village gathered at the foot of my incline and began a mournful, sorrowful, moaning chant that went on all night. It was a chant for the dead. Some left, others came. Children stopped talking to me when they saw me. They ran away, knowing that I was a dead man. People up and down the road that usually spoke and passed the time with small talk, ignored me. "Bua!", I'd say. I got nothing back. Scariest of all was when none of my students came to classes. I was avoided like the plague. Sometimes stray chickens would cross our property. Sam said that they were fair game so from time to time, we had unexpected chicken dinner. Even the chickens stopped crossing our yard. It went on for more than a week. I asked Abdul how long the curse was supposed to last. He laughed as usual and said that the villagers were surprised that I wasn't dead yet. Abdul laughed, obviously knowing more than I did. When I thought about the incident later, I understood how the curse could affect people in a frighteningly negative way. Perhaps had I been born in Sierra Leone; I would have acted in a different way. As an American, my perspective seemed to have affected the outcome. Admittedly, my nerves were beginning to fray after the first few days and nights. The one who is cursed begins to experience a sense of total isolation. In my case it went from isolation to paranoia. My mind kept telling me to stick with reason. In spite of my own beliefs, I was getting really scared. I thought about the Mau uprising in Kenya earlier in the century and how the natives invaded British homes in the night and massacred families in their beds. The victims never knew who their assailants were. It could have been their cook or their gardener or the driver. I thought about Sam and Lammie. It would have been just like Sam to hide under my bed, waiting for me. Then my sleep began to suffer. Next, my appetite disappeared.

At that point I had to slap myself back to reality. The power of the curse is that the people believe it based on what their environment suggests. Intuitively I felt just the opposite. The effects of my environment, though frightful, were determined by my state of mind, nothing else. I gave myself another mental slap and all was well. What I had to do was find the positive in the situation. It wasn't hard to do. Eventually everything returned to normal and my prurient interests were held in check during the next initiation season. The history of the village of Bunumbu would thereafter show that in the year of nineteen hundred and sixty-eight, a powerful Mende man from America, came to Bunumbu and repelled a Poro and Bundu curse. This great Mende man would come to be known as "Meestahlongbangbang."

APRIL 4, 1968

It was April 4, 1968, my mother's forty seventh birthday and I was in Freetown, a guest at the Brookfield Hotel where all the Peace Corps Volunteers stayed when they were in town. The BBC was on the radio and a group of us were jamming to Jose Feliciano's version of the Doors' hit tune, *"Light My Fire"*. Everybody was singing, *"Light my fire, light my fire, light my fire, yeah, yeah"*, when the radio announcer broke in:

"BBC SPECIAL REPORT: *American civil rights leader, the Dr. Martin Luther King, Jr. has been shot and killed!* Again, *American civil rights leader, the Dr. Martin Luther King, Jr. has been shot and killed."*

We all froze. Then instinctively we all gathered closer around the radio and turned it up. One special report after another confirmed our worse fears. Dr. King had been assassinated in Memphis, Tennessee. The thought of what would follow on the streets of America sent chills down my spine. Within ten minutes, every volunteer in the hotel was out in the court yard, discussing the bad news that had just come from home. We all crowded around tables that now held radios, all tuned to the BBC, as the broadcasts continued with the news of the tragedy. We were speechless. We looked blankly at one another as tears began to flow. We heard short clips from news stations around the U.S and around the world broadcasting news of the assassination. They were all the same. Our Dr. Martin Luther King, Jr. was dead. Soon reports of rioting began coming across the radio. Fires were being set in many cities across the nation and police were working hard to hold back mobs. Neighborhoods were being destroyed. The stories went on all night. We were all numb with disbelief. It was a day that I will never forget: Martin Luther King, Jr. died on my mother's birthday. Just as news of the King assassination was spreading through the city, we heard gunshots. Then there were more gunshots, then more and they were getting closer to the hotel where we were. Our immediate thoughts were that the King assassination had caused an uproar in Sierra Leone as well as other parts of the world. We were wrong. Things were about to get a lot more exciting at the Brookfield Hotel in Freetown.

THE COUP

During our training back in Washington, the volunteers learned about politics in Sierra Leone. It was good for us as visitor/residents to know something about the local politics. Siaka Steven was mayor of Freetown. In March of 1967 he was also declared Prime Minister of Sierra Leone. That was during the same time we started our training and got deployed. Stevens was as new to the office of Prime Minister as we had been to the role of Peace Corps Volunteer. He represented the All Peoples Congress (APC). He was in office literally only a few hours before he was ousted in a bloodless coup when the Armed Forces took over. Our training group might have been in Jamaica or Trinidad or even in the country while this was going on. However, a faction within the military took different actions and seized control of the government on March 23, 1968. The officers arrested their leader, commander, Brigadier David Lansana and suspended the constitution. They called themselves the National Reformation Council. The NRC was in control when we came into the country. The gunshots were right outside of the hotel now. Suddenly a staffer of the hotel ran out into the courtyard and broke the bad news that the Sierra Leonean Army was staging a military coup as we spoke. They had just taken over the government building and were going through town, shutting down places of business and taking charge of the city.

Suddenly soldiers barged into the hotel, guns out, asking who we were and what we were doing in Sierra Leone. Fortunately for us, they loved John F. Kennedy and were very favorable to Peace Corps. They assured us that no harm would come to us. We were rattled but safe. I learned that the NRC was being overthrown by another group of military officers calling themselves the Anti-Corruption Revolutionary Movement. This group restored the constitution and reinstated Siaka Stevens as Prime Minister. So far, two years had produced two military coups with more threatened. I was living right in the middle of it all. I could come away knowing that I was in a country where a man became Prime Minister twice in two years. Amidst all the turmoil in a letter dated Sunday, April 21, 1968 I wrote a letter to my parents:

"Hey, Folks!

I know that these *are very* troubling *times there at home with the death of Dr. King. And I'm sure you've seen on the news what's happening here. I have lived through a revolution. Yep, I was right in Freetown with other volunteers when the army took over the government and the country. It was just like in the movies: soldiers, machine guns, barricades, the whole works. They came right into our hotel but fortunately no one was hurt. Unfortunately, there were some people killed in a nearby town. I'm headed back to Bunumbu where it should be quiet and peaceful. Will write again when I get back up country."*

For the remainder of our tour in Sierra Leone, the military was a constant presence. Soldiers patrolled up and down the streets regularly. They weren't threatening to us, but their presence put a strain on the country. Back in the U.S., people were dying in the streets and neighborhoods were burning. As confused as I was about the events in the U.S., my students presented me with a thought-provoking question that I was hard put to answer. I had asked them why there are so many coups in Sierra Leone. Without giving me an answer, one responded with: "Why do the Americans kill all of their great leaders?" News of Dr. King's death had severely affected the people in the village of Bunumbu. Between the rioting at home and the coup in Sierra Leone, the adventurous life in the bush took on an entirely different meaning.

UNIION TEACHERS COLLEGE AT SAIC

With a coup and a curse behind me and things looking up, my attention was completely focused on my students' artwork. The School of the Art Institute of Chicago was a great place to have an exhibit. Mr. Gilmore should be happy to hear from me. It would give him a chance to 'make up' for not letting me into the school when I first applied so I was giving him another chance. It was a very good idea even from the Art Institute's perspective. It would not be the typical art exhibit. The work from Sierra Leone was fresh. I sent Mr. Gilmore a letter requesting his help in getting an exhibit at the School of the Art Institute. The letter read:

June 1968

Dear Mr. Gilmore:

I am proud to announce that through *my studies at the Art Institute, I have been able to spread some knowledge of the arts to other people. Here in Bunumbu, Sierra Leone (Union Teachers' College), I am the only faculty member of the art department. My job is to teach art to students who, in most cases, have taught school previously. Emphasis here is placed on exams; however, the solution found by most students is 'rote learning'. Thinking and real learning have yet to be experienced by many of my students/teachers. Few, if any of these students have ever had any art training, so art is a totally new field of study for them. Thus the situation arises where you find college students with perhaps four or five years of teaching experience but absolutely no art training I am almost tempted to evaluate the work on the level of children's art, and that may be wise, I don't know, but there is uniqueness in* the *work that clearly defines the limits of the African child and the African adult who has had no training. I have exposed my students to many different media, ideas and techniques. They have been aware of the vast array of materials found abundantly in nature; using these materials, art takes on some real meaning. The students have done water color, pen and ink, lino block printing, figure drawing, 2-D design; and stained glass using colored papers and paint.*

I would very much appreciate some assistance *in exhibiting some of their works. I will conclude and agree that this is much to ask, mainly because their standard of work is difficult to appraise. Your help in getting an* exhibition *at the School of the Art Institute would not only encourage these students and help them realize the value of art, but it will also indicate to me whether I am aiming in the right direction. At your request I will provide you as much information as you need. Will you please consider? Thank you.*

Sincerely,
Denver E. Long

My students asked why they should struggle to draw a straight-line free hand when they could use rulers. Or they questioned why they should read and study a book when they could just read it and memorize it. Why not just memorize everything? The realization was that the education system in Sierra Leone was not like that in the United States. It was based on an antiquated British educational system. My learning experience had brought me around the world just by having the courage to think and dream about going around the world. Americans call it creativity. We are never afraid to express new ideas. It was important for me to show and teach my students the importance of critical thinking skills. Understanding is a step toward wisdom. Westerners, especially Americans, question things, everything; nothing is sacred. We learn by doing and in the process tap into our other human capabilities. We think big; we think freely; we think because we can. In Sierra Leone students learned simply by rote. If one of my students was asked a question the same way it was printed in the text book, he would get the answer correct nearly every time. But if the printed information was presented to him with any changes in its order, he would not be able to tell what he had just read. He would not be able to think his way through the information. Their mental muscles had atrophied.

In such a learning environment I can just imagine the acuity of my average student's memory. My task was to help exercise and strengthen those mental muscles. The interesting thing was that the students had virtually no choice in changing their classes; they all had to take my classes in art and design as well as my English classes. Initially they protested. I heard one student say: "Meestah Long, in art you do not have to think atall, not atall!" I protested: "That is not true atall, not atall!"

Eventually they began to look forward to art and design classes and the good word got around the campus. When I wasn't in regular art classes, I was teaching English, writing and English composition to younger kids in the village who were, in many cases, related to my current stock of older male students. It was interesting when my teenage students were asking bold and daring questions like: "How far is it across America?" and "How do I write a book?" or "What is industrial design?" It was much easier communicating with the younger set because they thought I was a kid, too. I was "Meestah Long, Chicago, Al Capone, bang! bang!" Nobody ever said it any differently. There was no creative thinking in the student body. Creativity was dead. But the younger students began to appreciate the ability to study and ask me all kinds of questions. Ask any question. Then find the answer. Without exception, the older students' rote excuse was, "All work and no play make Jack a dull boy." I responded: "Yeah, Jack may be a dull boy, but he doesn't have be a dumb boy."

Back home Mr. Gilmore and the School of the Art Institute came through like real champs. In September of 1968 after months of preparation and correspondence, the art and design work of my students from Union Teachers' College was exhibited at the School of the Art Institute of Chicago. It brought attention to Union College, the village of Bunumbu and pride to Headmaster, Gwynn-Jones. When the students finally realized where their work was being exhibited, they were ecstatic. My family attended. My mother sent me photos of her, my father and sister standing there in the exhibit talking to, of all people, Dean Roger Gilmore. From all indications and the mail, I received from faculty and students at the Art Institute, the show was received very well and was a booming success. By late1968 Sierra Leone was my home. It was like I had been born there. I had not only adjusted to living in Africa, but I was thriving. Practically everything I needed was available. Most importantly I was making some difference in the lives of the students and children I'd encountered. It was a teaching and learning paradise. I had a tin roof over my head, a good roommate, two ridiculously silly sons, a good paying job and plenty of time to be as creative as I wanted. I could even travel. I also had dear friends who offered benefits. What was there not to like? Life was good.

As usual, it was Sam who brought new situations to my attention. One morning before heading off down the road to school, he looked at me, smiled and muttered something in Mende, then Krio, then Temne, just to piss me off. I didn't understand exactly what he said but I heard something like 'yamba' in the statement. I understood enough Mende to know also that he was referring to something behind the house. While Sam was at school, I went out back and looked around, not knowing what I was looking for. I tracked as far into the bush as I felt comfortable then returned to the house, having found nothing. When Sam came in from school, I confronted him. He laughed out loud and asked, "Meestah Long, do you like yamba?" "Sam, what the hell are you talking about?" I asked.

Once I understood what he was talking about, I answered, "Yes." That's when I discovered the gold mine behind my house. Sam knew everything. He knew plants and he guided me about twenty yards down the footpath, turned slightly and followed a slight down slope into some thick brush. "Voila!!!" Cannabis!!! Sam informed me that it was not there by accident; it had been planted and harvested before and it was very powerful. He took a thick green bud and broke it apart and rubbed his fingers roughly across the plant, exposing the sticky resin. He sniffed it and extended his arm for me to take a whiff. "Very strong!" Sam said. I had just hit the yamba jackpot. I had never smoked marijuana. I got a contact high the one time I rode in a car with Fred and the guys. Now I had a private farm and a gardener. And if Sam says it's powerful then I believe it's powerful. I certainly intended to find out. I could not have prayed for a situation like this but here it was. I renegotiated Sam's contract on the spot. He was not only getting a raise from me but those sneakers that we saw down at George the Lebanese's road side store were his.

SAM'S NEW CONTRACT

Sam had yet to complete the major portion of his new contract. His new task in addition to his regular duties was to take that shoe box from his newly acquired sneakers and keep in filled to the top with 'yamba'. He agreed to 'process' the plants back up in the bush and keep this our little secret. Once it was cut, it didn't take long for the sun to dry the plants out and make them ready for consumption. Sam ran his little business about twenty yards into the bush behind my house. I was struck as if with a bolt of lightning when it dawned on me who had planted the crop behind my house in the first place. He had had a business going in the bush behind my house long before it was my house, before I ever arrived in Sierra Leone. It was clear. Sam was the drug man though he never openly admitted it. When I asked about it, he only smiled and remarked about how good the yamba was. Sam belonged in the mob. It was during the rainy season and I had not yet touched any of Sam's product. In fact, I had, for a short time, completely forgotten about it. One night during a heavy rainstorm, when there were just the two of us in the house, Sam offered me a little present. I was flattered. He had rolled a joint with the product from his crop. It was a downpour, constant and heavy. Beaming over the success of his new contract negotiations, he suggested that we sit on the big round skin rug in the middle of the floor. The BBC and I were 'jamming' again with Jose Feliciano's *"Light My Fire"*. Sam snickered as we sat there looking stupidly at each other as he lit the cigarette. On my turn, I inhaled deeply and held it in like he suggested. Then slowly I let the smoke out, as instructed. The joint went between the two of us only one time. By the time he was handing it back to me, the skin rug was floating. I sat and stared across the rug at Sam. He was smiling from ear to ear and all I could see were white teeth. The rug was floating higher off the floor now. For a moment I was afraid to look over the edge, so I closed my eyes. Higher and higher I felt the rug rise until we were sailing through the night sky, over the rain and the jungle.

"Light My Fire! Light My Fire!, yeah!, yeah*! Light My Fire"!* We were on a magic carpet ride. I could feel the soft, warm wind on my face as we soared over a village, then another, floating like a bird under the beaming moon. Music was in the air, coming from nowhere in particular and everywhere at the same time.

> *"Light My Fire, Light My Fire!* yeah! yeah!" I gave myself over to the pleasure. *"Light My Fire!"* It was magic. Higher and higher we flew. *"Light My Fire, Light My Fire!"*

Then I opened my eyes. We were still sitting there in the middle of the floor with the radio blasting over the roar of the storm. We sat smiling at each other, and then broke into hysterics. Having had nothing to compare my yamba to, on a scale of one to ten, I rated it somewhere between fifteen and twenty. At night, especially during the rainy season, while I wrote in my journal and sent letters home, I listened to the BBC on short wave radio and rolled joints the size of Sharpie markers. With the back of my hand, I brushed away onto the floor, the eighth of an ounce or more that didn't fit into the joints. Why worry about saving sand if you own a beach? Sam saw to it that I was never out of yamba and I saw to it that Sam was never out of sneakers. It was a good deal. Those nights, listening to the BBC, writing letters, preparing lessons and listening to the constant concert of rain drops on the tin roof, were moments in a dream. I was in another world. I had a desk and chair and, on the wall, right next to me was my cork board full of photos. Right in the middle was a photo of Joan C. Johnson, my "Jamaican Doll". That was when I started writing the first few lines of the next great American novel.

SEGBWEMA

When Rick and I first arrived in the country, a major part of settling in was to activate checking accounts so that our monthly U. S. government paychecks could be deposited. Our bank was in the nearby hub city of Segbwema. Riding into town on a bright Saturday morning was a big deal for the students on campus. It was an even bigger deal for Sam and Lammie since they rarely had a chance to leave the village. Everybody looked forward to boarding the lorries and buses and taking off for a day of shopping, visiting and sightseeing in the city. We were fortunate enough to have a school minibus. Part of the new contract deal that I made with Sam was that he could come to Segbwema with me on alternating months when I went to the bank. On the other months, Lammie would get a chance to go into town. They both agreed to be my voices and guides whenever we spent time in town. We were like father and sons. Sam took me to all the places that I wanted to go but didn't know how to find. Back in Bunumbu, the four of us were just one big happy family. Rick and I went to work. Sam and Lammie went to school. Like a typical family, when we came home, we did our chores and sat down to dinner. Most of our dinner meals came from the kitchen at the college. If we didn't eat at home, we ate with the students in the campus cafeteria. Rice was the main staple. Over mounds of rice was cassava leaf stew. In the stew was bonga, a small dried fish that was another staple. On some special occasions the menu changed, and we'd have jollof rice or groundnut stew over rice. We generally just chose to eat at home. Lammie was making sure that rice chop dinner was always in the house. One evening rice chop dinners stands out. The four of us sat at the dinner table. Rick and I always sat at the ends of the dining room table with Lammie and Sam on either side of us. Just as brothers would do, they got into many verbal spats, screaming in both Mende and Krio so that Rick and I couldn't keep up. But their voices and body languages spoke volumes. Often Rick and I had to break them up across the table. As we sat, eating rice and discussing the day's events, breaking into laughter from time to time, one by one we all heard the same odd sound. We all stopped talking and eating to listen closely; the sound continued. It was a crunching sound. As if on cue, the four of us simultaneously bent over and looked under the table. Fang, our cat, was having snake for dinner.

One day I got home first. I went straight to my office as usual. Not long after, Rick came in and went right to his office, both of us ignoring the kitchen and getting right down to school work. Sam and Lammie came in and within five minutes, they were screaming for us to hurry and come see what was happening. If you can imagine a clogged sink full of dish washing liquid with hot water running into it for half an hour. You'd get suds, a mountain of suds. Imagine the suds rising three feet high from the sink basin. But instead of a mountain of white suds, there were ants, millions of ants. There was a mountain of 'foam' three feet high and overflowing down the side onto the floor and trailing right out the back door and out into the bush. There were millions of ants. They were clinging to one another creating a living bridge. Sam quickly showed us what to do as he warned us not to disturb them. Doing so would have put us all in big trouble because the ants would have scattered throughout the house. Instead, he retrieved one of the kerosene lanterns and carefully poured a trail of kerosene completely around the horde of ants. He made sure that every other doorway, every threshold was wet with kerosene so that if the horde split, they would not enter the house through other openings. The ants didn't cross a line of kerosene. When the ants were done, the kerosene 'border' guided them right out the back door and back into the bush. By morning the ants were gone. We learned that the ants were most dangerous at night when they can't be seen. That's why it was important to always stick to the footpath and carry a flashlight. If you stepped on a trail of fire ants at night without someone to help you, you'd be in big trouble. I was learning fast. The bush was alive!

THE BIG RACE

Life was good in the bush. Every day was a joy, especially since my 'son' had provided me with an unlimited supply of prime ganja. My relationship with Sam had grown to the point we even talked about him possibly coming to the United States to visit when my tour was over. I especially appreciated his keen, mature sense of humor. He was a survivor who deserved my respect and I gave it to him. We talked about overcoming obstacles and on the challenges that life presented-real serious stuff. Our biggest challenges were physical. It all boiled down to which of us was the most physically fit and athletic. Sometimes he won; sometimes I won. I was in top physical condition, so I'd take on all of his challenges. When the stakes finally reached the new sneakers level, we both got serious. I challenged Sam to race me from our front door to my art building. It took me about five to seven minutes to walk the distance. It was about one and a half city block in distance, but the path was through bush, up inclines, etc. If I ran at top speed, I could make it in about four minutes. I made him and offer he couldn't refuse. The first one to my building wins. If win, Sam works for free for a week. If he wins, he gets a new pair of sneakers and five Leones ($5.00). He was chomping at the bit.

At the starting line, we stood back to back at the front doorstep waiting for the count down. "On your mark! Get set! Go!". Sam was gone! He was gone! I heard the brushes rustle as he flew through the bush. There was no way I could beat him to my studio, and I knew it. Amazed at Sam's speed, I turned and went inside the house. I went straight to my stash box and rolled me the biggest, roundest prettiest joint ever. I took a beer from the refrigerator and headed for the front porch. Christo *Redentor* by Donald Byrd was playing on the BBC. I propped myself back in my big chair, popped my brew and fired up. After about fifteen minutes, I heard footsteps. It was Sam. I laughed about that race until I left Sierra Leone.

CHAPTER FOUR

Las Palmas Jingle Bells

My first Christmas away from home was spent in Las Palmas, Canary Islands, a Spanish possession, off the west coast of Africa, near Morocco. They experience tropical weather and have beautiful beaches; it was the place for young folks to be if you were leaving Europe during the holidays. From the north, students swarmed out of Spain, France, and Germany and as far as Italy to celebrate in the balmy air of the tropical islands. From the south we flooded out of West Africa: Sierra Leone, Liberia, Senegal, all headed to the party spot in the Atlantic. Lou and I went together along with a dozen other volunteers from across West Africa. One of the first people Lou and I met was Didier Alann, the Frenchman. Didier was cool, international. He was the same age as we were but worldly. Didier was very handsome, a cross between Dean Martin and Prince. Everything about him exuded confidence, yet he was comical and warm. He was bumming just like the rest of us, looking for a good time. Back home in Paris his family had money but for the time being, Didier was doing his own thing.

He became my most trusted friend while we partied and traveled around together. He spoke French, Dutch and a few other languages. When we first met in Las Palmas, he felt like an old friend right from the beginning. He was impressed that we came from America to live in the 'jungle'. I promised to visit him whenever I got to France.

Four of us rented two rooms at the Residencia Syria, Luis Mortre, 27 in Las Palmas. From there we moved to the Mar Azul on Paseo De Las Canteras, and closer to the action spots. Students from all over Europe and Africa converged on the tiny islands, if not Las Palmas then Tenerife Island a few miles away. There were more girls than guys on the island at one time than I had ever even imagined. That meant our favorability ratings sky rocketed. Chances of getting lucky shot through the roof. It was then that

I saw the most beautiful woman I'd ever seen in my life. She was purple-black with features that were cut from black marble. I stared. Her hair was black as night with a radiance that seemed mystical. Her eyes were piercing and deep blue. I was not the only one staring at her; she had captivated everybody she passed. Ethiopian, she was breathtakingly beautiful. It was hard for me to imagine a woman so beautiful that she literally leaves you speechless. Sitting in an open café under a bright sun, I was relaxing alone, when a group of young women gathered near the entry way. There were dozens of girls, girls everywhere. Most were students. The guys were outnumbered at least four to one. There was a big crowd forming near the entrance to the patio where I was sitting and over all the heads of the crowd, I could see Lou. He was right smack in the middle of all the hyper activity, talking and joking with everybody, especially the young women. They thought he was so charming. He was charming. As I continued to watch, he headed in my direction. In tow were two beautiful girls, one in each hand, one from France, the other from Belgium. If I had tried to write down what happened next and sell it as an idea, nobody would buy it; they just wouldn't believe it. I wouldn't have believed it. Lou introduced me to Rita and her friend Anna. As we were being introduced, Rita moved closer to the table and sat next to me. I reached out to offer my hand for support if she needed it. It was just an instinctive motion. She took my hand as we both sat back down next to each other. Lou began the conversation with one of his quips that got us all laughing. Lou ordered a round of drinks. The conversation grew as we got more comfortable.

Half an hour later Rita was still holding my hand. Somehow, we had come to know each other without the normal small talk. Lou and Rita's girlfriend, Anna both noticed that Rita and I had become fixated on one another. My new mate, Rita Curvier, was from Antwerp, Belgium where she had just left her family to attend university in France. She was twenty-one years old and studying European History in Paris where she became friends with Anna. They became dorm mates at school. Anna lived in Paris with her older sister who was a medical student. Anna was studying architecture. Both girls came from middle class backgrounds with well-educated parents. Of the four of us at the table at that moment, two of us had graduated college and gotten degrees and the other two were currently in college working toward degrees. Both young ladies were impressed at the fact that both Lou and I had graduated from college, left our country and chosen to go live in Africa. We seemed very mysterious to them. This was the first time I had seen Lou so content. He and Anna were the perfect couple. She was teaching him the rudiments of French. He wasn't doing very well. That only led to more humor as we ordered another round of drinks. I asked the girls why they would leave a crowd of hundreds of people from all parts of the world, in every color imaginable, and choose Lou, a black guy and follow him to meet another black guy. For a moment they pretended not to understand the question. But after a few moments of mumbling communications between themselves, they both broke into giggles then loud laughter. They never answered the question. Lou and I looked at each other and said: "Cool."

After that first day, the four of us were inseparable. There were parties every night of the week in Las Palmas with music a constant buzz in the air. Some parties were private, but the best ones were the ones where we arrived by 'accident' and nobody knew anybody initially. By the time the parties were in full swing, everybody knew everybody. Didier made friends easily. Girls were attracted to him like he was a movie star. He shared his good fortune with us whenever he could, introducing us to his friends, most of whom were girls. Our romances lasted for one week until it was time for us all to head back to our respective worlds. Before we left the island, Rita wrote down her address and phone number in Antwerp and asked that I promise to keep it in my passport so I wouldn't lose it. I promised. On the plane back to Freetown, Lou and I discussed our good fortune. He promised Anna he was going to visit her in Paris as soon as his tour was over. There would be so much to write about when I got back to Bunumbu.

Santa Of Rome

Life in Bunumbu remained normal until it was time to pack up for the last time. After two years, I was departing from the same location, Lungi International Airport in Freetown where I first arrived. Travelers, coming and going, came through Lungi. At regular two-year cycles, new volunteers entered the country as old volunteers departed, making the city a hub of youthful activity. During those active days, Freetown was booming, especially at night. It was a time of travel for everybody. Those headed out of country were headed for destinations around the globe. When meeting someone new, the common question was: "Incoming?" It was the time when lots of news and information was being exchanged as everybody got to know everybody. Incoming volunteers brought news from home; the old volunteers brought news from the bush.

For a week, parties abounded as the new volunteers headed to their posts up country. I was headed out. Word got around that there was an outgoing volunteer, me, headed for Italy, destination Rome. I did not know at the time that there was a Loyola University campus in Rome. Some of the new, incoming volunteers had friends and even siblings attending Loyola. They sought me out. If I'd deliver some gifts to friends and relatives at the university in Rome, they would pay me. My air fare was already paid so anything else would be extra cash. We cleared up the details and made a deal. Most of my personal belongings had already been sent home from Sierra Leone so I had only one piece of luggage; over the last two years, I had learned to travel light. The gifts were personalized with names and short messages from their senders but were mainly just small African souvenirs and trinkets. But the idea of my delivering a gift to a student in Rome who had a friend or relative in Sierra Leone was just too good to pass up. I not only had a destination; I now also had a mission. I was going to

Rome and play Santa Claus. The irony of my situation didn't escape me. I was going to deliver presents to little boys and girls who'd been good all year. I thought it would also be great if I could get lucky while I was in Rome because that was a part of my original dream. I had planned my itinerary from Sierra Leone back to Las Palmas in the Canary Islands to Rabat in Morocco, from there on to Lisbon, Portugal, then on to Spain. Many of us returning volunteers traveled together through to the Canaries and Morocco until we arrived in Spain. After Madrid, the group began to thin out as the destinations began to vary as some headed for home; others headed north, and some remained behind in Spain. But I was going to cross the 'The Big Med', the Mediterranean Sea and head straight to Italy. From there I was headed back through, Paris, London, Amsterdam and maybe Antwerp.

Thinking back about an industrial design project in school at the Art Institute, a classmate had taken a color photo of his project, a beautiful wooden bench that he designed and built. When I saw that photo and how beautifully simple the shot was, I decided that one day I was going to buy myself a good reflex camera and Amsterdam was the place to do it. I was going to buy an Asahi Pentax 35mm camera, just like the one my pal used in school. I could get it from the duty-free shop at Schiphol International Airport before heading back across the Atlantic Ocean for home. By the time I was ready to leave Madrid, I was really fired up because my next stop was Italy. I boarded an Alitalia airline, ready for the trip across the sea.

It was about nine o'clock at night as we descended into Fiumicino – Leonardo da Vinci International Airport also known as the Rome Fiumicino Airport, located in Fiumicino about twenty miles southwest of Rome's historic city center. When I looked out the window on our approach, I noticed it was raining. The view from the plane window looked like any other city at night but I was in Italy! The rain poured down as the plane descended. When we finally reached the gate and the plane's engines shut down, my heart started to pound rapidly. My heartbeat hastened as I left the plane and proceeded through the corridor to the luggage pickup. After a lengthy wait, the luggage finally started to drop from the carousel. I gathered my luggage and proceeded into the main corridor of the terminal building. Even at that hour of the evening the airport was bustling. I walked slowly as I drank in all the sights, sounds and smells of the airport.

Instinctively I walked into the first card shop I saw. I was standing at a card case in the airport just outside of Rome, Italy. That's when the reality struck me. I was in my dream again only this time it was not a dream; it was real. It was night as I had imagined long ago and it was raining, something I loved. I had to get a card sent home just like in the dream. There I was alone in the airport, crying like a baby. Two nuns were in the shop /they looked at me as I stood there with tears streaming down my face.

I was not afraid but frustrated and happy at the same time. In my dream there was a huge, bright cross hanging in the card shop, and it annoyed me, having no obvious purpose in a card shop so I did my best to ignore it in the dream, but I couldn't. People stared at me as I stood there crying. They wouldn't stop staring at me. My feelings were mixed. I was angry. I was sad and I was happy all at the same time. Then I would wake up from the dream.

The cross had to represent the two nuns who stood there staring at me, not knowing what to do. It was no longer a dream. It was real. I was alive, in the airport in Italy, looking for just the right card to send to my dad. I found a card and wrote: "Dear Dad, Need I say more? Love, Petie." Within minutes that card was out of my possession and on its way to the United States. I smiled as I strolled confidently through the terminal to the waiting buses outside. I had just made another of my lifelong dreams a reality.

Earlier in the summer, I had decided on a place to stay while I was in Rome. I rented a beautiful little apartment at the American Palace Eur Hotel, 554 Via Laurentina in the 'Jewish Ghetto' section of the city, near the city's famous Tiber River. It was located only a few yards from the metro train station. I thought the name was odd at first, but then I learned that 'ghetto' was not always in reference to the 'hood' back home. History showed that Jews had been isolated throughout Europe for many centuries, culminating in the German effort during WWII. It was a part of history. It was an immaculately clean apartment building and neighborhood. I think a cleaning service came every day and washed down everything: cars, buildings, streets, everything. I was very comfortable in my little apartment, in ROME, ITALY! There were inner courtyards to the complex of buildings in the neighborhood where clothes lines ran from the side of one building to another. Clothes swayed back and forth in the warm breezes. Looking up from the ground was like looking through a painting, colorful and alive with musical movements of the freshly laundered clothes. They hung from the top floor all the way down to just above the lowest apartment. I quickly settled into my little apartment and began writing a letter. Back home my mother had bought colored push pins to place on the map that hung in my room. My nephew, *Sputnik*, Jo's son, was about ten years old and able to follow my travels by putting a push pin on the map for every location that I had mentioned in my letters. That map must have been rather colorful.

My first night's rest in Rome was complete. I slept like a new born baby. The next morning was beautiful. It was warm and the sun shone brightly. After a big breakfast, I grabbed my bag loaded with the gifts and made my way to the Loyola University campus located on Mont Marie, the highest of the seven hills in Rome. I found myself gawking at all the sights along the way. Getting there was a challenge. Rome drivers were the worse drivers on the planet. The traffic hurling around busy monuments and parkways were suicide zones.

The sprawling Loyola campus was splendid. Immediately I could feel and see the effects of money, but I wasn't the least bit intimidated. I arrived on the campus at mid-morning and meandered around for a short time until I came up on a group of students who seemed relaxed, standing around talking and laughing. I approached them, introduced myself and explained that I had just arrived in Rome the day before from Sierra Leone, West Africa. The students perked up when I said that. As soon as they realized that I was an American Peace Corps Volunteer, the conversation lit up and got energized. They had questions for me about living in Africa. I had questions for them about living in Rome. We talked for nearly an hour and then after giving them some of my experiences, I explained why I was in Rome, at Loyola University. As I spoke to them, I took out my list of names of the students for whom I had brought gifts. They got excited, finding it hard to believe that I had come all the way from Africa to deliver gifts to them and some of their friends. As I off the names, two students, a young lady and young man both shouted out, "That's me!" Within the next hour, word had spread around the campus that a black guy from Chicago was there on campus to deliver presents from Peace Corps friends and relatives in West Africa. I was an instant celebrity. If Dad could see me now. I flashed back to the conversations with him when I promised him that when I got to Rome, the people were going to love me and take me in. These were rich kids and I was their special guest.

They took me into one of the buildings on campus and created a private party atmosphere where I read off the rest of the names and handed each student their present along with a personal note from the sender. By late in the evening I had met every student whose name was on the list and dozens more. One of the students I had brought a gift for was a gorgeous young lady from California. She was petite no tiny, short, dark hair and big brown eyes and a rich golden complexion. Her tan could only have come from lying in the sun, a lot. She looked like a tiny Liz Taylor. Her lips were blood red. I couldn't tell if it was from lipstick or wet paint, but her lips captivated me. I had never imagined a girl could be so beautiful. I wanted to kiss her yet even that seemed more than could hope for.

Her name was Candy; she was tiny and-stunning. I recalled a paperback book about a little vixen with fire red lips whose name was Candy; this one was real. She asked where in the city I was living. when I told her, she told me to move out and move on campus with them-free, until I left the country. It must have been love at first sight with Candy and me because less than an hour later, I was riding merrily through the streets of Rome in the back seat of a red convertible sports car with two beautiful young women. Candy was driving and her girlfriends Lisa, was riding shotgun. If only Dad could see me now. It was really happening. During the ride through town, my mind wondered back to the days at home when I boasted to my dad about the day I'd go to Rome and be welcomed and how I'd have mad, passionate love affairs with beautiful women in exotic places around the world. As I lay back, taking in the sights, I knew that his ride through the streets of Rome was a damn good start.

Once I moved into a dorm room on the campus, Candy and I became an instant item. Until then I had never thought of myself as a particularly desirable guy, not like Lou was. I was short, medium brown with a healthy, trim physique. I was in good shape; I even had a 'six pack'. But according to Candy, what she and the other girls found sexy about me were my muscular legs. I had muscular legs from having spent so much time at the skating rink on Sundays when I lived on Massachusetts St. All those afternoons at the rink were finally paying dividends. I had to admit that for my size, my legs were impressive, so I made it a point to always wear shorts-and it worked. I was just a normal twenty-something horny guy doing the best he could.

Candy's father was a big shot diplomat in Rome. Both her mother and father lived in a high rise building in an exclusive part of downtown. Candy had been in Rome for over a year, studying political science. I asked her what her parents would think if they knew she was with a black guy. She laughed and assured me that they would not take kindly to the idea. Back home they were very rich, hoity-toity conservative high society types. Candy was a little rich girl. I was hoping that she would really piss mom and dad off and go all the way with this black guy. There was a sinister joy in her voice and eyes when talked about angering her folks. I suspected it was spite that I heard coming from her. I thought that if she wanted to be with me just to spite her parents, who am I to object? She told me that she didn't always do what her parents wanted her to do. That was a joy to hear. Suddenly, it was deja-vu all over again. I asked why she would even want to date a black guy around all of her little rich white friends. She blushed and her laughter gave me my answer.

Once I hooked up with the students, I spent very little money. They fed me, took me to parties and showed me all the fun spots in the city. Candy and I went to the Coliseum together making a getaway from the group for a while. I was a part of the group for nearly a month. Then it was time for me to leave. The night before my departure, the students had planned a big surprise, going away party for me at, of all places, Candy's parents' high-rise apartment downtown. I was concerned about causing a problem and losing my ass. I was assured that the parents were out of the country on business travel and had left the apartment to Candy for emergencies. She always had access to the luxury apartment but spent little time there when her folks were in town. At the party, I was the guest of honor. The party was just fantastic. The apartment was on one of the upper floors of the building and it had a balcony that looked out over the sprawling city below. Next to me on the balcony, overlooking the city of Rome-at night, was Candy. She was wearing a very tiny, very red dress that matched her very red lips. I was ready to spread the paint. If ever there was a scene in a movie where a little vixen was displaying all her assets, this was it. No screen scene could have been this perfect. If I touched her, I'd burn my fingers; she was hot! If I rubbed against her, I'd sizzle. She was on fire. I figured: what's a little 'third degree burn', all over my body? Coming from inside the apartment we could hear The Beatles singing *"Hey, Jude"*. The moment etched itself into my memory. Another dream was coming true. Together Candy and I looked out over the city of Rome-then at each other. It was lust at first sight.

> *"Hey, Jude, don't make it* bad. *Take a sad song and make it better. Remember to let her into your heart. Then you can start to make it better, better, better, better!"*

The night was magical. Again, I was in an incredible, lust-laden, short term relationship that would end soon. Candy and I both acknowledged that we'd probably not ever meet again which made the night even more special. We were silent for a long time, enjoying the perfect moment, eyes fixed on one another. My mind was focused on what I wanted to do to her. We hadn't touched yet, but we could both feel the heat. I was as stiff as a crutch. And though I had argued with my dad to the contrary, this moment was perfect. We partied late into the night. When the party was finally over, Candy and I spent the night in the apartment. There are no words. Life was good.

A few days before I left Rome, I was able to call Didier Alann in Paris and let him know that I would be in France in a few days. He sounded excited. I left Rome smiling, having fulfilled another dream. What more could the future have in store, I wondered. Life is what you make of it. I spent the next month traveling through Europe with Didier. He was my guide and protector while I was in Paris. I stayed with him and his brother in a small, very classy and fashionable apartment. We could see the Arch de Triumph in the distance from where they lived. It was right in the heart of town, where they assured me "all the action is." They were right. After three weeks, I was worn out and ready for some rest, something I could not get there. I decided it was time to move on. My new camera was in Amsterdam waiting for me. It seemed the stars were all aligned because I phoned Rita in Antwerp and she answered the phone on the first ring.

When she realized who it was on the line, she started screaming. I was screaming, too. I told her that I was on my way back home to the states, but on my way, I was stopping for sure in Amsterdam to get my camera and maybe stop in Brussels. She sounded shocked on the phone, repeating that she never thought I would call her in a million years, but here we were, again. We were both excited about the chance to see each other again. During the conversation, I realized that it would be better if we both met in Amsterdam since Brussels was between Paris and Amsterdam, otherwise I'd be making two stops. But that was a lot to be hoping for. It would be such an imposition to ask her to fly to another country just to meet me. The flight time is only a few hours but still I didn't impose. As it turned out I didn't have to impose; things were getting better and better. Rita and Anna, whom Lou and I had met in Las Palmas, were themselves headed for Amsterdam the next day! It seemed that Anna's sister, Marie, the medical student, was going to be in Amsterdam with some of her friends from school for just a few days and demanded that Anna and Rita come and meet them there. Rita and Anna were leaving the next morning-so was I. The timing was perfect.

Ahead of time, Rita warned me that we might not be able to get together until the second day because of some big private party that she and her friends were committed to attending. It was a big dance party celebration for their first night in Amsterdam, so they had promised to attend. That was fair. Two days together instead of three would still be great. At the last minute, Didier decided to come to Amsterdam with me. That was a big benefit and I was joyous. He had been to Amsterdam many times before and knew the city. He also spoke Dutch. When we arrived at Schiphol International, we went directly to the Hotel Corona at De Lairessestraat 11 in Amsterdam where I had reserved a room before we left Paris. Didier even split the cost. He was a real treasure; I felt safe with him. There was no fear in him. If he wanted to do something, he did it. He reminded me of my friend Fred back home in Gary. Once we settled into our room, Didier got on the phone and got so involved in several conversations, in several languages, that I thought for a moment that he was a native of Amsterdam. For him everywhere was home. Again, I was impressed. He had planned our first night out in Amsterdam, but first we should eat and rest. It was about six o'clock p.m. We took his advice and after a hearty meal, we both crashed. We awoke around ten o'clock. I felt refreshed and ready to party. Once we showered and changed clothes, we headed for a night on the town. I followed Didier everywhere. I wondered what I would have done had he not come. I felt good, invigorated and excited to be in another exotic country with all kinds of new people, girls.

The city was alive. As soon as we hit the street there was activity in every direction. At a coffee shop we met the young folks from Amsterdam that Didier had been talking to on the telephone. They were good hearted and very friendly. I was introduced as Didier's friend and guest from the United States who had just come from living in the 'jungle' in Africa. He made me sound like Albert Schweitzer. From that moment on, I was part of the group. From the coffee shop we all headed to a party. Two of the guys in the group had cars so we piled into each and headed for the celebration held at an open-air venue a few miles from where we were. We could hear the music from some distance away as we approached the action. There were hundreds of people dancing and singing, having a wonderful time. It was a world peace party. Didier said, "Ok, let's party!", as he led me and the group into the festivities. It looked like every part of the world was represented in the crowd. I could hear different languages as we meandered through the crowd. There was an upbeat atmosphere enveloping the entire crowd. I followed Didier as he wove his way further and further into the crowd. Earlier in the day he told me that if we were lucky and he could locate them, I'd get a chance to meet some girls from Paris that he knew. Then from a distance he yelled out a name to someone ahead of him in the crowd. She was a beautiful young blonde. They greeted each other and hugged vigorously as they got reacquainted. They laughed about something in Dutch. After a few more moments of kissing and hugging Didier turned and introduced me to the young lady. She gave out a big smile as she came over and hugged me so tightly that I was caught completely off guard. Her name was Helga and she was one of Didier's ex-girlfriends. Now we were following Helga through the crowd to find her group of girlfriends. There were girls everywhere, of every color, size, nationality, of every description, speaking every language. I was in party paradise. Suddenly Helga shouted out to a group of a dozen or so young women ahead of us and they all turned to see us approaching.

To my utter astonishment, standing right in the middle of about twelve or thirteen girls was Rita. Our eyes met, stunned, our mouths dropped open as we froze. We both stood there in absolute shock and awe, staring right into each other's faces, tears beginning to run down her face. Without a word being said, we grabbed each other and embraced for a long moment. Several times we stepped back from one another to look at each other's face and then hugged again. By now the rest of the group was standing there with their mouths agape, speechless, looking at Rita and me, not knowing what was happening. They were wondering how she could just grab a complete stranger and hug and kiss him-right in front of everybody. After a few seconds it must have occurred to Didier who this young woman was, so he explained it to the rest of the group. Didier had met Rita and Anna when we were in Las Palmas during the summer break from Bunumbu. We never thought we'd be at the same party. Just like in Las Palmas, Rita and I spent the next three days together until it was time for us both to leave Amsterdam. Like so many other times in the past, I knew, and Rita knew that this would be the last time we met. There was only bliss.

From the time I left home up until the day I left the continent of Europe heading back home, I had 'fallen in love' every time my plane landed but that was all a part of the master plan. I counted at least six times. I had forgotten to be careful what I wished for. My attitude whenever I met a new girl was, 'just take me'. It worked. I left the Netherlands with a smile on my face and more precious memories in my heart. Out of all the excitement and merriment that I had experienced, there was something deeply comforting about fulfilling one dream after another based on effort and determination. I imagined what I could have done if I had had real talent or dare say, lots of money. But that was exactly the point. I wish I could take credit for saying it first but: "If I can do it, anybody can do it". I gained a degree of understanding about life, mankind, and the workings of the universe. In my mind few had come to understand what I had grasped. Suddenly I understood the mysteries of the universe. It was all so simple. It all boils down to one word: sex. As I saw it life was wearing while silk-or cotton panties. On the day of my flight back to the U.S. I bought my first 35mm reflex camera. As planned, I bought an Asahi Pentax; I was ecstatic.

CHAPTER FIVE

The Mystic Law

My total air fare from Freetown, Sierra Leone, through to the Canary Island and on through north Africa and Europe cost me $449. 97. The low fare was because of my Special Peace Corps passport. I was almost a celebrity. When I arrived back at Kennedy airport in New York, I got the shock of my life. Black men were wearing 'Afros'. Shouts of, "Black is Beautiful!", "Black Power! rang out everywhere." Three years earlier April 4, 1968, on my mother's forty seventh birthday, Dr. Martin Luther King, Jr. had been assassinated and the country was still in a political and social upheaval. The war in Viet Nam was still raging, soldiers were still dying and there were riots in the streets across America. Coming home to America was more of a 'culture shock' than going to Africa and living in the bush.

THE HANNUM EFFECT

After years of searching for answers about the meaning of life and my purpose in it, in 1972, Bobby Hannum, my old friend from the Art Institute days, introduced me to Nichiren Buddhism-again! I had heard of it several times before, but I had never bothered to investigate or try it. He told me that if I chanted Nam-myoho-renge-kyo, I would get whatever I chanted for, yadda, yadda. I thought he was crazy, and I told him so, not because it sounded strange to me but because that same Bobby Hannum had earlier been an active member of the Black Panther Party and we had always held strongly differing opinions about that organization's philosophy. To me anybody who was a member of the Black Panther Party was a militant, antisocial individual who was willing to kill another human being for a political cause; no such person could tell me anything about wisdom or gaining enlightenment. So, when I heard this newest presentation about chanting, the warning flags went up immediately. Nevertheless, Bobby, who had been just as vociferous as a Black Panther, extolling the virtues of armed rebellion and violent revolution was now talking to me about *'human revolution'* and *'conspicuous benefits'* that occurs when you chant Nam-myoho-renge-kyo. He went on to explain that the chant was the title of the Lotus Sutra, the highest teaching of Shakyamuni, the first recorded Buddha in history. It was all about the law of cause and effect; my belief was not a requirement. That struck a note. Despite my doubts, I could see that he was making sense. The name of the organization was the NSA or Nichiren Shoshu of America and its president was Daisaku Ikeda. The mission of NSA was kosen-rufu or world peace. It was explained to me that world peace really was possible. Kosen rufu was the condition in the world where people from around the globe are chanting Nam-myoho-renge-kyo. It stood to reason that if I chanted and became happy then sharing it with someone else, they too would become happy. From one person to another and another until everyone was chanting.

There was something different about Bobby. It was difficult to define, but his manner was easier, and I could see that his confidence came from his heart instead of from his ego where all of his previous arguments had originated. He seemed profoundly assured of what he was saying, and he had discarded his usual argumentative style for one of quiet certainty. I was impressed. Our debates continued like before, but they always ended up on the same subject, Nam-myoho-renge-kyo. He had been chanting for about a year. Bobby was built small like I was, but he was rather frail and sickly because of his long-standing bout with rheumatoid arthritis. He had it before I knew him. It was not uncommon for him to suffer from serious attacks of debilitating pain from the soreness in his joints. The knuckles on his hands, noticeably large were clear manifestations of his ailment. But where his spiritual dimension began was where his frailty ended; when he spoke, he demanded your attention because of the deep, penetrating nasal quality of his voice. His words were sound. I knew that once Bobby got to talking-about anything, it would be hard to stop him. I found myself talking less and listening more as he went on and on about Nichiren Buddhism and NSA. Its founder was a Japanese priest named Nichiren Daishonin who first chanted Nam-myoho-renge-kyo in 1253. I was impressed with his knowledge on the subject, but I was otherwise not yet moved enough to chant so I began my research. Initially the whole idea of chanting seemed absurd. I was a pragmatist supreme. I was not convinced of what he said but it was difficult to deny the fact that Bobby was looking healthier than he had looked in a long time. There was no question about that. It was one of those little things that I never mentioned, but let hang in my mind, wondering if it was just my imagination or if there was really something profound happening. He said that chanting would change my life, too. I said that I didn't believe a word of it. He responded: "I didn't ask you believe it; I just said chant". I couldn't argue with that reasoning. He explained that the law of Nam-myoho-renge-kyo puts people in harmony with the universe because it is the same law that flows through our bodies and throughout the cosmos.

He went on to say that when you begin to practice Nichiren Daishonin's Buddhism, you receive a mandala with Nam-myoho-renge-kyo written in Sanskrit down the center. That mandala is called the Gohonzon, and each member has one enshrined in his or her home. The Gohonzon, he said, represents the enlightened life of Nichiren Daishonin and our own enlightened Buddha nature. When we chant Nam-myoho-renge-kyo to the Gohonzon, he explained, we manifest that enlightened nature in our daily lives. The more we chant, the more change we experience in our lives and in our environments. I listened politely. It made perfect sense to me that I didn't have to believe a physical law for it to work. His explanation and logic felt a lot like the conclusions about life that I had come to when I was younger. It was difficult to argue with that logic, but I stubbornly refused to give in completely. There was something 'true' about this new philosophy I was feeling. I imagined that at a Buddhist meeting I'd see bald-headed monks in long robes and begging bowls, sitting around on the floor of a dimly lit room, mumbling mantras, showing people how to breathe through their fingernails or something weird. I imagined all sorts of strange things. But as we approached the meeting place, I could feel the vibrations coming from inside. Bobby just smiled. As we entered the room, we got a blast of energy like I had never felt before. The energy was in the air, the deep, rich, rhythmic harmony of thirty-or forty-people chanting Nam-myoho-renge-kyo was awe inspiring. The room was alive; it was filled with a positive force that was undeniable. From around the brightly lit room, I could see young and old, black faces, white faces, men, women and children. They looked just like me; they were regular, ordinary people. I remember thinking how it would be virtually impossible to be in the room and not feel uplifted. It was a totally new experience. In spite of my stubbornness, the joy I felt was so great that I thought I was going to explode. Bobby just continued to smile.

During the meeting, members explained what the practice of Buddhism was all about and why they chanted. Others, mostly new members, stood up and gave experiences they had since starting to chant. I held fast to my doubts. I was waiting for them to pass around the money plate, but they never did. It all just seemed too easy, I thought. New people introduced themselves to me after the meeting and they seemed genuinely interested in me. I started chanting and attending meetings with Bobby.

At one of my early meetings, a new senior in faith spoke. I had never seen him before and I wondered who this guy was. He spoke with authority about Nichiren Buddhism and NSA. I guessed him to be about my age. He was an African American just like me, a very powerful speaker with a sincerity about Buddhism that I could sense immediately. I wondered what there was about Buddhism that could make this guy so dedicated to such a relatively new religion, a religion that is virtually unknown to the black church-going community. He had been practicing Buddhism for about three or four years and was a chapter leader, encouraging other members. Then I realized why this guy was so much like me and why he held my attention besides talking about Nichiren Buddhism. It was because he wore tweeds and hound's tooth and herringbones. From the old high school style days of 'Gouster and Ivy League', this guy was Ivy League and I was impressed. His name was Darnell Pulphus.

When we first met, I had no idea he and I would become such close friends. He lived on the upper floor of the building where I attended my first chapter meetings. My chapter leader, Rene Robinson, held regular meetings in his apartment at 32nd and Calumet. Like me, Darnell was seriously into jazz and his apartment was proof that his record albums held more meaning that anything else in the apartment because you couldn't find anything else.

The small apartment was almost laughable in its disorder. But his albums were neatly stacked near his two huge speakers that sat on the floor.

As my practice grew and I attended more and more meetings at different locations, I began to see Darnell show up at more and more meetings, always leading gongyo, the meetings or giving guidance. Each time I saw him and listened to his message; I was more encouraged to continue practicing Nichiren Buddhism. He spoke with a determination and urgency that no one in the audience could ignore. When Darnell spoke, members listened. It was this trait about him that held my fascination and interest, wondering how a guy so much like me could be so fervent in his faith of Nichiren Buddhism. I wondered how he could be so absolutely convinced of the validity of the practice. We began to talk more and more as we met at the community center and other meeting venues. It was amazing to me to see such dedication and devotion to the practice of Nichiren Buddhism. I found it difficult not to be impressed by his passion. The combined efforts of Bobby and Darnell made a profound impact on my life and how I began to view the practice of Buddhism.

My attitude had been one of protest for months until Bobby made me an offer that I couldn't refuse. Our agreement was that I chant for one hour a day for one month, thirty days, attend meetings regularly and start reciting gongyo (daily recitation of prayers from the Lotus Sutra). That was all I had to do. The important thing to do was to chant every day for at least an hour. If, at the end of that thirty-day period, I did not have what I chanted for or see it coming into my life, he promised that he would not mention chanting to me again. The deal was made. I knew exactly what I would chant for, so I accepted the challenge with the sole purpose and intent of proving him wrong. I was sure that there was no way chanting could bring me what I wanted in thirty days. There was just simply no way.

The Mansion

Earlier I had discovered that two streets over (19th and Prairie Avenue) from where I was living, were old, well-kept mansions, holdovers from the turn of the twentieth century when the millionaires and business elite lived up and down both sides of the street for blocks. People like the Pullmans, Marshall Fields, Philip Amour, the Kimberly family and others had all lived there. In was the original 'Gold Coast'. The area was a quiet, secluded and a beautifully preserved historic district. One building had a 'For Rent' sign in the front window and I decided at that very moment I wanted to live in that mansion. The address was 1900 S. Prairie Avenue, the original home of Elbridge Keith, the wealthy businessman who built it in 1870. It was a three story, gray stone mansion with a coach house in the back. Elbridge Keith was one of three brothers. He owned a successful millinery business. His brother, Edison, owned a mansion just next door to the south. It was larger than his brother's but was demolished in the 1930's. Elbridge Keith founded and became the president of Metropolitan Bank. He was one of the rich guys. Now that I knew about Nam-myoho-renge-kyo, all I had to do was chant! I decided to chant for Keith House. I remember Bobby telling me not to waste time trying to figure out how things would work out. Instead I was supposed to just keep chanting and reciting the sutra daily, no matter what happened. When I told him what I wanted, he encouraged me to put Nam-myoho-renge-kyo to the test. So, I started to chant seriously for the mansion. The challenge was difficult because I did not have a job at the time, and I had no idea how to even begin approaching such a challenge except to just keep chanting. The building was empty except for a few clerical people who worked in the south wing on the first floor. The space was being rented out to one of the nearby businesses as office space. Every evening I walked around the property, picking up debris as I went along, all the time chanting Nam-myoho-renge-kyo. Every morning and evening I sat on the top step of the big house to recite the sutra from the little sutra book that Bobby had given me. I had no idea how but there was no doubt in my mind that something was happening to me; I could feel it. If nothing else, I was feeling much lighter and more joyful the more I chanted. I also learned an important principle in Buddhism from my studies and from the meetings that I attended. The term was 'esho funi' which means that when you chant, you awaken to the reality that your life condition finds expression in your environment. That was a fascinating idea to me. I pondered that. If I maintain a negative attitude, that condition will reflect in my environment whether I see it or not. But an enlightened life will allow me to perceive it. It made sense. This way I could see my own growth and development, called 'human revolution', as Bobby called it. When I started to chant Nam-myoho-renge-kyo, I kept this new principle in my head because it felt right:

"Your *life* condition *finds expression in your environment*".

I started chanting at least two hours a day, one hour in the morning, one hour in the evening and reciting the sutra on the top step of the mansion. It was usually around sunset every evening. One evening I was sitting at the top of the steps, facing east, facing east as I always did, soaking up the warmth of the sun setting in the west but reflecting brilliantly off of the huge plate glass window of the building across the street in front of me. When I finished reciting the sutra, I put the book away and closed my eyes to continue chanting, warmed by the reflected sun as I rubbed my beads. My eyes were closed for an extended period while I chanted. All kinds of things went through my head: ideas, questions, laws, music and a few kinky thoughts, were just starters. I was chanting from deep within, challenging the Gohonzon to prove itself to me and to show me something profound enough to get my undivided attention. "Show me the Buddha. Get my attention if you can.", I thought. I was in a deep, soft, rhythmic chant, eyes closed feeling very good. I was in another place, my mind alive and free as I continued, "*Nam-myoho-renge-kyo, Nam-myoho-renge-kyo*". Time stood still. "*Nam-myoho-renge-kyo*". "*Nam-myoho-renge-kyo*". Then I heard something.

I opened my eyes and looked down to the foot of the stairs. Directly in front of me stood seven or eight pale, skinny, zombie-looking people meandering aimlessly around in circles, back and forth on the sidewalk in front of me, their heads were weaving from side to side. They were rubbing their hands together. It was a real live, zombie thing. They were mumbling something incoherently. Some were on the other side of the street, shuffling aimlessly back and forth along the sidewalk. It was a scene out of a B horror movie. I looked down the street to the South and to the North to see if this was a movie set being filmed. This couldn't be happening. I was in shock. I didn't believe in zombies, but these people were either real zombies or real crazies. They appeared from nowhere. Since it was a secluded, residential side street, there was little chance of cars coming down the street, so a few of the figures stood in the middle of the street, painting the clouds and sitting on the nearby curb. These people were deathly white. I wasn't sure what I was seeing. They all muttered incoherently as they continued to walk around in small circles, rubbing their hands continuously, bumping each other as they circled. Some of them loped up and down in inarticulate motions, resembling robots in slow motion. Some snared nonexistent butterflies or stuffed handfuls of air into their pockets. There was an unseeing gaze in all of their eyes. My befuddled mind kept saying, "*Nam-myoho-renge-kyo*", but my eyes clearly said, "Twilight Zone".

Then it dawned on me that it was my chanting that had attracted their attention, but I wondered where they had come from. Not one of them spoke; instead they stared up at me as they passed back and forth, constantly mumbling incoherently. Then I realized they were chanting! They were chanting! Suddenly, to my surprise, like zombies again, they all marched away in the same direction and disappeared into the Marshall Field mansion on the other side of the street. I tried to ignore the whole thing but, I kept repeating: "*Nam-myoho-renge-kyo, Nam-myoho-renge-kyo.*" Did I just see that? My mind was racing.'

Esho funi: "*Your life condition finds* expression *in your environment,*"

I remembered. I'm crazy! I'm crazy! This means I'm crazy! I was freaking out. Nobody else was seeing this except me. What the hell was happening to me? I was flabbergasted. My heart and mind were racing. I was doing *shakubuku* (encouraging others to chant) with these people and didn't know it. They must have heard me chanting and came to investigate;

they were apparently trying to chant along with me as they strolled up and down the sidewalk. It was without a doubt, the strangest experience of my life. The people had indeed come from the Marshal Field mansion across the street. I later learned the Marshal Field mansion had been used as a mental facility.

I continued chanting consistently and doing gongyo. To my mind, nothing tangible had really happened except the weird 'zombie parade' and a few 'coincidental' things but I persisted. I was feeling strangely joyous. I continued to chant with vigor. Then I had an idea. This idea was strange, strong and reoccurring. It sounded absurd but it kept coming. It was the 'voice' and it was not whispering; it was shouting. It was an order. Loudly and clearly it said for me to call the real estate office and tell them that I was interested in the property! The absurdity of the idea only lasted a short time because I just did it. Without the slightest hesitation, I got dressed in my one worn suit, grabbed a few business cards, threw some letterheads into my brief case and I went down to the realty office, not having a clue as to what I was going to say. I just chanted all the way there.

Mr. Wilbert Hasbrouk was a restoration architect and business man. I met him at the realty office. His life's work was in the restoration of landmark structures, especially old gray stones. He was an elderly, soft spoken man who seemed to like me from our first meeting. He was certainly easy enough to like. Mr. Hasbrouk was also the owner of the mansion at 1900 S. Prairie Avenue. I was very businesslike, and we established a positive relationship right from the beginning. He spoke about buildings as though they were people. Buildings had personalities, and histories; they told stories. Just from our first meeting, I learned how to look at architecture and the old structures differently.

Mr. Hasbrouk's wife, Marilyn, owned an architectural book store. He was a major influence in the redesign and modernization of the old Polk Street Station in the Printers Row area of downtown. He talked a lot about the old structures of Chicago. His passion was the restoration of those buildings. Together we made two inspection tours of the mansion. He gave me a brief history of '1900'. On the first visit we walked through the front door and into the past. Its grandeur had remained all these many years later. It had been uninhabited for some time, except for the use of the downstairs main living room as office space. We did a walk through and agreed to meet again. Not once did the mention of money or leases or contracts ever come up. My chanting picked up considerably as I felt closer and closer to having my wish come true. I had originally gone to the real estate office because that's what the 'voice' kept telling me to do. I spoke with Mr. Hasbrouk on the phone some days later, but he didn't seem to be in any hurry. His mind was clearly somewhere else. It was when his mind cleared that I worried about. I could not afford to purchase or even rent the big house, but at least I had gotten this far. I was so close yet so far. I had chanted with real determination on being victorious.

Bobby didn't know it, but my attitude had changed; I actually saw my wish coming true, but I didn't tell him. It had been exactly three weeks from the time I challenged him until now. I had one more week to go. I saw no clear way to victory, so I chanted with even more conviction. Then one day Mr. Hasbrouk called, and I readied myself for the end. Instead, he said quite simply that he needed my help. He needed my help! What could I possibly do to help him? I assured him, before even learning what help he needed, that I would offer any assistance I could. He went on to explain how his work, his buildings, projects, business and financial activities required him to make some 'adjustments'. I didn't understand anything he said, except the part where he said he needed the 1900 S. Prairie Avenue property to be occupied full time. Occupied!! Full Time!! For insurance purposes, he needed a tenant and he wanted my help! In short, he wanted to know if I would be interested at all in moving into the building right away. I was stunned. I gave him all my help. I moved into Keith House exactly twenty-eight days after I accepted the challenge from Bobby. The first six months were free; then the rent was $200.00 a month. The rent covered not only the third floor where I had decided to live, but the entire building! And I needn't worry about security either because there was already a security service in the neighborhood that checked on all of the old buildings. The security patrolman had already begun to wave at me in the evenings as he drove through the neighborhood. He had seen Mr. Hasbrouk and me standing outside the building on occasions. The real estate company had already notified the patrolman that someone would be moving into the building. I was living in a real, genuine mansion, in a secluded section of town, and I had a private security service.

Not long after I moved into the 'Big House' Darnell and Riley moved into the coach house in the back. Along with two other Young Men's Division members, they kept the coach house alive with Soka Gakkai activities. Riley was a dog. He was a huge, sleek black short-haired mongrel. He was the stupidest, funniest dog that ever lived. Other dogs considered Riley stupid. Often you could find him out in the big field next to the property, chasing rabbits. There was never a chance in hell that he'd ever catch one but that didn't dull his enthusiasm. He slept on his back with his feet up on the wall. We all loved Riley but nobody seemed to know where he came from; he was just there. Riley captured my heart one day when I heard someone screaming and cursing at the very top of his voice: "You black $#(&%@big, you %@#!^%$#*^$*!! It was Darnell and he was furious. Apparently, Riley found Darnell's shoes to his liking so he ate one. As a practical joke, when Darnell's birthday came around I bought him a dog chew for Riley. It was in the shape of a shoe. Darnell didn't think it was very funny but the rest of us were in stitches. Riley loved the dog chew.

The mansion was one big wonderful benefit. Once I moved in, '1900' became the unofficial 'South Side Community Center Lite'. Meetings were held in my apartment on the top floor of the 'Big House' and activities were constantly being held in the coach house out back. During practices for culture festivals, '1900' became the rehearsal location for many of the performances. Our collective life forces as an organization were powerful and positive. On a big party night at '1900', the place was full of members. The security guard driving by had difficulty believing that there were so many people in the building without drawing attention to the block. Nobody was loitering outside. Even if we had been 'disturbing the peace', there was no 'peace' to disturb; the block was empty. The guard was impressed. That night the mansion 'rocked'. I don't think Mr. Elbridge Keith, the mansion's original owner, had ever partied like we did. I lived in a mansion without a job. I wondered how this could possibly be real. When I began the challenge, a friend who owned a moving company had wagered with me that if I got into that mansion, under any circumstances, he would move me in for free. He did not believe I was in until I took him to the building and with my personal set of keys, gave him a guided tour of the property. He was flabbergasted. He charged me nothing for the move.

Sometime later after the mental facility in the Marshall Field mansion across the street closed, I went to investigate the property. Through an open basement level window, I crawled in and was amazed at what I found. It was as though the occupants of the building all just got up and walked out, leaving everything just as it was. There were cigarettes still lying beside one of the many beds. Partly drunken beverages were still sitting there on side tables. The beds were all unmade. Food was partly eaten. It was like walking through a scene on a scary movie set. I learned that decades earlier, while still the residence of the Marshall Field family, someone had been murdered in that house. It was still a mysterious and haunting place.

Despite of the wonderful benefits I was receiving, it was not an altogether happy time in my life. There were many obstacles that plagued me during this period of spiritual and emotional upheaval. As I chanted, the obstacles became more acute, as if coming to the surface of my life. Very early on in my practice, I read a passage from my study material; and it stayed with me. Nichiren Daishonin said,

> *"Suffering and joy are facts of life. Suffer what there is to suffer; enjoy what there is to enjoy. Continue to chant Nam-myoho-renge-kyo no matter what happens."*

My personal relationship had deteriorated and was over. My life was in a downward spiral, meeting one big challenge after another, on and on. And the more I chanted, the worse it got. Eight hours a day I chanted, every day. But my practice was getting stronger and my faith was growing as I continued to attend meetings and get involved in many NSA activities. The pain didn't stop. It got worse; it was like a nightmare from which I couldn't awaken. Bobby encouraged me and explained the principle of '*human revolution*'. I was cleaning my life of some negative karma accumulated over a long period of time. I was growing stronger, wiser and more compassionate as a human being, he said. "It's called life training," he informed me. Life training my ass, I thought. During this very challenging period early in my Buddhist practice, my favorite aunt, my father's sister, Aunt Katherine died. It was as though she did it on purpose, just to throw me into the depths of despair and suffering. She lived happily all her life and insisted that all of us kids do the same, and then she just died. Her funeral was a happy affair. Nobody really lost control and cried, knowing that she would not have stood for it. She would have reprimanded everybody for wasting time and not having a party. Nobody cried, except me.

Aunt Katie had touched my heart when all of us kid cousins gathered on her farm in LaPorte, Indiana during the Christmas holidays. In those days, Christmas at my Aunt Katie's farm was like being in a Norman Rockwell painting. We always had deep snow; she had a barn with two horses and a sleigh. My Aunt Katie lived on a Christmas card. On one of those visits, Katie was surrounded by a bunch of us kids and advising us that marriage was more than just sex. We all giggled, not understanding her since none of us had ever had sex. From what we were hearing and the little that we did understand about it, sex was definitely the way to go. Katie assured us that once we, as married people, had lived through our spouse's farts, and bad morning breath, we'd see marriage and sex differently. Our laughter put the entire house in an uproar for the rest of the day. But now my life was coming apart at the seams and I felt like I was losing control. I chanted with more passion and determination to understand what was happening. Life could not get any worse. I was wrong.

A dear friend died violently. He was a very handsome guy, tall, dark with a thin mustache; he looked like a model. He was an avid gun lover and kept guns of every sort in his home. In his earlier days he was a real street fighter. Nobody intimidated him and he was afraid of nobody. His name was Larry, but we called him "Lank". Unfortunately, he was in an altercation years earlier where he shot another man. He didn't kill the other guy, but he wounded him so seriously that the man had to spend a lot of time in the hospital recovering and suffering from a lifelong physical disability. Many years later, that same man caught up with Larry, who, at that time was sitting in a booth in a bar, between two people. Before Lank could pull his gun, the other man shot him dead on the spot. Down inside I wasn't surprised at it happening. It seemed to me that the way Larry lived would surely suggest the way he would eventually die. I was saddened but not truly surprised.

Pilgrim Baptist Church

As a Peace Corps Volunteer in Sierra Leone, I became friends with a volunteer whose father was the pastor of Pilgrim Baptist Church in Rockford, IL. While we were still serving as volunteers, the congregation built a new church. It was a clean, modern design. The structure had slightly slanted walls that met at the top with a double span of roof between them. All white, the front of the church was like a huge blank architectural 'canvass'. The building was designed around that front panel. The church wanted a mural using a scene from the Bible. The final design structure would be done in mosaic tiles. My fellow volunteer friend, "Skip", told his father about me, informing him that I would be the perfect person to do the job. I was a college graduate with a degree in industrial design and that I was the head of the art and design department at Union College in Bunumbu, Sierra Leone. He also let it be known that I was planning to start a design firm once I got back home. He laid it on thick. Skip told me that his parents and members of the church were anxious to meet me when we returned home from Sierra Leone.

In June of 1973, after meeting several times with the minister and all the decision makers, I got the commission to do the church design-and installation. The church was a beautiful new structure, clean and sleek, reaching up to the sky. The mosaic tile mural would be about forty-eight feet high by twenty-four feet wide. It was a good-sized project and I was excited. At the same time, I was just getting seriously involved in my Buddhist activities. So far in my practice, my life had been challenging but rewarding. Everything that I had chanted for, I got. It was my first professional job as an independent industrial designer. The church members invited me to a Sunday service where I was formally introduced to the congregation and given the opportunity to tell them about me and speak about the project. The church was packed on the day I was introduced to the members. In my remarks I expressed how honored I was to have the opportunity to serve the members of Pilgrim Baptist Church and the African-American community of Rockford, IL. With all assurances provided for a successful completion of the project, I received a standing ovation. After the service, many of the church members approached me, asking about my experiences in Africa and what I planned to do in the future. It was all very flattering but, on the inside, I was conflicted: "Can I really do this job?" "Is this project in conflict with Buddhism?" At the same time, I was excited about just having the opportunity to work on such a prominent church in the black community of Rockford. It would be a great start to my career as a designer. After several meetings with the church hierarchy, reviewing the terms of the contract and design details, I started preliminary design work. I was so proud of myself for having come this far. I was being trusted by a community of Christians who were very proud to support a young black man, who was also a friend of the pastor's son, whom he had met in Africa. I was a 'shoo-in'. Even though the job would have been classified technically as 'architectural', I was still the man in charge. I immediately set to work on the scene from the Bible, Mark 15:21,

> *"And they pressed into service a passer-by coming from the country, Simon of Cyrene (the father of Alexander and Rufus), to bear His cross."*

It's a scene in which Simon, a black man from North Africa, is forced by the Romans to assist Jesus as he struggles with the cross. My first task was to research the man called Simon and the scene in which Simon becomes the first 'Saintly Christian'. I was back in study mode and I loved it. The library became my creative refuge. I spent weeks studying drawings from dozens and dozens of books, each presenting a different version of the scene. The final design was to be in color, but the challenge was to be as economical with color as possible; every different color represented a different color tile which affected the cost. I studied the Bible to get a feel for what the passage was saying. I always kept my sketch book with me and did dozens of sketches. Then the irony struck me. I was back studying the Bible, reading it more vigorously than ever before. My Buddhist practice was taking off, providing me with conspicuous and inconspicuous benefits and here I was studying the Bible. I was doing everything right with my practice. I was deeply involved in activities. Not a day went by that I didn't study the writings of Nichiren Daishonin and other study materials. And I was regularly introducing dozens of new people to the organization every month.

Finally, I arrived at a design that I thought would work best. After researching tile companies, I contacted American Olean Tile Co. of America for assistance. I made a business visit to the office and showroom, explained what my project was. The company seemed excited and impressed. My project was not the typical kind of job they did. When I checked the company's history and previous projects they had worked on, I was struck by the large number of projects they had to their credit. Some were vertical tile projects, but nothing like this church. We began a business partnership and agreed on the terms of the project, costs, time frame and other pertinent matters.

The contractors would supply the materials and any consultation. They also agreed to work with whomever my installment contractors were. The project was unique. I met with the company architects who estimated the amount of stress the mural would add to the front of the building. It would take more than an estimated one hundred thousand plus one-inch square tiles to complete the design. Once the weight and costs were determined, we agreed to do business. Once the church approved my illustration, my next step was to convert the sketch into a 'model replica' of the façade of the building, showing what the final façade would look like in small square tiles. Some three weeks later when I received a huge package from American Olean Tile, I was ecstatic. Inside was a quarter inch thick foam core board that measured about forty-eight inches tall by thirty six inches wide when unfolded. From my illustration American Olean Tile Company created a full color scale model of the front of the church with the approved design in place showing exactly what the finished project would look like. There was even a fine grid in the model that represented each individual tile. It was beautiful; it was perfect for my final presentation to the church. The members and I agreed that no construction work would begin until everybody involved had come to a common agreement on the final design. All I had to do was make one final presentation with the scale model before construction could begin. I scheduled a presentation for a Sunday morning, immediately after services. That meant that I had to be in Rockford early enough to attend the services to show respect for my clients. We scheduled the presentation for twelve noon. When I finally uncovered the scale model that was mounted on an easel, there was a collective gasp from the congregation. Then came approvals of *"Yes, Lord!"*, *"My Rock!"* *"Halleluiah!"*, *"Yes, Jesus!"*

It was déjà vu all over again. I was back in my childhood days at church. But now I was a new, strong, faithful, active, growing Nichiren Buddhist standing in front of a congregation of black Christians who were throwing praises at me like I was Gandhi. I thought about the Gohonzon and then softly chanted to myself *"Nam-myoho-renge-kyo"*. Once I made the presentation, there was an immediate and unanimous agreement from the membership. At that final presentation, something intriguing caught my attention. It was a very little thing. The model folded exactly across Jesus' neck. In the scene Jesus is on his knees looking up at Simon who was lifting the cross. Simon who is standing, looking down at Jesus is above the half way point in the mural. So, when the presentation is folded, Jesus' body is on the lower half board and his head on the upper board. Odd, I thought. I began to wonder if the Gohonzon was signaling me. Why would I notice such a little thing like that? I let the thought pass. In the back of my mind, I wondered if I was making profoundly negative causes, creating bad karma.

THE SOLILOQUY

I had done enough research in the Rockford, IL area previously to know the contractor that I was going to hire. It was Rockford Tile and Construction Company. For the company this was a big job, a creative project. The publicity of a young black professional designing the front of a new church in the black community was a good newsworthy story. Besides, it would give both the Rockford Tile and Construction Company and American Olean Tile Company plenty of positive local news coverage.

All the preliminary work was complete, and it was time for the actual construction to begin. As agreed, on a bright Monday morning, the construction company showed up at the sight and began building the enormous scaffolding. It took nearly two days to complete the structure that went nearly to the top of the church and covered the entire front of the building. It was a very exciting time for me and members of the church. Before the work began, the workers installed a huge rolled up tarp at the top of the building. They used the tarp to cover the design as they worked down the face of the building so that the design could not be seen until it was unveiled in a ceremony some weeks away. I was as excited as a kid in a toy store. No one was allowed near the work sight or scaffolding, except me. I was the boss, the chief honcho, 'the Man'.

The workers put in eight hours every day to complete the project on time and I was there with them every minute. I was even permitted to climb the scaffolding with the workers so that I could photograph the entire job from beginning to end, close. I had never felt so in charge of anything before even though I had nothing to do but take pictures and watch the professionals do their jobs. Well into the second week, the facial images on the mural began to take form. First it was Simon who came into view, standing tall over Jesus. A few days later, Jesus came into view. By this time the workers on the scaffolding were beginning to take a real interest in what the image was; they had only seen the scale model, so their curiosity and excitement grew as everyone else's did. By the time the mural was about half done Jesus' face came into full form. Close up it was about eighteen inches from the top of his head down to his chin. He also had a gold halo surrounding his head. It occurred to me that every day I was spending a lot of time thirty feet off the ground on a scaffold, under a heavy tarp, looking into Jesus' face. I decided to introduce myself: "Good morning. My name is Denver-Denver Long. What shall I call you? Ok, Jesus. This is my project. I'm from Chicago, Denver from Chicago. I used to read about you when I was a kid. To be honest, I thought it was unfair that they used to say that you could perform miracles, but Santa Claus couldn't. I always had a problem with that. But that's another story.

"What I really want to talk to you about is this situation you're in right now. I guess you realize by now that these folks plan to kill you. Look at how they're demanding that you carry that cross-the nerve. I wouldn't do it. I would tell them to go to hell. But you don't curse, do you? If you flatly refused to carry that cross, what would they do to you, kill you? What I wanted to talk to you about before this scaffolding goes down below your face is that I know a guy who will be in a similar situation just like yours in about seven hundred years, give or take. His name will be Nichiren Daishonin. He will live in Japan in the thirteenth century. He'll be in your future but trust me; he's somebody you should get to know. Check this out. Nichiren is a priest. And he propagates the chanting of Nam-myoho-renge kyo, the Mystic Law of life. And because of his activities, like you, the authorities decide to execute him by beheading. So, in the dark of the night, soldiers take him to a former execution grounds called 'Tatsunokuchi' and readied themselves for the execution. Nichiren declared to the heavens that no matter what, he would never forsake the Mystic Law. And just as the executioner raises his sword, the night sky lights up from a bright light that streaks across the night sky. The event scares the soldiers so much that they are afraid to carry out their duty. Nichiren is so in tune with the universe that it extends its protection to him. Then as a gesture of tremendous compassion, Nichiren encourages the soldiers to chant Nam-myoho-renge-kyo with him. Frankly what they plan to do to you is a lot worse than beheading, because what they're going to do to you is going to hurt-a lot."

News stations began patrolling the neighborhood. Reporters started coming around during the day while the work was underway. They couldn't see anything because the heavy tarp covering the building was half way down the wall. They all thought it was a wonderful project and that I was doing such a professional job. They assured me that I was certain to be going places in my career. By the time the final rows of tile were applied, the tarp had been dropped nearly to the ground and nothing of the design could be seen. The contractor and I agreed upon a suggested completion date so that the local media could be notified. Rev. Gilbert and the leaders of the church decided that on that same day, after Sunday services, they were going to have an unveiling ceremony. On the day of the unveiling, after church services, people gathered out front.

My mother was there, smiling from ear to ear. The local television station was there with reporters interviewing me. It was my fifteen minutes of fame. When the mural was finally unveiled, there was an audible sigh of delight and a long round of applause. It was magnificent. The sun even began to shine directly onto the mural as if on cue. I could not have planned a more perfect unveiling. The project had been completed on time and on budget. There was an extended round of applause. There had not been one hitch in the entire project. The pastor and the congregation all smiled at one another with their chests protruding as they continued to pat themselves on the back. The entire project from beginning to end went perfectly. It seemed impossible but it happened. My fifteen minutes of fame were running out, so I continued to bask in the attention for the rest of the week. I imagined new design contracts coming in from around the world: Paris, Vienna, Buenos Aires, Milan. My name, Denver E. Long & Associates, was destined to be headline news in design publications around the globe. They would all want me. I was trippin' like a big dog. *"Nam-myoho-renge-kyo."*

In Buddhism you learn not to be taken off track by the eight winds:

"Worthy persons deserve to be called so because they are not carried away by the eight winds: prosperity, decline, disgrace, honor, praise, censure, suffering and pleasure. They are neither elated by prosperity nor grieved by decline. The heavenly gods will surely protect one who is unbending before the eight winds."
("The Eight Winds" WND-1 794)

The wind of *praise* hit me like a hurricane. At the same time, I was doing the job I had chanted for. For the last month or so I had been spending some serious time with Jesus Christ, under a tarp. Just him and me. The entire project must have been karmic payback for all the bad stuff I had done in church. Maybe it was the 'The First Pussy' crack I made about Eve. Except for the spiritual confusion, my first architectural design commission as a professional was an overwhelming success. Then, as suddenly as it had begun, it was over. My fifteen minutes of fame were over and done. Months went by and the church project was still a glowing memory in my mind. Then I got an urgent call from Rev. Gilbert at the church. They needed my help immediately. I called the contractors right away and they agreed to meet me at the church the next morning. I drove to Rockford to offer any assistance I could. Apparently during a recent storm in the area, a lightning bolt made a direct hit on the church. More specifically, the lightning bolt had struck the front of the church. We all arrived at the church about the same time. When I saw the mural, I was stunned beyond belief. Lightning had clearly struck the mural; the black burn marks were visible from some distance away. To the architect, fire captain and others, it was not uncommon for high structures to be hit by lightning. To them it was just another lightning strike, until I pointed out something bizarre even to them.

I went to my car and brought out the American Olean and Tile Company scale model of the design and opened the presentation boards for them. Then I closed it and opened it several times to see if anyone noticed. Then suddenly one of the officials standing near me realized what had happened. Lightning had struck the mural precisely in the center, vertically and horizontally, exactly corresponding to where the presentation model folded. The upper half of the mural was perfectly intact. But exactly halfway down, right where the model folded and where the lightning struck, the huge mural had slid right down the wall of the church into a neat pile on the ground, beheading Jesus.

Curtis Mayfield

In 1973 Curtis Mayfield was hot. His tune *"Fred is Dead"* was playing all over the radio stations. 'Fred' was the sad story of a guy who sold dope and eventually died from an overdose. The message was so depressing that I got tired of hearing it. If I heard it playing, I would turn the station. Then one evening my sister called me from Gary and said, *"Fred is Dead!"* I responded with. "I am so damn sick of hearing that song I could scream". I could hear *"Fred is Dead"* playing in the background, driving me crazy. *"Fred is Dead; he ain't standin' on the corner now."* Jo said,

"No, FRED is dead!" Moments went by before I realized what she was telling me. She was talking about my best friend, Fred Mackey from Gary, who, like Fred in the song had just overdosed on heroin. He was doing drugs at home, on his bed when he injected himself with what was known as a 'hotshot', a powerful heroin mixture that went right to his heart. He was dead before his head hit his pillow. I was totally devastated by the news. It was the most intense emotional pain I'd ever felt. Fred Mackey, the poor little rich kid who lived a fast, furious life died just the way he had lived. He had admired my dedication to learning and education. He thought I was the smartest person he knew and would often say things to let me know that he had learned something new, like a new word. I would always recognize it and share a laugh with him about it. Fred had everything money could buy, but instead he would rather hang out with me and my father in our basement, on the sofa, and watch football or wrestle with my dad. The two of them were like two big kids when they got together. My father's big chair was off limits to mortals and everybody knew it. Fred would go to sleep in it.

I went to Gary. My father and I attended Fred's visitation service. We stood there together, looking down into Fred's face, not believing what was happening. In my mind Fred would awaken any second and start laughing as he often did when he pulled one of his ridiculously stupid pranks. I was hoping that any moment he would sit up and the joke would all be over. But he never rose; I was in deep, deep pain. If this was what human revolution was about then I understood it. It was one of the few times I ever saw my father cry and the first and last time ever that we cried together. After the visitation, my dad and I decided to hang out. Drinks were on me. We went to Junior Byrd's Restaurant and Bar on 18th and Broadway and drank until it didn't hurt so much. I was in my mid-twenties, home from my wild world adventure, building my life and having a drink with my dad. It was a comforting experience.

Afterwards, as we walked home, we smoked a joint. It was a first and it was wonderful. Approximately one month later, I was back at that same funeral home, visiting the same parlor where Fred lay only weeks earlier. I was standing in the same spot where I paid my last respects to Fred. This time it was my father who lay there exactly where Fred had lain. He had been shot. I was beyond depressed; in my mind, or what was left of it, I was going insane. I was numb. The mental patients that I had met out front of the mansion when I was chanting came to mind. I was crazy; this was not happening. Then one after another, three other close friends died. I continued to chant through my pain and tears. I remember the supreme irony of getting the keys to the mansion on the day of my father's funeral. It made the occasion of my move in even more memorable and bittersweet. The male figures who were important to me had all been taken in a flash. On the one hand I was profoundly affected by the spiritual changes in my life. On the other hand, I was in the deepest state of depression that I had ever known. There was no question in my mind that it started when I began chanting. I wondered if chanting had caused all the other events, too. I was losing my sanity and a breakdown seemed inevitable. Bobby was always there to encourage me; never give up he urged. He assured me that I would see a difference for the better. Easy for him to say, I thought. I was in the deepest depression of my life, not truly understanding what one thing had to do with the other. The encouragement I got was always the same: keep chanting no matter what happens. Often Bobby would come to the mansion and we would chant together for hours. He reminded me again that when you start to chant Nam-myoho-renge-kyo, you begin to clean up your life, not just your body, but your life, from the inside out, much like a garden hose that has been left out on the lawn all winter. In the spring when clean, fresh water (Nam-myoho-renge-kyo) is sent rushing through the clogged, dirty hose of your life, the first thing that exits is the dirt (karma) and residue that accumulated during the long winter (past lives). I gave him credit for his analogy, and we laughed about it. But the pain was still there; my friends died. I suffered. The negative devilish functions that assailed me were trying to discourage me from chanting and moving for in my human revolution. And if things weren't bad enough, "Miss Dorothy", Richard's mother died in her sleep and sent Richard into a deep state of depression. At that point in my life, I thought that I had endured as much pain as anyone could endure. I was wrong again because some time later I got word that Richard, my 'big brother' had also been killed.

CHAPTER SIX

Driving The 'Chattanooga Choo-Choo' To Kosen-Rufu

My Buddhist practice was growing, and my faith was getting stronger by the day. Early in my practice I got heavily involved in the art department and took responsibility for making big signs and decorations for all the activities that were happening in and around the city. Our activities were hectic but joyful. There were always meetings to attend, big festivals to prepare for and celebrations to plan. Oftentimes the events were in other cities or state or even other countries. Members eagerly joined in to contribute to the preparations. Dee Cooley, a Women's Division member, was my right hand and constant companion. She was always there to contribute, no matter the day or the hour. Together we spent many, many hours into the night painting signs and posters for upcoming events. I had recently gotten more proof of the power of chanting when I landed a job at a small insurance company. I had simply walked in the door and was hired right on the spot. But then, after only a few short months on the new job, I was faced with a huge challenge. NSA was presenting the *"Parade of Light and Hope"* in Honolulu, Hawaii. I asked Bobby if he expected me to take off from my new job, pay to fly to Hawaii, work and sleep in a warehouse for three or four nights to build a float, all for free! His answer was: "Yeah." It was not about the money; it was about making causes for kosen rufu. To me it was about the money: I had none.

Chicago's contribution to the parade, which was to be held at night, was a locomotive float which we named the *'Chattanooga-Choo-Choo.'* And because of my background and degree in industrial design, I was asked to design the float. I was honored and completely taken by surprise. I began researching all types of locomotives. Our float was supposed to be bright, colorful and joyous, reflecting the lives of all the young people who worked diligently for months preparing for this big event. I studied photos in black and white, and in color. I studied real locomotives and drawings, especially cartoon drawing and animations of trains. After two weeks of preparation, I began the rendering. When it was finished, I was proud of the outcome and even impressed with the energy that seemed to envelope the drawing. Copies of it were even sent to President Ikeda in Japan. It was approved immediately.

The challenge then was to build the float exactly according to my design and rendering. For the next month or so while members around the city, across the country and around the world designed uniforms, built their sets and practiced marches. Members worked tirelessly every night in a huge warehouse on the north side of Chicago, building the 'Chattanooga-Choo-Choo'. After weeks of sweat and toil, the first task was complete. The float was a real-life version of the rendering that I had done, right down to the gold trim on the huge wheels. The next task was to disassemble the train piece by piece, crate it up and ship the entire project to Hawaii for reassembly. It was a daunting task but, in the NSA, I learned that with harmonious unity (*itai doshin*), nothing is impossible.

Two immediate problems plagued me. I had a new job and could not take off and I had no money. Without the slightest hesitation Bobby told me to chant that my new employer would give me the time off. Then he said what I thought was absurd: when I ask for the time off, I should also ask my boss to give me an advance on my pay. "Are you crazy!", I protested. He expected me to take off from a new job and then ask for an advance. But I did it, explaining the purpose of the trip to Hawaii and what my responsibilities were. And to my absolute amazement my boss told me that taking the time off would be no problem and as for the advance, he would contact the paymaster and arrange for the advance to be given to me. My faith in the Gohonzon was growing through the roof. It seemed that everything I had chanted for I got! In the beginning I was told to chant for everything, every day, just chant abundantly daily. Those early days saw me putting Nam-myo-renge-kyo to the test. I chanted for the mundane things, just to see what would happen, things I am not at liberty to discuss. I always got surprisingly positive results. If all the other benefits resulted from chanting and being involved in activities, then this journey to Hawaii should be a real-life changer. And since I was the designer of the train, it was a given that I was to be its 'engineer' and 'drive' the train during the parade. All agreed. NSA members arrived in Honolulu in swarms. Members from around the globe came to perform and put on a show for the world to see. Everybody had a job to do. Members of the various brass bands practiced their tunes and marches as the Young Women's Division members went through their dance routines. The island was alive with thousands of members, all working together for kosen rufu. The energy that exuded from the many warehouses lined up alongside one another was contagious. There was hyper activity coming from every corner of the island. Carpenters, electricians and general handy men from different states worked diligently throughout the nights building their floats for the big parade that was only two nights away.

The Chicago warehouse was right in the thick of all the activity. Our crews arrived and immediately set about getting the float together; everyone knowing what to do. Each detail of the train was something special that members of the crew had created. The most remarkable and beautifully crafted piece was the train's headlamp that Mr. Oishi made by hand. He worked diligently the whole time, from Chicago right down to its installment in Hawaii. When he was finished, the entire crew looked at it with amazement. It was all wood, but it looked like metal. Behind the round lens piece, inside the light fixture, Mr. Oishi had installed a bright lighting system. It was beautiful. The cabin of the train was bright pink and powder blue with gold trimmings. The main water tank of the locomotive was powder blue with 'Chattanooga Choo-Choo' emblazoned across it-just like in the rendering. The wheels were red 'spoked' surrounded by powder blue and trimmed in gold. The pink smokestack stood ten feet, all the way up to its gold trimmed opening. There were the very special 'special effects' that we devised during the production stage of the project. Inside the cabin of the train were switches for us 'engineers' to use. At my disposal was the control panel for the two huge CO_2 cylinders of 'steam' that would billow from the smokestack. Next to the 'steam' switch was a control for the high-fidelity sound amplifier. Mr. Rogers, our 'sound engineer' had spent hours in railroad yards back home. He had recorded live activity in the rail yards with the sound of one locomotive overpowering everything else. That powerful sound was now the voice of the 'Chattanooga-Choo-Choo'.

And to top it all, along every edge, completely outlining the cabin and smokestack were thousands of tiny colored lights that were synchronized to rotate around the train. Mounted at the front, on each side of the engine were two flags, one of the U.S. and the other of NSA.

The time was drawing near for us to line up in the parade that consisted of hundreds of units. Most of us were not in uniform but still working on some final part of the train. I was still painting a part of the cow catcher when the drivers began to line up the floats even though we were many blocks away from the beginning of the march. It was getting dark and I still had not changed into my bright, iridescent pink and powder blue engineer uniform. Around our necks my fellow engineer and I wore bright pink bandanas with matching engineer caps. Following the train was the youth division's marching brass band. They, too, were decked out in variations of the engineer theme. It was finally time to stop painting and change into our uniforms. People were moving in every direction, hustling, bustling to get everything in perfect order. From a far distance we could hear music rumbling; some blocks away along Kapiolani Avenue, the parade was starting. Around us, engines were starting, band members began jumping into place and musical instruments were warming up to blast out their tunes. We 'engineers' boarded the train; the float driver was moving the float again, as we lined up behind a line of other units. It was nearly dark except for the bright, full moon that shone above. In silent anticipation I stood anxiously in the cabin as the float slowly began to turn again and proceed down the street behind the others. Then it stopped, waiting for the signal to proceed.

About a half hour later, it was our turn to go. The music and crowds ahead of us were at a fever pitch. The bands ahead strutted to their themes and did fancy unified dance routines as they marched along, getting loud applause from the enormous crowds. At just the right moment we were instructed to 'fire 'em up'! Before they could see us, the crowd heard the loud, realistic clanking of train wheels and railway horns. If you didn't know better, you would have thought that there was a real locomotive rolling down the street. Still the crowd could not see us; they just heard us approaching. As the driver of the float began to move into parade area, I flipped the switch and the multitude of tiny lights began to ring around the cabin in a stunning musical rhythm. I was amazed at how beautifully effective the lights were; we had only tested them indoors, under warehouse lighting. But now it was dark, and the crowds exploded in excitement as we moved into common view. I flipped the switch for the co2, and a huge bloom of 'smoke' billowed from the smokestack and the crowds went wild. I was in a magical fog. What I was experiencing at that moment was enlightenment. Everything was moving in slow motion; children ran out into the streets in attempts to board the train. Police, parents and adults struggled to restrain the youngers. People were screaming; camera flashes lit the night. I was driving the *Chattanooga Choo-Choo* to kosen-rufu, world peace. Visitors, tourists and NSA members from around the world were there in Honolulu, Hawaii crowding each side of the street. I was living in a slow-motion dream. It was at that moment that I thought about my dad.

"I want people from around the world to see my art and be moved by it"

I had said to him years earlier. That float ride was the most exciting ride of my life. Years later, when George Ariyoshi, governor of Hawaii in 1975, came to Chicago, he said that the people of Honolulu were still talking about the incredible *Chattanooga Choo-Choo*. It won the blue ribbon for first place in the parade.

The Wisdom Of The Lotus Sutra

Causes we make in the present affect our futures. Causes we made in the past effect our present. I was beginning to understand that better and better. Whether or not we chant, we suffer the consequences of our actions but chanting *Nam-myoho-renge-kyo* makes us aware of our actions and how to make the correct causes. I read that if you want to know what your life will be like in the future, look at the causes being made in the present. It all made sense, but it was difficult for me to always internalize. There was no doubt in my mind that I was undergoing some major changes. I could feel it, but I could not explain it or even talk about it to just anybody. Only those who chanted seemed to understand. It became clear that there was no one who could do anything to change my situation except me and to blame others for my suffering was not only futile, but ignorance in its simplest and most blatant form. I began to understand what it meant to take responsibility for my own life. As I sat in front of my new altar, chanting to my new Gohonzon housed in its new butsudan, (cabinet holding the Gohonzon), in my new mansion, the world outside seemed dark and threatening. I had just received the greatest benefit, yet I was still deep in the world of Hell. I resolved to keep chanting, no matter what! One morning as I was completing my morning prayers, I was overcome by a sense of extreme well-being, of peace.

My life had been at its lowest ebb. In that lowest of states, I understood what a leader meant at one of the meetings when he said that there was enlightenment even in the world of Hell, the lowest of the Ten Worlds. That leader had explained to me that the Ten Worlds were not physical places, as expounded by provisional Buddhist sutras, but were the fundamental conditions of life that exist within everyone, Buddhist or not. From the lowest to the highest, they are Hell, Hunger, Animality,

Anger, Tranquility, Rapture, Realization, Bodhisattva and Buddhahood or Enlightenment, the highest life condition. Hell, the lowest of the ten is the state of life in which people suffer and can do nothing about it, a seemingly inescapable life condition. A person in that condition suffers every moment. In the world of Hell, people have no power to influence the environment, no hope for the future, and are suffering either physically, spiritually or both. I had been in the world of Hell. Emotionally I had been at that point where the only direction left to go was up. When I internalized that fact, my depression began to lift like a fog. I chanted more and more, remembering the garden hose analogy that Bobby had related to me. *Nam-myoho-renge-kyo* was running through my life and it was no longer important to think about suffering. It was more important to challenge the obstacles, change what I needed to change to improve my life condition and get on with the serious business of living a happy life. From that moment of realization forward, I began to understand my life. The subsequent joy became permanent.

I started challenging every obstacle. I chanted for others who were suffering. One after another the things that I chanted for manifested. They never actualized the way I thought they might, but they always occurred. I saw new members begin to deepen their faith as benefits flowed into their lives. My faith was growing stronger every day. Despite myself and my questionable attitude at the beginning of my practice, the power of the Gohonzon had impressed and empowered me. As I developed my practice, I read everything I could about the law of cause and effect; I studied diligently. Flashbacks of my childhood church days occurred: *"Have faith in the Lord", "Trust in Him!"* It all seemed so clear to me now. In the beginning I didn't believe that chanting worked; but I couldn't deny that something was indeed at work in the depths of my life. I had made a major step forward in my spiritual and emotional life.

The Vow

I made a vow. I would dedicate the rest of my life to propagating Nichiren Buddhism if one special desire was realized. I needed proof positive that everything that I had experienced was not just one coincidence after another, so I chanted for something so very special that I dare not discuss it with anyone. I chanted for the Gohonzon to bring a part of my past into my present. Having been in the lowest of the Ten Worlds, with the deaths of so many close, dear friends, I understood what it meant to make a vow. If I got what I was chanting for this time, I would dedicate my life to propagating Nichiren Buddhism. I decided to challenge myself and deepen my faith in the Gohonzon and be victorious in my pursuit of enlightenment. I got the mansion I had chanted for and many other benefits since my practice had begun, but now I needed unquestionable proof of the power of the Lotus Sutra and the practice of Nichiren Buddhism. Without any further delay, I put it to the Gohonzon. It had been seven years since I completed my Peace Corps service. I was sitting in a mansion in front of my altar, alone, chanting to the Gohonzon. I was chanting for Joan from Jamaica, my "Jamaican Doll" to come back into my life. I chanted specifically for her to be sitting on the two pillows right next to me in front of my altar. I had no idea where she was or even if she was still alive. We had not communicated but once in all those years and that was right after I left Jamaica and went to the University of the West Indies for further Peace Corps training; that was in 1967. All contact had been lost. For all practical purposes, she was just a warm memory. I began a daimoku campaign.

I was reaching the end of the first week of my eight-hour a day daimoku campaign. I had not missed a single day of doing gongyo. A week later near the end of June, while I was chanting, my telephone rang. It was Joan, my "Jamaican Doll". I was stunned. First I thought it was a prank, but nobody knew about my challenge and surely nobody knew about Joan; I hadn't said a word about it. Her accent convinced me. I was dumbfounded. I stammered and stuttered: "Where are you? How did you find me? Where did you get my telephone number? What are you doing now? How did you find me? Where are you?" I was in a state of shock. The last time we had seen each other was at her house in Kingston at the *"Rock-Steady"* party she gave for me when the volunteers were leaving Jamaica, seven years ago. I had not yet realized the significance of the time span. When I finally calmed down, Joan began to explain to me that for the last 'couple of weeks', she had been thinking about me. I told her that for the last 'couple of weeks' I had been chanting for her. She was calling from New York where she lived. She had moved from Jamaica in 1968, a year after I left. She was taking a vacation on her job and she had planned to visit her cousin in, of all places, Evanston, Illinois. Referring to the map and noticing how close Gary, Indiana was from the Illinois state line, she thought of me. She wondered if I still lived in Indiana.

The crazy letters that I had written home from Jamaica led her right back to me. When she decided to contact me, her first call was to the Indiana Bell Telephone Company. The irony hit me like a blast. It was the old Indiana Bell Telephone Company from my precocious childhood that had come back into my life and brought Joan and me back together. After two calls of 'Longs' in the directory, Joan got my father on the phone. It did not take her long to convince my father who she was since he and my mother had already heard and read so much about her in my letters. But Joan's accent did the trick. My mother, happy to help, gave her my Chicago number. When I finally put the telephone down, mouth agape and in total shock, I stared at the Gohonzon for a long time. In the late afternoon of Sunday, July 7, 1974, (the seventh day of the week, the seventh day of the month and the seventh month of the year, exactly seven years to the day of July 7, 1967) and the hour that I had walked into her office at the Jamaica School of Agriculture as a new Peace Corps Volunteer, channeling Clint Eastwood, Joan was sitting on the two pillows next to me in front of my Gohonzon, looking very much like a miniature version of Angel Davis. We sat there quietly at first. I explained to her that I was practicing Nichiren Buddhism and had been chanting *Nam-myoho-renge-kyo* for her to come back into my life. She found it hard to believe but I assured her that it was true. As I began to chant to the Gohonzon, Joan chimed in softly. We chanted into the evening.

East Meets West

At 5:20pm on Saturday, January 31, 1981 Chicago's Union Station was buzzing with activity. Over five hundred NSA men, women and children began boarding a new Amtrak train bound for Dallas, Texas. The new train was eight cars long and NSA occupied. Each car was a neighborhood; each set of seats was a household. The train was alive. The members in each car began chanting softly and continued for the next hour or so. Each car agreed to do gongyo at the same time so that there would be complete harmony on the train. After gongyo, families and members ate their prepared meals and continued the lively chatter throughout the train. After dinner the conversations really began. Celebrations erupted. I could walk from one car to the next, like walking down the block, meeting friends and neighbors. The celebrations went on. The next day, February 1st, we pulled into the Dallas Reunion Station. I had no idea of the significance of the name Reunion Station until we headed back to Chicago.

We were welcomed by the Young Men's Division Brass Band, members from the Dallas area and the Drum Corps of the Japanese members who had come from Japan to support this cause for kosen rufu. As we exited the train, the band played, and a line was formed on each side of us as everyone applauded; we happily marched and danced into the station. From the entrance of the station all along the corridors inside, leading to the main terminal, Japanese members were lined up to greet us and shake our hands. The big surprise came when we entered the big hall of the main terminal where, to our amazement, were more than a thousand members greeting us with a spirited version of their hometown song: *"Deep in the Heart of Texas"*. After a brief meeting with the General Director, and other dignitaries, the members took recess for a few hours to have lunch and prepare for the *"East Meets West"* culture festival to be held later at the Reunion Arena, just across the street from the station. The program opened with the dynamic Fuji Fife and Drum Corps. Their spirited play and unity had the entire audience on its feet giving full approval to the performance. The next part of the show surprised members as well as non-members because riding out on horseback in full samurai warrior costume, representing 'the East' was Toshiro Mifuni, the famous Japanese actor (Torinaga) of *Shogun* fame. Riding out onto the stage from the opposite direction in full cowboy attire, representing 'the West' was Patrick Duffy of '*Dallas*' fame. Both Mifuni and Duffy were practicing Nichiren Buddhists. The two riders met in the middle of the stage and shook hands. This brought an extended standing ovation from the audience. The program continued with one outstanding presentation after another. The festival was magnificent. Heading back to Chicago, we were all exhausted. It felt good to sit down and relax as the train slowly left the station headed back to Illinois. The entire trip and festival were a complete success. The ride back was more subdued than the ride down. Having expended so much energy shouting and screaming at the festival, most of the members just laid back and engaged in low key conversations as they enjoyed the soothing sounds of the train rolling along the tracks. I felt rejuvenated as I strolled down the aisle of one car and into the next, greeting members as I went along. All along the aisles you could hear lively conversations about the festival.

As I continued my stroll, I heard someone in a conversation say "Gary". I immediately responded, "I'm from Gary!" When I located the section, the comment had come from, I approached it and repeated, "Hey, I'm from Gary!" There was a group of young women engaged in a very lively conversation, laughing and having a wonderful time. Mixed among them were three small children, two playing amongst themselves. The third, a beautiful little girl of about three years old, stood there on the seat just staring at me. Our eyes locked as soon as I walked up. Her stare intensified as I introduced myself to the group of young women. Strangely I felt I knew this little girl but that was impossible. Everything about her seemed familiar, her sandy brown hair, her gray-green eyes and most of all, her attitude, her stare. Stranger yet, she looked at me like she recognized me. We both stood there, eyes locked on each other when a friendly female voice said, "I'm from Gary and you look familiar". I introduced myself to the group and let them know that I was born and raised in the 'Steel City' and that she looked familiar to me, too. In quick response, the young lady asked, "Do you know any Morisses?" Braggingly, I replied, "Yeah, I know some Morisses: I know a Michael, a Craig, Crosby, a Shane, a Kim, and a Denise. They lived down the street from me, across from the Stewart House on 15th & Massachusetts Street. Our eyes met and locked as I shouted, "You're Denise, aren't you?" At that moment I could tell she recognized me because she paused for a moment, stood up as she approached me and gave me an enormous smile and said, "No, Denise is my older sister. I'm Kim!"

I screamed, "KIM!" It was my little Kim from 15th and Massachusetts St whom I had not seen since she was three years old. We gave each other a huge bear hug. I had Kim laughing to tears when I told her how she used to treat me when she was three years old. Never a word would she utter to me; she would just stare at me, exactly the way the little girl standing on the seat was staring at me now. Kim was twenty-five years old with a daughter of her own and her daughter was the little girl standing on the seat staring at me. Her name was-Kim. It was deja-vu all over again. Big Kim and I laughed until it hurt. Kim excused herself from her friends and we sat together and talked for hours as the train rolled on toward Chicago. Kim had begun practicing Nichiren Buddhism only a year or so earlier and this was her first trip with the organization. She gave me her address and phone number and we promised to stay in touch. The reunion took me back deep into my memories and how she had affected me when she was a baby and how I had promised her that we would meet again and become friends. I had kept my promise. My life surely had a purpose. Her daughter, Kim, Jr., who was three years old, stared at me the whole time, never said a word to me.

On July 7, 1983, exactly sixteen years from the day I walked into her office channeling Clint Eastwood at the Jamaica School of Agriculture, Joan and I were married. And though I am not into numbers, I can't ignore the fact that on 07/07/07 we celebrated our twenty fifth wedding anniversary. We had two ceremonies: one in New York for her family and friends and one in Chicago for mine. Joan moved to Chicago the same year. We got our first apartment on Dearborn Street in Printer's Row in downtown Chicago and began our lives together after years of long-distance dating. By this time, I had plenty experience. I had worked as an industrial designer, as an artist, taught at dozens of schools in the Chicago Public School system and worked as a contract teacher. I had spent several wonderful years with Urban Gateways where I even wrote a program that was taught in the schools. My resume was expanding.

CHAPTER SEVEN

Class Of '39

In 1989, Blue Island Community High School celebrated its 50th class reunion for the graduating class of 1939, my mother's graduating class. The reunion was held at a country club south of Chicago. My wife, Joan, my sister, Jo and I escorted my mother to the affair. Other than supporting my mother, I had only one reason for going and that was to meet the one and only Mr. Frank D-i-N-o-v-o. It was a very long shot, but it could be worth the effort. We arrived early and found our table. We relaxed and enjoyed the music. Passersby stopped at our table as they recognized my mother and reacquainted themselves. We walked around the huge ball room, escorting my mother as she met more old high school friends. She introduced us to those classmates she recognized or to those who recognized her. So far, there was no DiNovo. After a while, we returned to our table to continue our celebration. Our table was vibrant, animated and full of laughter. Jo was being her usual self. My mother was having a wonderful time when she suddenly said, "I think I see him." "Where"? We all shouted in unison. She directed our collective gaze to a table about twenty-five feet directly ahead of us. A man sat alone at the table. I suggested that mom not say anything but walk by and make very sure that he was 'the guy'. She did. He was. When she returned to our table, I said, "My turn."

I left our table and slowly approached the table where the lone man sat. As I got closer, he looked up, smiled and we both spoke. I asked, "Hello, how are you?" "I'm fine, thank you.", he replied. "Are you Mr. DiNovo, Mr. Frank D-i-N-o-v-o from Blue Island High School?", I asked politely. He looked at me, surprised that I knew his name, wondering who the hell I was but he responded softly, "Yes, I'm Frank DiNovo, and you are?" As I sat down across the table from him, I extended my hand to him and introduced myself as we shook hands. "My name is Denver.", I said.

There was silence. He was clearly confused, at first. "My name is Denver Long. You went to school with my mother at Blue Island Community High School.", I added. He relaxed momentarily. I picked up a napkin from the table and wrote *Nam-myoho-renge-kyo* on it. I turned the napkin around so that he could read what I had written. "Have you ever heard of *Nam-myoho-renge-kyo*?", I asked. "Heard of what?", he responded as I had expected. *"Nam-myoho-renge-kyo"*, I repeated. "Here try to say it with me", I urged. He studied the napkin and stuttered, *"Name-miho-rengee-kio, Namo-mioho-rengee-kyo"* and finally, *"Nam-myoho-renge-kyo"*. "My mother's name is Irene Long; it was Thomason when you were in school together. Maybe you remember her. She had an older sister named Aisalee who also went to school with you at Blue Island High School from 1935-1939.

My mother and her sister were always together; some thought they were twins", I added. I could see his mind churning. He was working hard to process all the information I was giving him. He listened quietly as I continued. "I went to school, the Art Institute of Chicago with Katherine, Kay, your daughter. As I spoke, I reached across the table and spread the photos of my mother out before him, the same four pictures that Kay had shown him twenty-four years earlier. They were the same photos that had nearly given him a 'heart attack' when Kay discovered that he had had a 'woody' for my mother back in high school. He squinted at the photos for a moment then reached into his breast pocket and brought out his glasses. He picked up the pictures again and studied them carefully. The transformation on his face began slowly. His face got redder and redder as he flipped through the pictures one by one. He swallowed self-consciously. The memories raced through his mind and exploded. He turned bright red when he realized who I was. He looked up at me and we stared directly into each other's eyes for an eternity. We said nothing. His eyes made it clear that he completely understood. I slowly gathered the photos, stood up and reached out my hand again. He didn't get up, but he slowly reached out his hand and we shook again, this time for an extended period since I held on to his hand longer than was necessary. He was speechless. "It's been a real pleasure meeting you, Mr. DiNovo", I said sincerely, smiling politely as I turned and walked back to my table. I glanced back in his direction and he was still sitting there, motionless, staring at me, stunned. My prediction had come true. I had shaken Mr. DiNovo's hand, twice, something Kay said would never happen. I had earned some real bragging rights and an opportunity to show Kay that, as I had said earlier, nothing was impossible. She would have to congratulate me.

Googling The Past

Thirty years had gone by since Kay and I were in school together but from time to time we'd hear from each other. Then in 1994 I got a card from her. She was living her life as Mrs. Katherine Kay Laube. She had married a photographer, Ed Laube, a white photographer. I know we both chuckled at that. I remember her telling me about him while I was in Sierra Leone. In her letters she related how they had started dating sometime after I graduated and moved overseas. Kay assured me he was a very nice guy who had wanted to date her even before I left the country, but he knew that she was already in a serious relationship. She was now a fashion designer and photo director, traveling much of the time and working full time with her husband in his commercial photography business. I remembered using her as my model when we were in school and I was learning photography. It was good to know that she was happily married. In the card was a beautiful color photograph, taken recently of her two adopted children, a girl and a boy, Mary and Ed, both Korean. As predicted, she had become a mother to many, but not too many. Her card read;

"Dear Denver,

My folks told me that they ran into you and your family at the class reunion. I meant to write much sooner than this. Life is such a whirlwind for us right now. I'm enclosing a photo of our kids. Edmund is10 and Mary is 9. Among other things they keep us really busy these days.

My job in commercial photography keeps me traveling out of town about two weeks out of every month. I'm Chairperson of the Zoning Board in town and am on

the board of two other organizations. I can't seem to stop
volunteering for things. I guess I feel that life is pretty short
and there just isn't enough time to do all the things I would
like. College *days at the Art Institute seem so far away now.*
How are you? What are you doing with your life now? Hope
your family is well.

All my best,
Kay DiNovo Laube,
And Ed, Edmund
and Mary."

She knew I would get a laugh out of her Korean kids; that was why she
sent me their photo. It was an old joke we shared from school. I had always
joked that she would have mixed babies, Italian and black, but mostly
black. Our son's name would have been something like Frank Giuseppe
Leroy Michelangelo Mario Jessie Antoine Leon Long. The 'Frank' part
would be in honor of her father, Frank. I knew that Mr. DiNovo thought
that any son we had would be called, "Booger!". Kay's tears flowed like a
river when she heard that one. She laughed a long time about us having
a son named "Booger!". I was happy to get the card and photo. I decided
to reach out and give her a call. The last time we talked, we ended up in a
fit of uncontrollable laughter just like in the old days at school. It took me
years, but I finally decided to get in touch with her just to say:

"Hello, Kay, hope you and *your family are doing well*
and thanks for thinking about me and for sending me the
photo of your two absolutely beautiful 'unmixed' children."

I started with Google, looking for Mrs. Katherine Kay Laube. To my
amazement she not only lived in the Fox River Grove area but was, in
fact, the Village Board President. I was impressed. I had plenty of ammo
to kid her about. I couldn't wait to let her have it. Her extensive list of
personal accomplishments went on: she was the Girl Scout leader and the
Chairperson in both Cub Scouts and Boy Scouts. I was in tears laughing
when I thought about the Halloween party we attended as students at

the University of Chicago, when I was dressed as a nerdy Cub Scout and she was my 'hot' den mother. I couldn't stop laughing as I read on remembering what I had said about her being the wet dream of every teenage boy in town, scout or not, and perhaps a few of their dads. I had no doubt that was also true. To top it all, she was a founding member of the Fox River Grove Lioness Club, and, as I had also predicted, the envy of every mother in town. My crazy predictions were right on the money. Everything that I had kidded her about in school had come true. The final prediction was the one that really blew my mind. The Village had planted a tree and placed a boulder with a bronze plaque at its base at Picnic Grove Park Playground and the Lioness Club, which Kay was a founding member, donated two park benches that were also installed at the playground. She got a bronze plaque in a playground. I had predicted a building, but she got a playground. I read on but I had not predicted:

"Village President Katherine "Kay" Laube passed away suddenly on Monday, September 15, 2008 after a long battle with cancer." And just like in the old days at school, my tears flowed.

MARY LAUBE

One evening at the end of 2018 I was on the internet and the name Mary Laube crossed my eyes; I thought nothing of it. I saw it again on my phone's "Messenger "app. Whoever she was, she was sending me a message. I opened it and the text read: *"Dear Denver, I hope this message finds you well. My name is Mary Laube. I am the daughter of Kay Laube (formerly known as Kay DiNovo). I am an artist/professor currently in Knoxville TN. I was doing some research on my mom's time at SAIC and came across your book, Professor Buddha. I was amazed and moved by your story. Chapter 10 is the most detailed account I have of her and I wanted you to know how meaningful this is to me. I remember a long, long time ago she told me about you, and it didn't occur to me until I was finished with the section on the DiNovo Sanction in the book that you were the one in my mother's story. I understand the potential awkwardness of me contacting you out of the blue, but I wanted to ask if you would be interested in having a conversation sometime. Below is my contact information. Thank you again. Warmly, Mary Laube.* I was flabbergasted! She was the little kid in the photo that Kay had sent to me in her card. She must have been all of eight years old at the time. She was now thirty. Without much hesitation I responded with: "I am absolutely astonished! I am searching for words to say. I quickly loaded up the photo of her and her brother. The photo was all I knew of Mary Laube. I included my telephone number in the text. She said that she would be available for conversation on the next day, Wednesday. I sent a morning text that said: "At your convenience".

A little time later my phone rang. I was excited. It was Mary Laube. Our voices reflected out mutual excitement. She explained how she had amazingly come across my book Professor Buddha with a story about her mother. We shared the amazement. Mary had moved to Knoxville, TN about two years ago to take an art professorship at the university. Immediately she reminded me of her mother and her dedication to the arts. Without a doubt Kay would be completely dumbfounded to know that her adopted daughter and her boyfriend from the past have somehow come together. To complete the profundity of our meeting, I told Mary that I would also 'adopt' her. From one artist/professor to another, I welcomed her into my life as my new "daughter".

CHAPTER EIGHT

Robert Morris College

My friend Margaret taught at RMC and attended night classes at DePaul University.

We developed a good relationship. She found me interesting, someone my age with so much vitality and determination. She needed heartfelt encouragement for the problems she was dealing with in her life. I encouraged her to chant. She appreciated the uplifting conversations we had because one evening she said that if I were interested in teaching part time at Robert Morris College, she would give them my name. I expressed my deep appreciation and within a week I was contacted by the school and asked to come in for an interview. When I left the school, I had the job. I taught college classes during the day and took college classes at night. It turned out that upgrading my credentials was exactly what RMC was expecting of all the teaching staff. College teaching requirements were getting stricter. A graduate degree was the minimum requirement for teaching anything. My new boss, 'Dr. Deb' understood that I was back in school and she was very understanding. I began my duties teaching art/design classes. Then I taught writing, then English and whatever else came my way. RMC and I were a good fit. I had been there about a year, loving the experience and the growth that I was experiencing. One evening while I was preparing for class, I noticed a job posting. I took the notice and read it very carefully. It had just been posted that day. The notice read:

Position, Director of Upward Bound
Level: 13 (Full Time)
Department: Academics

JOB DESCRIPTION

RMC seeks applications *for the new position of Director of Upward Bound. This is a federally Funded program beginning October 1, 1995 scheduled to continue through September 30, 1999. This position relies on continued federal funding.*

The Director reports *to the Vice President for Academic Affairs and is responsible for the daily operation of an education enrichment program for high school students which includes a six-week summer program with a residential (one week) component. Primary duties involve the Implementation of program activities and services to meet specified goals, curriculum planning recruitment of 50 students from five local high schools, financial management of grant funds, faculty hiring, training, supervision and evaluation of program. Qualifications include: A Master's Degree with related teaching/academic experience. Experience working with student from a disadvantaged background important. Good oral and written communication skills essential.*

Interested *applicants are to discuss* this *position with their supervisor and then contact Stella Rifton in the Human Resources Department at (312)836-4870 no later than Monday, September 11, 1995.*

I took the bulletin directly to my supervisor and expressed my interest in the position. As instructed, she told me to talk to Stella in H.R. I met with her and she made note of my interest in the position. She gave me an application to complete. I completed and returned the application immediately. When I left Human Resources, I went directly to see 'Dr. Deb', the Vice President Academic Affairs. My presentation was dramatic, desperate and ridiculous. When I entered her office with the bulletin in my hand, she smiled and asked what I needed. "This is my job! This is my job! I can do this! Look, this is my job!", I repeated. She looked startled at first, not understanding what I was talking about. When I handed her the job posting, she started laughing and told me to relax. We sat at her desk and discussed the new position. My enthusiasm filled her office like air freshener. There was no way she could give 'my' job to someone else. Our conversation became the interview. She questioned me, looking to see if I had any hesitation or reluctance in responding. I had no reluctance or hesitation; the job had my name on it. She reviewed my resume and past work experience. Then she asked, "Do you think you've had enough experience to do this job? It is quite a challenging and time-consuming assignment." Again, I thought, "I've bought bush beef, held hands with straight men in public places and repelled a death curse. I think I can handle this job." She instructed me to bring her three professional references and then she would review all the applications and decide. I immediately contacted my staff colleagues at Urban Gateways where I had previously been a contract artist/teacher. In three days, I had collected the required number of professional references needed. There was a long moment of silence as she scanned through the letters then looked at them with more scrutiny.

". . . He is vibrant and amusing"; "Denver is a professional. . ."; He left a distinct impression in the heart and minds of both students and parents... they loved him"
Junita Rushing
Associate Executive Director

". . . He has an outstanding professional attitude."; "He is an excellent candidate." "You are fortunate to have Denver as a candidate."
Michael Barlow,
Assistant Director of Program Services

"I know that Denver would make an excellent Director"; "Denver has shown himself to be a creative, dedicated and very capable professional."
Ina Burd
Assistant Director
Program Services

With a broad smile on her face, she looked at me and asked, "How much did you pay for these? I smiled back at her as I left her office, with my new job. I was the new and the first Director of Upward Bound at Robert Morris College. The program was a federally funded TRIO program. Part of my job responsibilities was "financial management of grant funds." It meant that I had to report to Washington once or twice a year, in person to explain how, when, why and where the money was being spent. I was proud of myself. I gave myself a mental pat on the back, seeing another dream come to fruition. I had always wanted to say: "I have to fly out to Washington in the morning on company business." Now I could say it and mean it. I was so excited about this aspect of the job that I took advantage of every opportunity to tell a friend or colleague: "How's the new job going?" I could say, "I love it; it's keeping me busy. In fact, I have to fly out to Washington in the morning on government business."

The year was 1995 and on my first day as Director I was shown to my new office. As I was being led to my office, I thought it strange that we were going down stairs to the lower level of the school. My 'office' was a bare desk in a far corner of the basement between the furnace room and the janitorial supplies. I was so proud of that desk because it was my desk, the desk of the first Director of Upward Bound Program of Robert Morris College. My desk didn't have a telephone on it or a telephone jack nearby. I was literally starting from 'scratch'. No one had done it before, so it was all up to me. Armed with my stack of federal rules and regulations manuals, I looked forward to the challenges that were straight ahead. I was pumped up. The happy flashbacks from childhood visited me. My dad and I had had this conversation when I was about ten or eleven years old. He already knew then, as I had constantly reassured him, that I was going to be a professor with wisdom and compassion beyond all comprehension. I remembered him laughing, not at me but with me. It had become my goal, no my mission, to encourage others to realize that the happiness they sought did not come from outside themselves but from inside. My students were my best audience. My new job meant that I would be personally responsible for helping to shape lives and provide a new richness in education for hundreds of young people. This time it was I who made the decisions.

It took about a week to get a telephone and get set up in my 'office'. I had to create a work plan and a schedule. In preparing my plan of action and schedule, visions of Bunumbu returned and I was momentarily back in the bush. It had also been up to me then to make the decisions and start from scratch at Union Teachers' College. If I could survive and even thrive in Bunumbu where everybody spoke Krio and Mende, I was confident I had the advantage communicating with students in Chicago who all spoke English. Included in my stack of documents and instructions was a list of the five public high schools from which I was to recruit my program's fifty students. For the next few weeks, I was on the telephone calling the schools and making appointments to visit and make presentations to all interested juniors. The schools were all very obliging in helping me set up my presentations. On average I selected ten students from each school. My schools were: Curie, Senn, Roosevelt, Clemente and Lane Tech. Interested students had to complete applications, submit grades and be interviewed along with at least one of their parents. The parents also agreed to be an active part of the program. When the parents are involved, the students perform better. In this case the parents were excited to take part, to know that their children had been selected to be in such a program.

Within the first two months, I had selected nearly ninety percent of the students, hired teachers and staff and drawn up most the of the program's curricula. During our first orientation, the program was explained in full to those students who had questions; rules and regulations were also discussed. Student attendance was crucial for successful completion of the program and grades in school had to be maintained at a certain level. Failure to maintain required grade levels in school and you are out. Then I shared what to the students was bad news. All participants in the program would have to wear a uniform. A compromise in store. With my assistance, the students could design the uniforms and with my approval, the program would pay for them. Everybody agreed. After several meetings with students in the program who designated themselves the 'design committee', the colors for the uniforms were decided; white shirts/blouses, navy slacks for the boys and navy skirts for the girls and burgundy sweater vests for all. Every student would also wear a tie that complimented the uniform. The outfits were conservative and at the same time sporty and smart. A bonus for the students was the that I designed a logo patch that was sewn to each sweater, giving the students the look of an exclusive prep group. At the first mention of having to wear a uniform, most of the students balked! But after seeing the uniforms and wearing them, they slowly began to show real pride in being a part of something special. It wasn't long after the program started that there was a waiting list of students from the five recruiting schools. Parents were particularly excited about having a student in Upward Bound, knowing that to remain in the program, that student would have to do well in school.

Most of the classes were held on Saturday mornings at the Robert Morris College downtown campus. Some were held in the evenings. To successfully complete the two-year program students had to keep their attendance up, always wear their uniforms to class and pass all the required courses. In return the program offered a stipend every week, field trips and a residential component which meant that they would live on a college campus during the summer. I took responsibility for the young men; three female teachers took responsibility for the young women. The job was designed just for me. When I was having 'men only' discussions with the boys, I remembered the days at Union College in Bunumbu when I had to explain things to the adult male students who had their own ideas about education and learning. Here at Robert Morris College I had the benefit of parental input.

While the program grew and gained enormous popularity, I was constantly in 'learning mode', always looking for answers from other Upward Bound directors at other colleges around the city and state. I learned very early on that the way my budget was spent was pretty much up to my own discretion. The key point was that to be safe, I had to make sure that I kept accurate records and that whatever money I spent, was spent on the kids in the program. More important: I should spend all of the money provided in the budget. If there was money left at the end of a year, Washington would assume that I didn't need it and that amount would be cut from the next budget year, so with the help of other directors, I learned how to maximize every dollar.

The Upward Bound program targeted inner city, low income minority students who were unlikely to attend college. So, Project College Bound was created. Much like the Upward Bound Program, Project College Bound was designed to provide students with the skills and motivation necessary for success in post-secondary school; it would also simulate a college-like experience so that students in both programs could learn what to expect when they find themselves living in a dormitory. Unlike the federally funded Upward Bound Program, this project was sponsored by Robert Morris College, thus freeing it from the rigid guidelines and restrictions of a federally-funded program. I established a close relationship with Robert Morris College. Faculty and staff provided consultation and expertise in the educational curricula. The students also participated in various cultural, social and educational activities included field trips to learning institutions, museums and other places of educational interest. At times the students were taken to restaurants where the boys would have to wear ties and the girls would have to wear appropriate dresses. The senior participants took part in workshops designed to help them learn the importance of properly completing applications for college, successful interviewing techniques and how to prepare effective resumes. Since the seniors were closer to graduation, they received extensive tutoring to increase their chances for success as they applied to colleges. Many had already expressed interest in attending Robert Morris College. All the student activities were scheduled so that they did not conflict with the students' high school calendars.

The six-week Summer Program, lasting from the beginning of July through the middle of August, gave the seniors the opportunity to experience dormitory living, hands on classroom assignments and career speakers. I was fortunate to get Roosevelt University to participate in our program and house our students for their dormitory live in experience. Enrichment courses as well as fun-filled activities completed the Summer Program. Some of the younger students had never been out of the city; some had never even been to downtown Chicago. All my efforts were directed toward broadening the students' vision of what their lives could be. I wanted them to see the city, do things and go places they had never considered. To this end, I made geography a required course for every student. In the process I found that some students had no idea where Brazil was. Many didn't know what continent they lived on. Canada was part of Europe and Africa was a country. I saw eyes begin to open as they studied the world maps the program provided. Many became excited when they were able to locate countries in different parts of the world and connect them with the news of the day. Then I had a grand idea.

Every month we held parent/teacher/student meetings where we discussed the program, answered questions from parents and gave a progress report on student participation. To further encourage and instill the idea of learning more about the world they lived in, I announced that to successfully complete the program and with the help of the parents, I would pay all the fees for each student to apply for a U.S. passport. Eligible students had at least one full year to complete the obligation and there would be no input or assistance from me or the Upward Bound program; success depended on the initiative of the student. When the proper forms were completed and photos were needed, I would provide the funding. Some students seemed shocked; others elated. Parents were generally overjoyed. And without a hint of what was to come, the passport idea became the basis for one of the greatest success stories of my Upward Bound experience and it took me right back to my Gary childhood memories and my vow to see Rome.

GABBY

Of the fifty students in the program, thirty-five were girls and fifteen to sixteen were boys, all between the ages of fifteen and seventeen years. Most of the students were either African American or Hispanic while the Asian students came in third. The teaching staff was reflective of the student body, one teacher from each of the student ethnic groups. All women, they represented the diversity of the student body and provided the much-needed closeness that some of the young women in the program sought. One such young woman who entered the program after its second year was Gabriella. She was a very quiet, very reserved little Hispanic girl. If you didn't see her, you wouldn't know she was in the room. With soft blonde hair, she kept to herself and spoke in near whispers whenever she was called on to say something. Having met her mother, I could see right away where she got her shyness. I made it clear to the students at the beginning of the program that if they ever had any problems that they needed to discuss; I'd always be available. Some took advantage of the opportunity to bare their souls to me in private conversations. After hearing the personal problems that many were having at home and at school, it was easy to understand why they performed the way they did. For too many, their problems prevented them from seeing beyond their present circumstances. To imagine living in another land or going to a college away from home just seemed impossible to most. The staff and I worked diligently to change that mindset and to show that they could accomplish anything hey set their minds to.

Gabriella who we called Gabby, was different. She had a dream and she shared it with me one morning when she approached me and asked if we could talk in private. Once we were alone, she told me her dream in a voice so soft that I had to ask her to repeat it. Afraid to share her desire with the other students, Gabby confessed to me that she wanted to go to France. I was surprised and delighted. I gave her a big hug and she responded with the biggest smile I had ever seen from her. I told her that I would do everything I could to encourage her and to make sure she accomplished her dream. Like in my childhood, I remembered how much I lived in my head and putting all the details into my dream, making sure that I constantly nurtured it with pictures and books and music and anything that would keep the dream alive. I shared my story with Gabby and from that exchange she began to confide in me. My advice for her was to learn as much as she could about France: learn the language, the food, the people, the cities, customs, learn everything: "Become French", I said. .

In addition to her always neatly pressed uniform, Gabby began wearing white knee-high socks that stopped just short of the bend in her legs. On her head was a matching white beret. Her beret and knee socks were always immaculately white and became her trademark. To my utter astonishment, whenever she spoke, and she talked more now than ever, she pulled out a little black book, a little black French translation book. Gabby was learning French. Before she said anything, she opened the book and attempted to say it in French. We were all impressed. Her entire personality began to sparkle; she began to talk more openly to the other students and big, broad smiles became her new calling card. When my superiors heard about it, they gave me and the program high praise for the obvious benefits it was providing the students. I had high hopes for my students.

In my mind's eye, it was me in this Upward Bound Program, dreaming about my future and how I was going to get to Italy. From my vantage point, it seemed easy to get to France, but I could just imagine what Gabby was going through. What I had learned from childhood was that when you begin to live in your dream that's when it becomes real. Like me, Gabby was strolling the streets of Paris in her mind, enjoying the sights as she laughed and joked with her friends. I was Gabby; she was me. Living a dream means that the environment must respond to you in that very same way.

With I did all that I could to encourage her to 'live' in France every day; she was becoming a little blonde French girl right before our eyes.

One Saturday morning she and I got into a conversation about college. Asked where she wanted to attend college, she didn't know. In fact, she questioned the whole idea of being able to go to college. I suggested that she apply for college in France; there was absolutely nothing she had to lose. She agreed and together with my help and her mother's devoted efforts and insistence, we helped her complete dozens and dozens of forms and applications and more forms. For some I even paid the fees associated with applying. As if by destiny, my decision to require students to apply for a U.S passport was perfectly timed. In addition to the dozens of pages of documents she had to complete, she was also applying for her first U.S. passport. Upward Bound was changing lives for the good. The program grew and became a beacon of RMC's enlightened environment for high school students. I moved up to the fourth floor to a real office. I had my own computer, telephone, desk; the office even came with a window. The program was doing wonderfully; grades were improving, parents were happy, my boss was happy and again I was living in a dream. To demonstrate our progress and growth, I decided to take the students on a trip, a trip to our nation's capital, Washington, D.C. When word got out that the program was taking the kids on a plane to Washington, D. C., attendance improved dramatically, attitudes changed for the better, conversations became polite and an undercurrent of excitement permeated the campus. Not one of the students had ever been on a plane.

Planning for the D.C. trip demanded my full attention. There were so many details and time suddenly seemed to speed up the closer we got to departure day. Three of the female teachers were going on the trip along with me and about forty-five students. I sought out advice from other directors about which hotels to consider and what agendas to prepare once we landed in the capital. Most of the students going on the trip were young women, so my primary concern was for their safety and protection. With that in mind, I referred to my much earlier training as a Young Men's Division member in NSA. As a YMD, it was always important to maintain harmony and to work together with those participating. The idea was to promote unity that reflects the principle of many in body but one in mind (*itai doshin*). The safety and protection of every individual member was the foremost concern whenever the organization went on a 'movement' to promote world peace. Working together to protect one another was the outstanding hallmark of the organization's youth divisions. In the case of Robert Morris College and Upward Bound, traveling across the country as a group required the same kind of attention paid to safety and protection. I held regular meetings with all the young men in the Upward Bound Program, emphasizing the importance of respecting and protecting the young women in the program. For the boys to learn to accept the responsibility of protecting their classmates as brothers and sisters was a big step forward in the building of their characters; they chose readily to welcome the opportunity to show their maturity. It was just as important for the girls to act accordingly when traveling with the group, too. The female teachers were there at every turn to assure that proper conduct was always adhered to. By the time the trip rolled around, we were ready and well prepared. Hotel reservations had been secured with the students having chosen their own roommates. Flights had been arranged for the group and sight-seeing agendas had been completed. To top it all, when we departed, we were all attired in our 'traveling whites' uniforms. Everybody in the group was wearing white jeans with matching white shirts emblazoned with the RMC Upward Bound logo and matching white caps. It was truly a multi-racial group and I was so proud to be its director. In our preparatory meetings it was decided that since most of the group were girls, then there would be two boys assigned to each group, along with one teacher. The boys were to act as chaperones and the girls were expected to cooperate. When traveling around the capital, no one was to ever travel alone. If anyone broke the rules and conducted themselves in an improper manner, I assured them that, with or without their parents' consent or approval, I would personally have them arrested and executed.

At the airport students wandered around in their respective groups waiting for our flight to be called. Many strangers approached us, asking who this well-mannered diverse student body was. When told that we were Robert Morris College's Upward Bound students bound for Washington, D.C., they were very impressed. People were taking our pictures, talking to the students and asking questions about the Upward Bound program.

I was chanting softly for most of the day as we waited to board. Then our flight was called, and students began jumping up and down, the girls hugging one another. Each student marched onto the plane as though they were receiving an academy award. I felt overwhelming pride in what we were about to do. Once everyone was seated and settled on the plane, I could almost hear the rapid heartbeats from the rear of the cabin as I strode down the aisle making sure everyone was on board. Eyes were wide, nervous conversations shot back and forth across the aisle, from row to row at breathtaking speeds. Excitement and fear both filled the enclosed space. From time to time, I looked back into the plane to make sure everybody was ok. Suddenly we were moving backward, away from the ramp and for a moment all talking stopped. Eyes scanned the small windows as they darted around the cabin to see how fellow students were coping. As the plane roared down the runway, hearts raced; there wasn't a sound in the cabin. I looked back into the cabin and laughed as some of the students' faces strained to reflect the fear as hands grasped armrests with desperation. Many knuckles turned white. I think many of the students reaffirmed their faith in God as we climbed higher and higher. Once the plane leveled off, little changed. The students were taken aback by the sensation of being motionless. There were still some white knuckles. I laughed halfway to the capital. But by the time the plane landed at National International Airport in D.C., I was among a bunch of pros. When our bus pulled up in front of our D.C. hotel, the young men on the bus, knowing what to do, jumped off the bus first, before the girls. They quickly off loaded the luggage so that by the time the last girl and teacher had exited the bus, all bags were lined up along the curb, ready for pick up. The hotel had been notified of our scheduled arrival and was ready for us. Once all of the students had entered the hotel and proceeded to their rooms, the hotel manager approached me and said that he had never, ever seen such a large, well behaved, polite, and diverse, group of kids. I gave him a list of every student in the group and how their families could be notified in case of some dire emergency. We talked about all the tourists in Washington and the tremendous number of students that travel to the capital every year. Over the years, the manager had seen hundreds of thousands of students. His hotel catered to colleges and high schools. In our conversations about education, he asked me what my discipline philosophy was. I said, "Immediate arrest and execution." We both laughed.

Up to this point, nothing more could have been asked of the students. They were magnificent. The planned agenda indicated that at this point, everyone, once settled into their rooms would gather for lunch in the hotel dining room and then go out for an afternoon of sightseeing. A set time was agreed upon to meet back at the hotel at the end of the day. We divided up into four groups of about eleven students with one instructor and at least two boys per group. I took the fourth group and then we all went our separate ways.

Back at the hotel that first night, after everyone had eaten dinner, the students started partying. Our Upward Bound group had nearly the entire floor to ourselves so that we wouldn't cause any disturbances to the other occupants of the hotel. There had been no need for concern. Every room occupied by the students had its door open so that there was a constant flow of visitors from one room to the next. There was music and dancing and laughter that started the moment we arrived back at the hotel. From my room, I could hear the celebrations going on down the hall and around the corner, but they were surprisingly controlled considering the number of young people who were participating. Suddenly a group of students were knocking on my door begging me to come and dance with them. I agreed on condition they got the teachers to dance with us, so they did and the party went on. My time to leave the party came upon me so I thanked the students for such a good time. I reminded everybody, especially the boys, that there would be no roommate swapping, as we all laughed, and I said good night.

The next few days of the trip were just as marvelous as the first day. Whenever we ended the day back at the hotel, the students exchanged stories about the museums they had visited and the monuments they had seen and even some politicians that some of them had seen. The trip to Washington was a complete and total success as every student in the group agreed.

The flight back to Chicago wasn't nearly as scary as the one was to D.C. By now the students were much more confident about themselves since they had come on the trip. When our bus finally pulled up in front of Robert Morris College late in the evening, the young men on the bus knew exactly what to do as they jumped into action, unloading the luggage and lining it up along the sidewalk. All the waiting parents were truly impressed with the order, harmony and joy that they saw in the students as they disembarked. We had all returned home safely having shared, for some, a three-day experience of a lifetime.

Weeks had passed since Gabby sent off her forms and applications for scholarships, admissions, tests, passport applications, photos and other required documents. A big part of her challenge was that her parents, especially her mother was not that well versed at reading and writing English so Gabby relied much more on a relative and me to get all of her required paper work completed. And then one Saturday morning she came to class beaming with joy. Her passport had come in the mail the day before. She was so very proud that she passed it around the classroom so that everyone could see it. And in the photo, there was Gabby looking a bit nervous but donning her white beret and a timid half smile. Her accomplishment had only served to inspire the other students to hurry and get their passports because rumors of Gabby traveling overseas had begun to spread around the program. Then week by week she received one piece of good news after the other. First, she received word that she had passed her battery of tests that were required before she could seriously enroll in any college, whether foreign or domestic. Then, after having sent applications to a half dozen schools, she got two letters expressing interest in her coming to study in Paris. On this particular morning, Gabby showed up at school with her mother, both of them crying. I was immediately concerned about what she had been through. As I approached the two of them, Gabby spoke for her mother as she handed me a letter and a package. When we all thought that it couldn't get any better, she had won a scholarship to study abroad. I was caught off guard by the way the good news had been brought to me. I read the letter that said she had been granted funding to study in Paris for the term of one full year. In the other package was a brand new neck tie that her mother had bought for me to show her deep appreciation. Her mother reached out and hugged me, crying as she did. Gabby reached out and put her arms around the both of us, as I reached out and embraced the two of them. There we were, the three of us, standing in the middle of the hall, all hugging one another, and all of us crying like babies.

Gabby went to France and lived for a year and what made the story even more amazing was the fact that before she left Paris, her mother was able to travel to France and visit her. How that happened is still a mystery to me. She sent me a post card letting me know that her dream had come true and that had it not been for me and the Upward Bound Program at Robert Morris College, she would never have made it. By the time I moved on from Robert Morris College, three students had not only gotten passports but had traveled outside of the United States, one later permanently moving to Spain. I was living my life all over again vicariously through these students, knowing that the little spark inside that begins to burn brighter and hotter when nurtured, was truly within all of us. It only took something or someone to point it out.

DePaul University

My hunger for learning was still going strong in1993 so at the golden age of fifty, I had enrolled in graduate school at DePaul University's Lincoln Park campus. It had been nearly twenty-six years since I received my bachelor's degree in industrial design. DePaul's graduate program was called MALS, (Master of Arts in Liberal Studies). It was a program specially designed for older adults who wanted to continue their education and receive a graduate degree. Master of Arts in Liberal Studies was a name that seemed fitting to me and since I wanted to know something about everything; I felt this was a perfect match. Part of the application process was a personal interview with the director of the new program, Dr. Charles Strain. I contacted Dr. Strain and together we agreed on a convenient time to meet. A day and time were set for our meeting, so I spent some time doing as much preparations as I thought was necessary. On the day of the interview I dressed very conservatively and smartly. I wore a navy blazer with two shiny brass buttons, neatly creased gray trousers, a brilliant white shirt and a red tie with tiny white polka dots and a pair of polished black Cole Haan loafers. I also had a briefcase. There was an air of patriotism about my outfit. I stood in front of the mirror checking out my outfit. I looked good and felt very confident about the upcoming interview. I was not the least bit nervous.

I arrived in the lobby of the Schmitt Academic Center on the Lincoln Park campus of DePaul University with about seven minutes to spare. My meeting was on one of the upper floors and my timing was perfect. I stepped onto an empty elevator and pressed the button for my floor but just before the doors closed, one man jumped onto the elevator. He looked like he might have been a professor. He was Caucasian, about my height with a mustache, a neatly trimmed beard and horned rimmed glasses. We acknowledged each other's presence as he stood to the other side of the small enclosure. We both realized it at the same time because the hint of a smile softened his face. Then I smiled but neither of us said a word about our observation. We were wearing exactly the same outfit; I mean exactly the same. It was as though we had dressed together that morning so that everything would be identical. He wore a navy blazer with the two shiny brass buttons, a brilliant white shirt and a red tie with tiny white polka dots, gray trousers and polished black loafers. When the elevator doors opened, he nodded politely and smiling, stepped off the elevator into the hall. I was so amazed that when the doors closed, I realized that I should have gotten off on that floor, too. I rode up another floor and waited anxiously for the elevator to go back down to my floor. It was just about time for me to be walking into Dr. Strain's office. As I exited the elevator, I took note of the signage that directed me to the right department. I found the office that said, 'Dr. Charles Strain, Director of MALS' program. I entered the outer office and announced myself to the young lady sitting behind the desk, informing her that I had an appointment with the director. She said, "Oh, yes, Mr. Long, Dr. Strain is expecting you", as she directed me to an inner office door. She told me to just go right in. When I entered the office, Dr. Strain, who was sitting behind his desk, rose, reached out to shake my hand and with a grand smile, introduced himself. We both started to laugh openly. He was the same man I had just met on the elevator, wearing my outfit. The ice was immediately broken as we sat and began to discuss my interests and the graduate program. Perhaps from my appearance or maybe my manner, Dr Strain informed me that I was exactly the kind of adult student that the program was intended for. He then granted me unconditional acceptance and welcomed me into the program. The program was to last approximately three years if all the classes were taken when scheduled, at which time, I would have to write my graduate thesis. From the beginning, I decided three years was just long enough to be back in classes as a student, so I switched my mind to 'student/study' mode. Like the days of old, I got crazy focused again.

Dr. Dennis P. McCann Ethics and Economics

When classes began a week or so later, I had purchased all my books and study materials for my first class. In the early class orientation about the course and the program, it occurred to me what an absolute irony I was a part of. Here I was, a fifty-year-old black Buddhist, attending a nearly all white Catholic university and sitting in a class with all white, teens, twenties and thirty-somethings. I was the same age as the professor, if not older. But none of that mattered to me; I was there to continue my education. During the term, my assignments were exciting, and I took pleasure in delving deep into the reading and study materials. As was my nature, I asked questions, lots of questions. On a couple of occasions when I raised questions about some topic or argument and got involved with class discussions, a few of the younger students claimed to be offended by my position on the topic. In one case, a young woman who held radically different views from me, was so upset that I was not a Christian that she stood up and stormed out of the class.

It didn't take long before my religion became known to the students. Asked by some why a Buddhist would attend a Catholic university, I responded that I was there to get a Master of Arts degree in Liberal Studies education, not to become a priest. It seemed to be the perfect environment and I thrived in it. The classes were vibrant, and my professors seemed to enjoy the exciting exchanges that I initiated in them. In fact, my professor of *Ethics and Economics* told me that if he could fire up his classes as well as I did, he would be happy. When I was asked by a curious student how and where Nichiren Buddhism began, I asked permission from my professor to recite a research paper I had done which would address that question. And though it was a lengthy paper, he granted me permission to read it to the class. My paper went on to answer the student's question.

A Research Paper Tracing the History of the Soka Gakkai In Modern Day Japan

In these few pages I will explore the subject of religion in modern day Japan and specifically the history and growth of the Soka Gakkai, the lay organization of the Nichiren Daishonin sect of Mahayana Buddhism. The process will necessarily include a discussion of the political, social and economic conditions that prevailed prior to its inception and those similar conditions that have contributed to its subsequent growth. The primary sources of reference for this effort are: *Japanese Religion in the Modern Century* by Professor Shigeyoshi Murakami of Tokyo University, translated by H. Byron Earhart; *The Human_Revolution* and *A Youthful Diary* by Daisaku Ikeda, third and current Soka Gakkai International President. *The Human Revolution* is President Ikeda's fictionalized account of his early days as a youth division member in the Soka Gakkai and his subsequent rise to presidency under the tutelage of his mentor and second SGI President, Josei Toda. *A Youthful Diary* comprises excerpts from a private journal kept by Daisaku Ikeda as a young man, recording some of the reflections and struggles of his early days of faith. These excerpts are serialized in the Seikyo Times, published by NSA Publications Department, Santa Monica, California.

Other secondary reference sources are *Religion in Contemporary Japan* by Ian Reader and *The Buddhist Tradition in India, China and Japan* by William Theodore de Bary. The beginning of this century marks the emergence of Japan as a modern industrial and commercial success story. Even so, no considerations can be given to this development without factoring in the religious influences that played a major part in the creation of modern Japan. We can trace the source of modern Japan back to at least the Tokugawa period (1600-1867); but it was in 1868, under the Meiji Restoration that the impetus for Japan to enter the modern world was provided. Before the Meiji Restoration, Japan had been a rural and agricultural nation, feudal in its political description. But this feudalism was relinquished in favor of a symbolic emperor. Instead of the dictatorship that existed under such feudalism, a parliamentary style government was established. Consequently, urban and industrial development began as trading centers grew.

It should be noted that the Meiji Restoration saw Japan abandon the two hundred years of isolationist policies that preceded 1800, while at the same time entering the world scene as a result of defeating both China in the Sino-Japanese War of 1894 and Russia in the Russo-Japanese War of 1904. From our vantage point of 1900, we can see that Japan has just completed one war and is facing three more conflicts: the Russians, which they defeat; the 2nd Sino-Japanese War in which Korea is annexed; and the total devastation of World War II in which the United States dropped the atomic bomb on Hiroshima and Nagasaki, followed by the American Occupation. Japan combined both industrial and military strength to become a major international power; education was at the center of the general plan for bringing these two forces to bear upon international markets. Underlying this economic, political and social evolution was religion, specifically, the time-honored Shinto tradition, even though Shinto was found to be impractical as the center of the new government. It was, however, partly responsible for the restoration of the symbolic emperor and the removal of the feudal dictator, and until the defeat of WWII, and the Occupation, Shinto played an important role in Japan's educational development and government. Though Buddhism had been an integral part of the government during the Tokugawa period, it was abandoned in favor of Shinto at the beginning of the Meiji era. But in spite of its defeat in favor of Shinto, Buddhism had already shaped such a strong alliance with Japanese patriotism that it provided the impetus for the advent of extremely reactionary political policies. Although strong Confucian influences existed in the educational system and provided the political thrust of the Tokugawa regime, it was rejected. Later, Shinto was declared a non-religious practice and, representing the ethics of the nation, was the only religious tradition that could be taught in schools. In general, the customary practices of Shinto and Buddhism were weakened by the social changes occurring in Japan, particularly those occasioned by the shift of the population from agriculture to industry and from rural areas to the city. This weakening of Buddhism and Shinto tended, at the same time to lend strength and popularity to the new religions, even though the new religions were not completely free to organize until the end of the war in the 1945. Until then even Shinto and Buddhism were subject to persecution and government control. A new era in Japanese religion began at the end of World War II.

Religious freedom became a reality for the first time while at the same time the state support of Shinto was eliminated and state support for any religion was ceased. For the first time religions were totally free to organize, even though there was some degree of difficulty in determining just what constituted a religion; such difficulties arose as a. result of eliminating those who would attempt to avoid paying taxes as a tax exempt organization. This changing atmosphere for religion in Japan created an unsettling condition that went far beyond the relative strength of organized institutions. Religion had been an integral part of the long, continuous effort to build national unity and a successful economic base for the country. There seemed to be a social crisis: both Shinto with its religious values and Neo-Confucianism with its ethical notions had been used to instill a sense of national identity and personal motivation in the young students. After the war, all forms of thought control and coercive participation in religion were abolished, leaving a moral void.

The prosperity that Japanese capitalism experienced after World War I fell into a serious decline, eventually becoming a worldwide postwar disaster. Previously prosperous industries deteriorated. The working class, farmers, laborers and managers found it more and more difficult to make a decent living with the rising prices, attendant factory strikes, and subsequent riots centered on the price of rice. As if these social conditions were not enough, an earthquake destroyed the center of Japan's military, political and economic center, Tokyo in 1923. Persecution continued and by means of the Peace Preservation Law, the Japanese government maintained its oppression of any socialist movement in the country. By the 1930's fascist movements began to gain power, at the same time defending the position of the farmers and an overall quest for political change. In its pursuit of foreign expansion, the Japanese launched a full-scale war on China, seizing Manchuria. These were the circumstances under which a fascist emperor system was formed; they were also conditions that fostered the growth of many new religions. At the core of these new religions were the small business owners and the new lower middle class. "The new religions of this period, according to the 1924 survey of the Ministry of Education, totaled 98 organizations-65 Shinto, 29 Buddhist, and 4 Christian." (Japanese Religion in the Modern Century, Murakami, p.83).

When Nichiren Daishonin first declared Nam-myoho-renge-kyo in 1253, he undoubtedly cherished the entire world, in his mind. Of course, his view and understanding of the entire world could hardly have exceeded the limited boundaries of Japan and nearby coastal regions. He stated in various writings that his actions corresponded exactly to the predictions of Shakyamuni Buddha's Lotus Sutra. One of his clearest and most powerful statements appears in *On the Buddha's Prophecy*. It begins with a reference to a passage from the twenty-third chapter of the Lotus Sutra, "In the fifth five hundred years after my death, accomplish worldwide kosen-rufu and never allow its flow to cease." Kosen-rufu is the Buddhist term for world peace. In this gosho (writing) he expresses his great joy as well as his certainty that his teaching would spread all over the world without fail.

Nichiren Shoshu (the priesthood) has handed down the pure lineage of Nichiren Daishonin for seven centuries up until today. Now his teachings are spreading throughout the world. The essential spirit of the Soka Gakkai (value-creations society) has been that Nichiren Daishonin's disciples should dedicate their lives to fulfilling his will for the establishment of world peace. With this deep commitment, the successive presidents of the Soka Gakkai have struggled to bring up able individuals, give guidance on faith, apply Buddhist philosophy to all fields of society, and courageously carry out far-reaching plans to spread the teachings of Nichiren Daishonin. In 1940, the Religious Organizations Law, which had as its objective, the control of religion and mobilization of religion for the war effort in Japan, was enacted. According to this law, the various denominations of the Nichiren tradition were advised to unify under the Nichiren sect, but there was a movement in the priesthood, led by Nikko Shonin, its founder and disciple of Nichiren, to oppose this order. In direct opposition to this movement was the Soka Kyoiku Gakkai, (which later became the Soka Gakkai). Its leader, Tsunesaburo Makiguchi (1871-1944), was an educator who had long been the principal of an elementary school in Tokyo and developed a distinctive educational theory of pragmatism called "value creation". In 1930, together with Josei Toda, also a faculty member from the same school, he formed the Soka Kyoiku Gakkai as a study group mainly for elementary school teachers. In 1937 the formal inauguration of this movement took place in Tokyo, after which all efforts went into religious activities.

It is interesting to note that Tsunesaburo Makiguchi and Josei Toda, the first and second presidents of the Soka Gakkai came from the ranks of the elementary teacher, a profession that was not known for its production of leaders and those who spoke out in spite of government repression. Noteworthy also is a comparison that can be made with Thomas Rohlen in his *Japan's High Schools*: "And the teaching profession was not democratic: Teachers were followers rather than leaders. They were poorly paid and received far less compensation than other government officials of comparable rank. As members of the national civil service, teachers were responsible to the national government in Tokyo rather than to the local community in which they served. The right of teachers to organize associations was severely limited by the government; teachers' associations were government-sponsored, subsidized, and controlled." (Rohlen, p. 64) Yet in spite of these conditions, one of the largest new religions in Japan had its beginnings in the elementary school. Attention must be given to the scant treatment given by H. Byron Earhart when he describes the process of initiating new members into the newly formed organization. Little explanation is given to one of the most important aspects of practice in the Soka Gakkai. His description is only superficial, in that he does not go further to explain the purpose or principles based on the Lotus Sutra that underlie the action of shakubuku. As a result of this oversight, the reader can find no connection between the practice and how the small group grew to become the large, vibrant organization that it has become. He writes: "Through aggressive proselytism they organized elementary school faculty, shop owners, and salaried workers into discussion groups for "life renewal" with practical results; they studied the concepts of benefit and punishment in the Lotus Sutra, and the theory of value with its emphasis on beauty, gain, and the good. And they were told of the actual evidence (magical this-worldly benefits) gained from the objects of worship of the Dai Gohonzon (a mandala in Nichiren Shoshu's head temple Taisekiji, near Mount Fiji." (H. Byron Earhart, p. 108)

The real explanation and compassion that is conveyed in the practice of shakubuku can be understood better by Daisaku Ikeda, who, as Shin'ichi Yamamoto in his story, *The Human Revolution*, records the words of then president, Josei Toda: "If we are to live the life of Buddha in today's society and cherish a real love for the world, then we have to practice shakubuku. There's no other way. Shakubuku is the ultimate means of achieving personal happiness, the most direct route to world peace and the master key to national prosperity. Therefore, I say that shakubuku is the highest of Buddhist practices. Because it is carried out for the sake of human happiness, because it deals with what Buddhism terms "man's salvation from suffering," it is in keeping with an enlightened state of life. Those who do shakubuku must never forget the spirit of mercy. Shakubuku is not a religious debate, nor is it a membership drive. Shakubuku means to put into practice the mercy of the True Buddha, Nichiren Daishonin. He who does shakubuku becomes Buddha and carries on the work of Buddha. Don't forget this." (Ikeda, p. 56)

It is my opinion and conclusion that if we are to accept and make efforts to understand the growth and development of an organization, make strides in understanding any past event or series of events, then documented, first-hand accounts are to be preferred. I find it no different in this situation that the validity of accuracy of the accounts given by the person who experienced them gives the reader a much clearer picture of the circumstances and problems that surrounded these historical figures. I say this without the slightest intention of swaying one's belief or defending this or any other doctrine. In light of this position let me present to the reader the private thoughts of the man who now heads the Soka Gakkai, Daisaku Ikeda. I would assume, as perhaps any court would, that the personal entries in one's diary are to be taken at face value. Written some 40 years ago during the social upheaval that plagued Japan, these entries and private thoughts give us some insight into the mood of the nation. These excerpts are from *A Youthful Diary*, most of which are written while Ikeda was a youth division leader and studying under the watchful eye of then president Josei Toda.

1950

Though five years had passed since the end of the war, the standard of living had not yet returned to its prewar level. Small and medium-sized businesses suffered greatly in the stagnant economy. A government economic report issued on June 30 claimed that the standard of living had risen to only 76-78 percent of its prewar level. Consumption of staple foods had recovered but that of other commodities, especially clothing, was still low, it said; people spent only 30 percent of what they had before the war on clothing, making do with the items they had on hand.

Sunday, July 9. Clear.

"Cool all day today. Mr. Toda and I keep struggling desperately. The business is obviously failing day by day. Anxious about Mr. Toda's health deteriorating. No one but I can succeed my teacher, Mr. Toda."

Sunday, July 16. Cloudy.

"Mr. Toda's business seems to be in grave difficulty. I see bad signs both inside and outside the company. Went to work today too. Rested a little in the morning. It tears my heart to see my co-workers leaving the company. Who is going to stand up and take responsibility both in the business and the Gakkai? My mission grows heavier and greater."

Tuesday, August 15. Fine and Clear.

"Anniversary of the cease fire. My heart flooded with a thousand emotions. Cherry trees blossomed (reminiscent of the cherry blossoms in the story of the Makioka Sisters by Junichiro Tanizaki) and red leaves fell, snow lay on Mount Fuji and the summer sun beat down so quickly, five years have passed. Hard times for the company. We have reached a crisis. The directors conferred until 10:30. More employees seem to be leaving. My responsibilities are heavy, heavy indeed. Who will build the coming era? who will be its driving force, who will set its direction? Read Tolstoy's *Confessions*."

The strained economy drove many smaller companies into bankruptcy. The Tokyo Construction Credit Association, established by Josei Toda to recoup the losses of his earlier business venture, was forced to suspend operations on August 22. Mr. Toda, then general director of the Soka Gakkai, decided to resign his position in order to prevent any possibility of his personal difficulties casting a shadow over the organization. He announced his intention to resign on August 24, following a lecture on the Lotus Sutra. Young Daisaku Ikeda exerted himself in winding up the company's affairs and continued to protect Mr. Toda in every possible way." (Seikyo Times, p. 16-17, November 1983)

After my presentation, I went on to explain the schism that developed between the priests led by chief priest Nikken Abe, and the lay organization led by President Daisaku Ikeda. By 1990 the membership in NSA was growing tremendously. However, Nikken Abe insisted that the membership abide by his interpretations of the writings of Nichiren Daishonin. In essence he demanded that all the members follow his path which meant that the members had to go through the priesthood to receive any benefits from the Gohonzon.

He demanded that all the members continue to contribute alms and donations to the priesthood as was the custom in Japan. He was imposing his authority over the entire membership of NSA in direct opposition to the teachings of Nichiren Daishonin. The membership instead continued to follow Daisaku Ikeda. As a result of this division and refusal of the membership to follow the priesthood, Nikken Abe excommunicated the entire NSA membership. In response to the excommunication SGI (Soka Gakkai International) was formed with Daisaku Ikeda as its president. From that point on, the SGI began to grow in unprecedented fashion. Since then the SGI has grown to one hundred and ninety-two (192) countries and territories around the world.

THE CLIMAX

My presentation was clearly intimidating to many of the students but that wasn't my intention. I had been practicing Nichiren Buddhism now for at least twenty years and I asked some of the same questions from the past and some new ones. But now I already knew the answers. The professor and the majority of the students were approaching this course, its materials and ideas from a Christian perspective, and I understood that. In my mind I thought: "Been there, done that". I, on the other hand, was viewing the entire universe of religious thought from my perspective, as a Nichiren Buddhist having been a Christian. My life's course had been such that I was in the perfect situation to share some insights about what I had learned.

Dr. McCann was professor of Religious Studies and he found himself on many occasions caught in the middle of heated discussions, having to decide what position he would have to take during the discussions. He seemed truly excited to come to class and watch the interaction between the class and me. Often times many of the students would agree with me; but that was a terrifying realization for some of them because it meant that beliefs they had previously held for so long had been challenged and brought into question Not all of the discussions were mild; some got heated. There were nights when those who were 'committed' Christians and I would draw rhetorical and philosophical 'blood'. The hottest of the debates came one night when the two words: *sex* and *Jesus* came up in the same sentence. From the beginning of the year I had been challenged by some angry students about, not so much my beliefs but about my alleged dismissal of their beliefs. It wasn't that I was dismissive. I was simply explaining and defining my beliefs and by doing so it threw their religious/philosophical positions into question. And more often than not, it would be the other student who would make 'eye opening' statements in spite of him or herself.

During the class, which had grown since the start of the term, every pertinent question that I had ever asked since *The Mystery of the Porch Door* had been answered.

I told them my Santa Claus story. I told them my Delaney Methodist Church story. I told them about Reverend Davis and Alvin Plummer. I talked about the religious curse experience I had had in Bunumbu. But on one particular night, sex interjected itself into the conversation when I asked if Jesus was a man or a god. They all knew to choose carefully. When it was agreed upon that he was a man, I asked if Jesus had ever had sex; Adam had had sex. I suggested they all think of where we'd be if Eve had said no. The men in the room were immediately on my side. The barrage of counter attacks, all from the women in class was furious and relentless. Their position was that sex was the only thing that men think about. Most of the guys in the room verbally agreed with that. Dr. McCann laughed hysterically and interjected from time to time, obviously trying to remain neutral. "Men need sex" was the premise the male students defended. Coming from the women, we heard: "Sex is not everything!" "Jesus was pure!", "He was a prophet and didn't need sex!" "He wasn't into sex!" That comment nearly brought the house down.

Asked to think about the role that sex plays in religion and religious matters, those in opposition to me were caught off guard. I argued the facts that Jesus was a thirty something Jewish guy who was 'born' without his mother and father having sex. It was 'immaculate'. He was illiterate because he couldn't read or write. He drank wine, didn't shave, didn't have sex with women and was into sado-masochism. One young woman shouted out: "Men don't have to have sex to make them great!" Loaded with venom, that comment was aimed directly at me. Without thought or hesitation, I said, "I agree but even Gandhi was getting laid." Not because of that comment but I got an A for the course and I was beginning to form an idea of what my thesis was going to be.

Dr. Frida Kerner Furman Great Ideas, Business and Society

My three-year program was winding down and I had only one or two more courses to complete. I had decided that my thesis would be on the growth of Nichiren Buddhism in Chicago within the African American community since I had begun to practice. I decided that it would be titled:

THE SOKA GAKKAI INTERNATIONAL
TOWARDS THE 21ST CENTURY

Nichiren Daishonin's Buddhism in Chicago's
African American Community:
Reflections on Twenty-Five Years of Socialization (1970-1995)

One of my final and favorite classes was called *Great Ideas, Business and Society* held by Dr. Frida Kerner Furman. This was the second class that I had taken with her and we both knew what to expect from one another. She knew how I worked, and I knew how she taught. Because the name of the course and its content materials seemed so dry and mundane, I decided to go out on a limb and present a paper that would both address the issues at hand and at the same time inject some personal, enlightened insights into it. The first thing that grabbed Dr. Furman's attention about my research paper was the title: <u>Senate Subcommittee Investigating the Nature, Meaning, and Consequences of Social and Political Equality</u>. Rather than just do a run of the mill paper, I decided to take philosophers from different time periods, different countries and of different moral persuasions, put them all in the same room as members of a subcommittee, discussing topics like democracy, politics, morality, religion and see what happened. On the subcommittee were: Nicola Machiavelli, Thomas Hobbes, John Locke, Jean Jacques Rousseau and Alexis de Tocqueville. In these hypothetical gatherings tempers began to flare as soon as the proceedings got under way with one participant attacking the ideas of another and causing the entire gallery to burst into momentary turmoil. Like scenes in a hostile court room, shouts of "Order, Gentlemen, Order!" heated the atmosphere. And to make matters even more challenging, I added women to the audience so that any chauvinists would have to address the concerns of the women who were present, women who had the right to publicly protest. The most powerful outspoken voice from the women was that of Angela Davis.

At closure, the interpretations and summation for the subcommittee's findings and conclusions were done by Nelson Mandela. Dr. Furman was delighted with the paper and totally impressed. On the last page of the paper she wrote:

> *"This is a very good paper, Denver. You do a fine job of analyzing and explaining the authors' views and you inject a note of much needed mirth into it. Take care. I enjoyed your class participation."*

I received an A for the paper and an A for the course. In June of 1995, I graduated from DePaul University and received my MAL degree. It was still my objective to land in a college level class as a professor, but Robert Morris College would have to do for the time being. After graduation, in support of my application for admittance into a Ph.D. program at the University of Chicago, Dr. McCann wrote me a letter of recommendation which read:

> *From: Dr. Dennis P. McCann*
> *Professor of Religious Studies*
> *DePaul University*
>
> *Re: Letter of recommendation for Mr. Denver E. long*
>
> *I write in support of Denver Long's application for admission to the Humanities-Art/Design program at the University of Chicago. As an alumnus of the University (PhD., Divinity School, 1976), I can personally testify that Denver has what it takes to make a significant contribution as a student at the U of C.*
> *Denver was a student in the MALS/MBA course that I did in Ethics and Economics. The section in which he was enrolled focused on a work in progress, a student evaluation of the anthology or primary source materials that has just*

been published by Eerdman's Publishing Co., "On Moral Business; Classical and Contemporary Resources for Ethics in Economic Life" (1995). I mention this because Denver was extremely helpful to me, at a crucial stage in the development of this work, in his comments on the various readings, and their suitability for classroom instruction.

The man, unquestionably, is a leader. *He is an intellectual, a rarity in academia these days. He is lively in classroom discussion, outspoken and yet eager to mentor his junior colleagues. He is quick witted and yet* invariably *well prepared, well-disciplined in his work and study habits. He is also extremely good in his written work. Imaginative, and yet very much to the point.*

Having obtained his first undergraduate degree in 1967, I suspect that he is now in his early fifties, as am I. He brings an impressive wealth of experience *and personal learning with him to any academic program he pursues. He has not lost a youthful appetite for fresh ideas. Intellectual conversation with him is a form of play. In my view, it's almost a miracle for someone his age to still be possessed by an Eros for inquiry. He has the gift, and over the years he has cultivated it well.*

I believe that Denver *is returning to school in hopes of becoming Professor Long. He wants to teach at the university level. I know that I relish the opportunity to have him as a colleague. He has already demonstrated considerable promise as a student and* teacher. *I sincerely hope that you will enable him to fulfill his academic aspirations by admitting him. He was a genuine credit to our MALS program her at DePaul and I am confident that he will be no less to the University of Chicago.*

Denver Long has my sincere admiration *and respect. He has my highest recommendation. I commend him to you without any reservation. If you need anything further, please call me at 312 325-7000 ext. 1287.*

Sincerely,
Dr. Dennis P. McCann

Dr. Furman wrote:

Director of Graduate Studies
The University of Illinois at Chicago
106 Jefferson Hall
929 West Harrison Street
Chicago, IL. 60607-7018

Dear Graduate Studies Director,

It is with pleasure that I write this letter of recommendation on behalf of Denver E. Long. I first met Denver when he took my course, Great Ideas, Business, and Society, during spring term, 1993 as part of this requirement for the Master's in Liberal Studies Program. This is an ambitious and demanding course spanning centuries of Western thought-from Plato to Max Weber-on economic and moral dimensions of social relations. Most students who take this course have not had much exposure to the subject matter in their undergraduate careers, but Denver displays an impressive enthusiasm and hunger *for learning. Denver outdid most others in this regard. Not only did he always come prepared to participate actively in class discussion, but what I found so impressive was Denver's seemingly unending creativity. His angle of vision was always unique and inventive, whether in oral exchanges or in his written work. He understood the traditional and perhaps more prosaic issues that emerged from per shared reading, but he always wanted to move in another, more original direction. And he did this with grace and good humor, never appearing overbearing or obnoxious. In fact, it was clear that he was friendly with other students in the program and he enjoyed their respect.*

I have kept in touch with Denver in the intervening time. I know he has enjoyed the teaching he had done at Robert Morris College. *That experience has* inspired *him to seek an advanced degree so that he can continue to devote himself to teaching in the areas of humanities, literature and art and design, in which he already has considerable experience. I have no doubt that Denver will do very well in all facets of graduate school-he has all the necessary skills to succeed both in school and in his chosen profession-and then some. In short, I enthusiastically support his application to your graduate program.*

Sincerely,
Frida Keener Furman, Ph.D.
Associate Professor

American Family Insurance Company

In1997 I left Robert Morris College to go into business. I decided to give entrepreneurship a try, so I opened the Denver E. Long Agency, Inc., a franchise of the American Family Insurance Company. I wasn't sure at first why this idea appealed to me except for the fact that it offered plenty of opportunity to learn, travel, to grow as a businessman and to make more money. It also afforded me more time to be involved with my Buddhist activities. Except for temporary stints in insurance companies when I first returned from overseas, this was a far cry from where most of my experience lay.

I was invited to interview at the American Family suburban office in Burr Ridge, IL. I was to meet with District Manager, Ray Petrocelli. The interview went well as I was very impressed with him and him with me. I was invited to join the company as a new agent, and I accepted. What I did not know at the time was that Ray was one of the leading managers in the company and that his district, District 808 was one of the top producing districts in the company. I was being recruited into a district that was to insurance what the Championship Chicago Bulls were to basketball in the 1990's. Ray Petrocelli was the Phil Jackson of District 808. And an agent whom I grew to respect and admire was Joe Kobel, the top producer in the district and one of the top producers in the entire company. He was the district's Michael Jordan. I was going to be working with real professionals and the idea both excited me and scared the hell out of me. These guys were some of the best in the business.

Initially I was hesitant because my heart wasn't fully in it but when I began to get more involved with locating an office and completing the extensive training that came with being an agent, I started to get enthused. But even then, it wasn't the kind of enthusiasm that I held for education and higher learning. Once I made the commitment though, I put my whole being into becoming a successful businessman. And like most of the other endeavors in my past, my agency started from scratch. For months I worked to get my new office open and in presentable condition as I regularly attended training sessions in outlying suburbs of Chicago and at the home office location in Madison, WI.

Finally, I was open for business. My first two weeks as a businessman were frightening. I had done everything I was instructed to do by the company professionals who assist new agents in setting up their offices. But for nearly two weeks I sat at my brand-new desk, staring at my brand new telephones that never rang. I found myself lifting the receivers from time to time to see if there was a dial tone; the telephones were working just fine. Then slowly calls began to come in and slowly business began to build. I was fortunate enough to find a young lady who was initially a potential client who ended up being my trusted and dedicated office manager. Her name was Myia Featherston-Jones and when she came into the business, everything changed. I started to grow by leaps and bounds. It seemed that she was just exactly the person I needed to run the office while I was out doing business and I grew very fond of her. Myia took care of my office and business the same way Sam took care of me and my house in Bunumbu. She knew how to talk to potential clients; she knew how to answer questions from existing clients, and she knew exactly how to calm down anxious clients. She got even better at her job when started attending training sessions at the company headquarters. Myia and I were a winning team and our clients were beginning to tell others about us. Located in the heart of Hyde Park, on the campus of the University of Chicago, The Denver E. Long Agency, Inc. was off to a good start. As with any business, there are goals to be set and met. My agency was no different. The biggest difference was that the company, American Family Insurance set basic goals for every agency to reach. Without goals there could be no growth and without growth there would be no business.

The first two years of growth were slow and steady. Training was an ongoing part of the business so both Myia and I were learning more and more about the business as we went along. Most agents set their aims at becoming Agent of the Month and Agent of the Year; but achieving All American was something that signified that you had made it as a successful agent. Qualifying for All American meant that the agent earned free, all-expense paid trips to where ever the company was scheduled to go in a particular year. The really big accomplishment was to reach Life Diamond status, a level reached from life insurance sales. With Life Diamond status came many rewards and acknowledgements from top company officials in addition to receiving a Life Diamond ring. By year seven of being an agent, I had made All American status for four consecutive years and in the fifth year, I had made Life Diamond. I attributed my accomplishment to lessons I learned from Ray, who became one of the most impressive people I had ever met. Regarding my training in life insurance sells, he once told me something that I never forgot. He said, "Once you've made your presentation, stop talking and just listen. The one who speaks next, looses." I have kept that bit of advice in my life and have found it to be of tremendous benefit in other areas of life.

Not only had I made All American and Life Diamond but in 1999, just two years after joining the company, my picture was on the cover of the company's agent magazine, the *All American*. For months afterwards, agents from all over the city gave me the blues for having just joined the company and landing on the cover of the magazine. As a consequence of earning the respect and honors associated with All American and Life Diamond, I received my diamond ring, earned free trips to the Bahamas, Orlando, Florida, Las Vegas several times and to British Columbia. My wife Joan and I traveled every year like we owned a travel agency. But the biggest and most important aspect of opening an American Family Insurance Agency had nothing to do with selling insurance products. My biggest reward and impact on the public was my ability to do shakubuku. My Buddhist practice was vibrant and strong and every new person I met while in business, I saw either as a client and/or a shakubuku. Every week I was inviting and taking dozens and dozens of new people to the Chicago Culture Center to learn about Nichiren Buddhism. At one point, a friend and fellow member told me that he had 'reserved' a section of the seating for 'Denver's people'. There were Sundays when I had as many as eight to ten new people with me, introducing them to the practice of chanting Nam-myoho-renge-kyo. I had not forgotten my vow to propagate the Mystic Law. So many of my new and old clients were beginning to chant and see changes in their lives that oftentimes their coming into the office would be to discuss personal matters in their lives that had nothing to do with insurance. My passion for introducing people to the Gohonzon was limitless. One young woman who had been a client of mine since my agency opened, confided in me that she was reluctant to chant for what she really wanted because she was told that her desire was impossible to fulfill. After many private conversations about chanting, she finally told me that she had a physical condition that doctors said would prevent here from ever having a baby, something she wanted more than anything. I encouraged her to chant more with faith in the Gohonzon and to continue doing morning and evening gongyo. She also got involved in her district activities and started attending meetings at the Chicago Culture Center and introducing new people to Buddhism. Her attitude changed drastically after a few weeks of dedicated effort. For months I didn't see her, fearing she had given up her practice.

Exactly six months went by when she called me and asked if we could meet. I chose a popular watering hole near my office in Hyde Park. As we sat and talked, she smiled and said, "I'm pregnant." I asked if she was sure and she relayed to me how her doctors were at a loss to explain how her previous condition had totally changed. They were as amazed about the pregnancy as she was. She later gave birth to a healthy, handsome son. That experience only strengthened my faith and made me reaffirm my dedication to continue spreading the word about Nichiren Buddhism. My decision to become an agent was destined to change the lives of many people with whom I had come in contact. On October 6, 2007 the Soka Gakkai presented me with the *"Treasures of the S.E.A." Award*. The award read:

"For your great compassion in sharing your experience *in your journey of human revolution with members and non-members at home and abroad. You* are *a wonderful treasure to Southeast Area. Congratulations"*

Westwood College

After ten productive years as a successful agent with American Family Insurance Company, my desire to get back into the classroom was too great to ignore. When word got out that I was interested in teaching again, one of my clients immediately gave me the name of a program director at Westwood College in nearby Calumet City, Illinois. I called the school, met with the General Education Director, Mrs. Sheila Roe-Boston, for an interview. During the meeting I was asked to make a short class room presentation to demonstrate my abilities as a teacher. She had convened a small group of faculty members for the demonstration. The presentation went well as the group of faculty members expressed some delight with my confidence and expertise as a teacher. When the new term started, I was back in the class room where I belonged. My schedule started out light with only one or two classes. I was being tested to see what contributions I could make as part of the faculty. My first classes were English, College Writing and Literature or Public Speaking. I was back into the books, and I loved it. As new terms began, I got more and more classes until I was teaching a full load of six classes.

I was now being called Professor Long, just as Dr. McCann from DePaul University had foreseen. I understood why very early on, I had a liking for the 'Ivy' look from my days growing up in Gary, Indiana. I liked tweeds, bow ties, cardigan sweaters and button-down shirts. My life had been preparing me, sort of a dress rehearsal you might say, for when the right time came. The things that I liked as a child growing up were all a part of 'designing my uniform' for later life. I thought about the little plant cutting in the window. I knew why I had asked so many questions as a child, adolescent and as an adult. I understood now. I came to the realization that if I was alive, I was important. My earlier life experiences had prepared me and guided me to my real mission. If only my dad could see me now. He knew back then that knowledge alone was not enough to make me happy. Wisdom was needed.

I had gained both knowledge and wisdom. The important thing was to know what to do with the vast amount of information that was accumulated. The benefits of the practice that I adopted years ago as a Buddhist were manifesting in my life and now, I saw and understood them. Everything that I had ever set my mind to had been accomplished. I was a professor at Westwood College. Having said that, I knew, too, that it was at Westwood College where I would carry out my mission. What I had to teach was needed there and it was much more than English, College Writing, Literature and the Humanities. My reputation as a tough professor grew quickly. Buddhism came to Westwood with me. I understood how delicate it could be to have faith in a practice that differs so drastically from the norm. Nearly all of staff, faculty and student body were Christians of one denomination or another. There were a few Muslims but primarily Christian and me, the Buddhist.

I made no proclamations, no demands, and no in-your-face refutations. It didn't take long for my students and me to connect. We openly discussed their studies, their questions and other concerns. When they learned that I was a Buddhist, questions came at me from all directions. I explained the basics and moved on, avoiding any possibility of students complaining about the subject matter. Not everyone was open minded. I based all of my lessons on the fundamentals of Buddhism. That, on its surface sounds threatening but in fact is quite the contrary. Using the fundamentals of Buddhism in the classroom only means utilizing the tools of reality that exist right in our midst. One such tool is reason; some others are tolerance, compassion and the rarity of curiosity or a seeking mind. The students began to understand this on a deeper level and began to truly appreciate an active and invigorating learning environment. My classroom opened a universe of inquiry for the students that I took pride in. We Americans take for granted that we are effectively communicating when we talk but oftentimes all we must do to be effective communicators is to listen

DENVER E. LONG

TO THE PRINCIPLE'S OFFICE

The fundamental law of Nichiren Buddhism is Nam-myoho-renge-kyo and the Law protects those who propagate and practice accordingly. From the first day of my classes at Westwood College, I strongly encouraged all of my students to ask questions. In fact, I used the phrase, "Ask questions until you understand." That didn't necessarily mean asking me, but to continue asking questions until the answers were found. Students were delighted with that notion and often wondered aloud how I could possibly know so much. During one of my humanities classes, the subject of religion came up with questions to me about my religious beliefs. I told the class that I was a Nichiren Buddhist. Then I briefly explained what the practice was about. Most of the students in the class were fascinated, having never known a 'Black Buddhist'. Like most, their idea of a Buddhist was of a bald, potbellied guy sitting in a lotus position. I clarified most of their misunderstandings. In that humanities class, we discussed disciplines like art, music, religion, dance, architecture, etc. A vibrant discussion ensued with most of the class taking part. But there were a couple of dissenters, protesting that the class and I were denigrating their religion by questioning and dissecting certain aspects of religion. I often reminded students that a critical thinker was one who always asked questions about any given topic when studying that topic. The annoyed students went to the newly appointed Director of Student Affairs with a complaint about me and the class talking about Christianity and Buddhism. They were also upset that most of the class was actively participating and asking quite relevant questions about both religions. Not long after, I received a notice to come to the director's office to discuss the matter. When the two or three disenchanted students heard that I had been called to the office, they were gleeful about my apparent plight, telling others that I was going to lose my job or at least get reprimanded and maybe even be forced to apologize to them. I arrived at the director's office, was invited in and offered a seat. As I sat down, she turned away from me, closed her office door, and turned around to look me right in the face and together we both exploded into laughter.

The director was a new Women's Division SGI member who had just started practicing Buddhism a year or so earlier. She knew that I had been practicing for years. During the course of the term before she became a director, she had sometimes sought me out to ask me questions about the practice. Our meeting ended in laughter, but I had to walk out with a straight face to avoid any suspicions. The complaining students never knew. From that day forward, no student ever complained about any of the discussions again. That was perhaps due in part to the fact that an excerpt of my graduate thesis from DePaul University, the story of how I met my wife, Joan, had been published in a book entitled, *The Buddha Next Door*, the sequel to *The Buddha in Your Mirror*, by Middleway Press. When I received my copy of the book, I immediately showed it to my Program Director, Mrs. Boston, whom I had grown to like very much, and she was pleased to have a new instructor come in with some published work to his credit. What does she do?

At the faculty meeting, she holds the book up and starts talking about how "Denver has brought a new standard of professionalism and excellence to the faculty, yadda, yadda, yadda" and "We, the faculty should work harder to get published, etc. Please take a minute and stop by Denver's classes to congratulate him." By now every faculty member in the room was glaring at me with tight smiles and courteous nods of their heads. I wondered what Nichiren Daishonin would have done in a similar situation. Sometimes during my classes, I wrote phrases on the board like: "Questions are the answer" or "Learn everything about everything" or "A sword in the hands of a coward is useless," hoping to spark critical thinking efforts in the class. Initially the students thought I was weird for asking the class to explain what they thought such phrases meant. In the context of the subject of humanities, almost anything could be discussed. My intention was to have the class get deeply involved in conversation about things they never thought about, have them start to ask questions about anything, everything. No subject was 'off-limit'.

I had discovered that even when the opportunity availed itself, most of the students were reluctant to get 'invested'. In one writing class a young lady said aloud, "Mr. Long, you make us do all this writing and reading of our stuff out loud. It's embarrassing!" She continued smugly: "Why don't you read some of your stuff out loud?" The entire class broke into laughter. But I said, "Ok, Ms. Taylor, I will do just that and since you brought it up, you can come up front and read it for us, out loud!" I handed her my copy of *The Buddha Next Door.* The room fell silent as she began to read. Then she read the part about chanting Nam-myoho-renge-kyo. And just as she read the last few words, a deep male voice in the back of the room shouted out: "Yo, Dr. Long, what is Nam-myoho-renge-kyo?" "Yesss!" I thought. Later that evening I heard the highest compliment ever paid to me. I was walking down the hall, passing a group of my female students going in the opposite direction when we all spoke: "Hello, Ladies", I said. "Hello, Mr. Long", they all responded. Then one of the young ladies looking back at me and laughing aloud, shouted: "Professor Buddha"!

The Past Returns

In 2017 several messages were sent to me on *Messenger*. Initially I ignored them because I couldn't identify the sender. The messages continued for some weeks until I decided to open one and see who and what the urgency was. The messages were from a Dr. Greg Bond, a professor of history at the University of Wisconsin, School of Pharmacy. I wondered why he would want me. His posting left a number and an email address. I reached out and finally contacted Dr. Greg Bond. Dr. Bond is a researcher of African-American pharmacists of the late nineteenth and early twentieth centuries. Guess who he was doing a research project on-Leo V. Butts! My Mr. Butts from the *Owl Drug Store* on 15th & Massachusetts St! The University's School of Pharmacy had been doing research on Mr. Butts but hit a brick wall when trying to find out more about him in the store when *Owl Drugs* was thriving in the early to mid-nineteen fifties. I asked Dr. Bond how on earth he found me. To my utter surprise he said that during his desperate efforts to find more, he Googled Leo V. Butts whose name popped in my book, *Professor Buddha*.

It turned out that I was the only person living who knew Leo V. Butts personally when Leo V. Butts was a legend. He was a legend that I knew nothing about as a kid, and I was with him nearly every day. When I think back about my days in the store, he came to the neighborhood about 1950 and opened the *Owl Drugs Store* in 1951. I had no idea how old he was; at ten years of age if he was over ten, he might as well have been a hundred. We were together in the store nearly every day and all I knew was that Mr. Butts was a very kind man. He was a big man-with big hands who treated me like I was his son. I never knew who he really was.

Dr. Bond and I, both amazed at how we met, discussed his research project. We established a communications link. He asked if I had any photos or stories that I could share with him for the project so, with honor, I wrote a short article about what I remembered working for Mr. Butts at *Owl Drugs*. During our communications, Dr. Bond sent me documents, newspaper articles and even Mr. Butts' master's thesis from the University of Wisconsin, written in 1920 where he was the first African-American to graduate from the University of Wisconsin's School of Pharmacy. What I never knew was that Mr. Butts was a real pioneer in college sports, academics, civic leadership and pharmacy. He was a civil rights activist before I even knew what one was. His story left me flabbergasted. The man that I knew as a kid was a real-life hero in the community and the African-American community at large. Born in 1898 in Madison, WI, he attended Madison High School in 1913. He was an incredible athlete in football track and basketball. What really struck me about Mr. Butts' story was that his father was born into slavery. I've investigated Mr. Butts' life and the contributions he made to society during the time I knew him. It was Black History-live! I lived among giants and never knew it. Life is good.

Postscript

The Gohonzon of Nam-myoho-renge-kyo had been in my life from the very beginning; I just didn't know it at the time. I know it now. It was there in the tiny plant and it was there in me. I came to know it as the 'voice', my invisible friend. Even before I was born, the mystic law of life (myoho) was at work. In my life it manifested in me as one who asked questions, the cause for obtaining answers. Asking questions is a vital part of critical thinking and in Buddhism is called a 'seeking mind'. A critical thinker questions everything. Now, after forty-two years of practicing Nichiren Buddhism, I can see that from the beginning, the Gohonzon was always there. And in honor of those dedicated years of practice, in October of 2012 I received the SGI-USA Distinguished Pioneer of American Kosen-Rufu (DPAKR) Award, signed by my mentor SGI-USA President, Daisaku Ikeda.

The day I asked about the plant was the day I opened the double doors to my mind. I was four years old when I began my journey and I have pondered the causes I might have made before I was born to come into this world so demanding of the truth. *"Seek* and *ye shall find"*, *"Cast your bread upon the water"* are true causes, not magic. Improbable as it may seem, this 'mystic' principle called Buddhahood is, as I suspected as a child, within us all. I knew very early on that happiness had little, if anything to do with all the 'attachments' and distractions of the world 'out there'. I could go anywhere and be with anybody I wanted to be with right in my little room which was as big as the universe. I went to Africa, Italy, Australia, Space, Another Time in History; I went on cruises with famous people from the past, all for free. I slept in castles, navigated great oceans. Famous people came and visited me right there in my room. Maybe that's what Jo was hearing all those years. I can laugh now because for all those years she thought I was in my room talking to myself.

Recently, while doing my research, I asked Jo for an update on some of our friends from childhood

from the old neighborhood and she brought me up to date, informing me that one of my 'best' and

'favorite' childhood friends of all times, Alvin Plummer had passed away. I was sad to hear that, knowing how much he had helped me grow and understand the importance of facing life's obstacles.

I hadn't seen him since childhood, but I knew I would miss him. He taught me that obstacles are

part and parcel of life, period.

A few years after Joan and I got married and were living downtown in Printer's Row, I was sitting outside a cafe across the street from our apartment building on South Dearborn Avenue one afternoon. The café was a few doors down the street from Mrs. Marilyn Hasbrouk's Architectural Books store when a guy walked out and headed my way. He was looking through the book he had just purchased so he didn't see me immediately. Then I recognized him. Just as I was about to say his name, he looked up and saw me. Our eyes locked and our jaws dropped. It was Marty from my Peace Corps days.

The last time we had seen one another was in Sierra Leone, some seventeen years earlier. We gave each other a bear hug. We were both dumbstruck by the possibility of running into each other in such a random way. He was just visiting Chicago and had heard about the Hasbrouk architecture bookstore. We reminisced and laughed about events of the past, especially my world adventure with two quarters in my pocket that he reminded me of. Marty was leaving the city within the next few hours, so his time was limited. We shook hands and gave each other another hug as he turned and walked off. My dear friend Marty turned out to be none other than the now world-renowned artist and sculptor, Martin Puryer.

Printed in the United States
By Bookmasters